Public Expenditure
Allocation between competing ends

Public Expenditure

ALLOCATION BETWEEN COMPETING ENDS

EDITED BY MICHAEL POSNER

CAMBRIDGE UNIVERSITY PRESS

CAMBRIDGE

LONDON · NEW YORK · MELBOURNE

Published by the Syndics of the Cambridge University Press
The Pitt Building, Trumpington Street, Cambridge CB2 1RP
Bentley House, 200 Euston Road, London NW1 2DB
32 East 57th Street, New York, NY 10022, USA
296 Beaconsfield Parade, Middle Park, Melbourne 3206, Australia

First published 1977

Printed in Great Britain at The Pitman Press, Bath

Library of Congress Cataloguing in Publication Data
Main entry under title:

Public Expenditure.

Includes index.
1. Expenditures, Public — Addresses, essays, lectures.
I. Posner, Michael.
HJ7461.P82   336.3'9   76-53522
ISBN 0 521 21555 2

Contents

Contents

Preface

The authors are collectively grateful to the Royal Economic Society who organised the Conference to which the papers in this volume were presented. They are also grateful to the participants at the Conference for the lively and useful discussion – and the Editor would like to mention James Meade as a notably helpful discussant who added light as well as distinction to our proceedings.

The Editor thanks his fellow members of the original organising committee – Maurice Peston, Alan Williams and Keith Norris (the last named was the Royal Economic Society Conference secretary); Chris McKenna, for work on the index; and the officers of the Press for their kindness and diligence in the process of production. He also points out with some satisfaction that 5 of the 16 authors were serving as economists in the Civil Service when these papers were written, and another 5 have served in that role before or since. All the authors are of course writing in their personal capacity, but the fact that they have been able to write so freely is modest evidence of the growing 'openness' of our bureaucracy.

Pembroke College   M.V.P.
Cambridge

PART I: FRAMEWORK

1

Introduction

M. V. POSNER

This book, arising from a Royal Economic Society Conference at Pembroke College, Cambridge, in the spring of 1974, is about the pattern of expenditure in the public sector. It excludes, at one end, the problem of financing expenditure, the size of the budget surplus or deficit, and the factors which determine the growth of public expenditure through time. At the other end of the scale, this book is not about the problems of nationalised industries, nor the control or planning of their operations. (It also excludes, for more obvious reasons, the question of once for all increases in the *scope* of the public sector – nationalisation and all that.) Our interest is in that huge middle ground comprising the work of the great 'spending departments' in Whitehall – the Department of Education and Science, Department of Health and Social Security, the Department of the Environment and so on. How much should be spent on individual services, how the merits of different programmes may be assessed, and what advantages there might be in shifting resources from one line of activity to another – those are our chief interests.

The chapter by Ian Byatt provides a clear exposition of the main analytical processes involved, and can itself be read as an introduction to this volume. In my own introductory remarks to the Conference at which these papers were discussed, I ventured a very simple minded exposition of the sequence of decisions which are in some sense 'necessarily' implied in the decision making process.[1] At any point of time there is a set of programmes and commitments in the public sector, flexibility in which is slight in the short run and perhaps not all that much greater even over a five year period. Ministers do have however a certain amount of 'play' and can determine (within limits which are narrow at first but become wider later on) current basic expenditures. These will comprise for the most part wages, salaries, transfer payments and consumption of currently produced materials from the private sector. Given the expectations about the growth of the economy in the medium run, and the discount rate used for assessing 'economic' investment expenditure in the nationalised industries in particular, the machine will generate a set of bids (from decision makers operating under devoluted powers at the grass roots) for capital expenditure of various sorts. The total of current expenditure on existing programmes plus this 'economic' capital expenditure will then be struck, and compared with the resources that might be available to the public sector if, for instance, the 'burden of taxation' in some sense is to be kept constant over the planning period.

A major set of decisions on economic strategy is then called for, treating the requirements of the public sector as one of the competing calls on national resources and trimming in particular the balance between personal consumption (in particular 'privately financed personal consumption') and public expenditure over a run of years according to the political tastes of the Government of the day. If it is broadly believed that taxable capacity can or should be increased, then there will be, hopefully, something 'left over' for new spending commitments; if, alternatively, it is hoped to reduce the burden of taxation through time, the aim might be to trim existing programmes rather than increase them.

In formal terms, it should be possible to vary the rate of discount used in assessing capital spending proposals, so as to reduce or expand this particular call on resources. According to the naive view of the supporters of the test rate of discount[2] the discount rate in fact reflects two simultaneous decisions by government: a decision about the desirable rate of productive investment and economic growth generally, competing with consumption and other calls on resources today; and a decision that, after appropriate corrections for the imperfection of the capital market and all that, capital resources should not be used in the public sector if their 'true return' is less than that in the private sector. (The reader will have to decide whether this naive approach stands up to the elegant analysis in John Flemming's paper, and I offer some views on that question below.) If this approach were broadly accepted, it would be open to Ministers to raise the test rate of discount if they felt that the calls of private or public consumption should have priority, for a run of years, over the calls of capital investment expenditure. The defence of this naive approach is, to translate and adapt the old latin tag *vox populi, vox dei*, as follows: 'Ministers in making decisions about the path of consumption and investment are expressing their understanding of the electorate's time preference, as shown by its willingness to accept tax burdens, make wage demands, and vote against unpopular Chancellors through the ballot box.'

Conceptually, this use of the discount rate as a regulator of investment expenditure could be extended to the tightly defined area of public spending itself – quite apart from the obvious effect on the capital programmes of the nationalised industries. To some extent the building of hospitals and schools is alternative to spending on the salaries of nurses and school teachers or text books, and this type of investment expenditure could be governed by some discounting test, just like the building of new power stations. But it appeared from discussion at our conference that the scope, even in principle, for this type of 'capital rationing' is relatively slight, for two main reasons: first, much capital expenditure *generates* rather than *saves* current expenditure – new language laboratories in schools need more and better trained teachers, not fewer teachers; and secondly, programme objectives (for instance kidney transplants for all who would profit by them) tend to imply an inflexible package of capital and current expenditures.

So, in practice, even if it were appropriate to use the discount rate or some other form of capital rationing as a fine tuner of the total of government expenditure, the scope for this type of tuning may be slight.

Regulation of the path of public expenditure therefore has to be pursued along three possible paths. First, programmes can be accelerated or retarded in a wholly traditional way – perhaps the best example is summed up in the initials 'PRSLA' (postponement of the raising of the school leaving age) announced in the 1968 expenditure cuts. Secondly, the objectives of particular programmes can be reassessed *ad hoc*, with the aim of releasing or absorbing resources in the desired amounts. Or thirdly, the objectives of particular programmes can be specified in more concrete detail, so that decisions can be made about the level of government expenditure in full knowledge about the implications for the attainment or shortfall from clearly stated objectives.

It is this third way of deciding on the level of government expenditure which has most bearing on the main issues discussed in this book – the choice between the different components of government expenditure. In order to allocate additional funds as they become available to, say, the alternative purposes of education or social security, Ministers really need some guidance as to what they are buying at the margin by devoting additional dollops of expenditure to these two different programmes. I think most of us accept that broad decisions between an addition to our defence capability, on the one hand, and the health service on the other, can only be made on political grounds by politicians, although even under those circumstances a clear statement as to what might be achieved by £100 million spent on the alternatives would, to say the least, be helpful to Ministers. But the choice between expenditure on education and the health service is a matter on which more technical advice and considerations may intrude: e.g. special classes for slow readers in primary schools may to some extent be alternative to financial assistance to mothers of poor families designed to enable mothers to spend more time with their children and less time earning money. The interesting and important issue which we were concerned with at our conference was the detailed description of the ways in which economists and other technicians might help in marshalling the evidence on which these decisions must be made, and the limitations to economic techniques necessarily imposed by harsh facts.

To take another example. There are many children who need publicly assisted care – orphans, the poor, the deserted. There are many ways of caring for them – fostering, adoption, special schools, subsidising natural parents, the employment of social workers to help mothers, family allowances, day nurseries, play groups. The problem of policy is to choose how much to spend in total and how to distribute the money among the several programmes. If the outputs of the different activities were unambiguously the same – units of measurable child happiness – the problem would be merely mechanical: calculate the ratio of resource cost to output at the margin for each activity, adjust the relative size of each activity until these ratios were identical, and get the politicians to decide how much in total they wish to spend on child welfare rather than, for instance, defence.

But the outputs are *not* homogeneous, and from this fact stems many of the problems considered in this book. Fostering of deprived children produces a different 'output' from, say, a minimum family income guarantee: Who is to compare the return from £1 million spent on the two alternative programmes? Economists cannot go to Ministers and ask – 'please give us a *formula* for equating given dollops of the two alternatives', because it is precisely on this sort of problem that Ministers seek guidance. Nor, however, can an economist merely impose his own judgement. Between these extremes, what can be done?

The chapter which bears most directly on this problem is Jeremy Hurst's, but we came back to it again and again in the discussion of the papers by Mark Blaug and Anthony Harrison among others. Mark Blaug chose to investigate one small facet of expenditure – the Arts Council – and found it possible to arrive at fairly concrete policy conclusions about the balance of expenditure in its budget. In discussion some of us thought that, because he concentrated on only one facet of public support for the arts generally, he was neglecting wider implications and analysing imbalances which would appear less striking when set in a wider framework. Another objection to his analysis was the implicit valuation of very different outputs (opera in London versus concerts in the provinces) that he was brave enough to attempt. But these two classes of objections (although some of us did not see this entirely clearly at the time) were contradictory: If the canvas covered by a study is very small, most of the problems of the valuation of different outputs begin to disappear, because the outputs are in fact very similar to each other; so the more we urged Blaug to widen the area of his study, the more, implicitly, we were urging on him the necessity for that very valuation of highly different final outputs which in our next breath we were preparing to deplore. Blaug of course stuck firmly to his guns, and rightly so.

Harrison offered us an excellent account (pp. 133–58) of the classic problem of the valuation of road users time in the assessment of road improvement schemes. It is not possible to go to Ministers or senior civil servants and say — 'please, how do you value time saved by the building of a new by-pass?' Nor can you go to them, cold and unprepared, and ask — 'is the time saved by holiday drivers avoiding the centre of York on their way to the East Coast as valuable as the time saved by business commuters travelling from the West Midlands to London?' It is possible, with skill and good timing, to urge Ministers and senior officials towards certain decisions on this sort of analytical issue, but in doing so economists have a duty to explain and emphasise the answers that thus get built into the assumptions. Hurst's paper emphasises the very large amount of ground work which needs to be done before any of these rather grand questions are asked at all. In many areas of social spending the mere description and analysis, the establishment of a suitable information system, is too little advanced for any rational decisions to be arrived at. A description of the outputs and a specification of the objectives of different activities is an immensely laborious task, and itself will take us somewhat nearer a situation where reasonable decisions can be made. But this sort of work does not avoid the ultimate difficulties.

Alan Williams and Robert Anderson (both from York University, not by coincidence) both tackled this central issue of value judgements though from different angles. Williams' approach is from the theory of compensation, and from the standpoint that 'potential compensation is not good enough: actual compensation is required' which is one of the more useful conclusions of modern welfare economics. It is fair to say that his paper is more useful in posing the questions than in finding the answers, but that is more than half the battle!

Anderson provides us with an analysis of the criminal justice system which by common consent is somewhat near the frontier separating that which is possible in this field of economics from that which is impossible: it remains a question of judgement whether the frontiersmen of the Anderson variety are brave explorers of new territory, or alternatively have gone beyond the pale! To many of us at the conference, it seemed that his analysis of crime and punishment in economic terms gave too little weight to 'moral outrage' as the social reaction to crime — an implication which Anderson did not intend and to some extent removes in his revised contribution to this book. But how *should* police forces dispose their constrained resources in helping to prevent, say, on the one hand crimes against property and on the other crimes against the person? One way to answer this question is to observe how, as a matter of fact, police forces *do* operate – implying that by studying the 'revealed preference' of public bodies we can show the public what is being done on their behalf and ask whether they consider the implicit decisions correct. Another way is to proceed directly by questionnaires or by other methods to find out what the public really think – and it was here that for some of us Anderson's paper, in reporting (in the Table on p. 245) the work of some American investigators, approached black comedy in its equation of one motor car theft to five rapes! But surely Anderson is right, and deserves all our support, in attempting to assess the 'pay off' from police or penal systems, taking account of both the objective costs and the subjective costs of those actually involved.

At times during the Conference proceedings some of us were tempted to retreat from the more ambitious aims exemplified in some of the papers to mere 'cost analysis' – displaying the cost of various alternatives, and leaving the choice to others. But most of us – rightly in my view, but perhaps dangerously – are not prepared for such a retreat, such an abdication. By constant probing, niggling, displaying of the facts, pressing for 'marginal' evaluations, asking 'Do Ministers (or the public) *really* think this or that relative size of programme is justifiable?', a gradual zigzag course towards improved decisions can be hoped for. Such a path can certainly lead us astray – the opportunity for big changes may be missed, and large choices between different 'packages' of measures are avoided or left to political parties to press. But this seems to me correct, provided that the role of economists precisely *in* the political parties is also acknowledged: the more that economists in the public sector work on small canvases, avoiding the very difficult cross-evaluations, the more their colleagues outside have the duty to sketch in larger choices with all the difficulties and problems that that might give rise to.

The papers by Ray Rees and John Heath provide, it is hoped, a definitive analysis of some of the main strengths and weaknesses in the major cost–benefit analyses which have recently caught the public eye – the studies for the third London Airport and for the Channel Tunnel. Gerry Corti in his chapter draws attention to some of the main elements in their analysis, and I will not here repeat his succinct exposé. But since the whole of this book is in a sense about 'cost–benefit analysis' I would like to venture some comments put in my mind by discussion at our conference. A great deal of the work which goes on in this field is not done by or read by economists: it is concerned with 'planning', largely of land use, and mostly under the head of the so-called 'structure plans'.[3] Under this new scheme, the large county authorities formed after local government reorganisation are charged with the task of preparing, discussing with the public, and ultimately presenting to a public enquiry, rolling ten year plans for the development of the areas for which they are responsible. The structure plans are not concerned with the traditional problems of the building of particular roads or the development of particular housing estates or industrial developments: rather the emphasis is on the broad brush, the general drift of developments and the disposition of the foreseen increments in population and employment. Should, for instance, the main development be within the old centre of the county, should it be in the string of old market towns which lie on a circle around the old county centre, or should it somehow be connected with the development of a new link with industrial areas in adjacent parts of the country? How will the new developments tie in with the supply of public utilities, how will shopping centres and transport needs be developed? What, above all, will produce the 'minimum cost' for any particular quantum of new development, and what amount of new development will be in some sense 'optimal'?

These questions are of course far easier to ask than to answer. And yet in every county hall across the country earnest groups of planners are struggling with alternative answers, and preparing them to discuss with the public and interested parties in a whole series of consultative operations. Many of the problems of the traditional, formal, economists' cost–benefit studies arise here once again. How sound are the projections of population change and employment change? How robust are the solutions proposed to possible variations in these basic assumptions? How will the interests of different groups of citizens be affected by developments, and how far will it be possible to compensate those who lose? What valuation should be placed on various types of amenity? In a situation where many costs which the community incurs are not charged as prices to those who force these costs on the community, how can rational allocation succeed? If minimum cost is sought, what rate of discount should be used, and should all expenditures be costed at the same discount rate?

We need not be excessively trade unionist, we economists, about the staffing of this sort of exercise. Few of the people involved have formal economic training, and this is no bad thing provided that a common approach can be distilled and sensible routine instructions can be issued. The discussion at the end of Rees' paper of the so called 'Manual of Cost–Benefit Analysis' is therefore particularly welcome, as here we see for the first time economists striving to systematise and reduce to a routine some of the more conceptually difficult procedures of their subject. But equally, I think economists have something to learn from the techniques of structure plans as they are being developed, the essence of which is, put unkindly, its 'public relations aspect'. The public living in the area to whom the plan refers are drawn into the discussion of the planning procedures, and their opinions and preferences are at least to some extent genuinely taken into account. A duty devolves not only on the local authority but on the Secretary of State for the Environment to ensure that public opinion *has* been heard, and the planning process is seen explicitly as a process of resolving differences of opinion and interest. The trouble with much of the work done in the central government machine is that it is not published, and, if it is published at all, is served up as a set of answers to questions rather than as a continuing, almost 'do it yourself' approach to which the audience is invited to contribute. I recall from my early Treasury days that it was at one time hoped that the computerisation of the economic forecast would lead to a fruitful dialogue between the technicians who produce the forecasts and the senior officials and Ministers who used it for policy optimisation purposes. The technicians could explain the properties of their model and the implications of the assumptions that they made, and the clients could investigate the results of changing the assumptions or the nature of the model relationships. This has had some limited success in practice and something of the same sort clearly needs to be developed in the relationship between 'cost–benefit analysts' in public sector resource allocation work, and their bureaucratic and political masters. The interesting implication of Harrison's chapter is that some of this interaction does in fact take place, but I believe it to be a lesson of our Conference that much more effort needs to be directed towards this end, thus simplifying and making more fruitful much of the economists' work. This is a point which is made strongly by Heath, who would throw 'Ministerial' preferences into the same general melting pot as those of the public.

I now turn to the four technical papers by Ed Mishan, Maurice Peston, John Flemming, Paul Burrows and Wynne Godley. I shall try to put these papers in the context of the general issues discussed in this book. I have already referred to the problem of capital rationing, and the plain man's justification for the Treasury test discount rate. While the trade off between current and capital expenditure may not be as important as economic literature sometimes suggests, almost any exercise in cost–benefit analysis calls for some discounting or bringing streams of expenditure to present values. I think it not unfair to many of the extremely sophisticated practitioners in the public sector to say that our views on appropriate discount rates are at present in complete disarray. For some classes of problems (for instance the depletion of natural resources) we seem to be coming to the view that microeconomic techniques are inappropriate, and prefer to deal with such counters as 'absorptive capacity' (for instance in the Norwegian use of their North Sea hydrocarbons), or 'preserving economic power for our grandchildren' (as in the Saudi Arabian case).

But there are some problems where old-fashioned discounting just has to be used. And we do not know which is the right rate. As far as can be publicly known, the civil service still does at least some tests at the 10 per cent rate first introduced in 1968. This is clearly an 'opportunity cost' of capital in some sense, and is usually strongly opposed by those who prefer a 'social time preference rate'. It is generally believed by all participants in the dispute (but not by the present writer) that the STP rate is well below 10 per cent. Those who would press the use of an STP rate, however, acknowledge that it may be necessary to go in for 'capital rationing' of one sort or another, and they therefore acknowledge that it may be appropriate to work with a shadow price of capital goods which is above their market price.

The combination of an STP type discount rate and shadow pricing of investment goods leads to resource allocations which, in principle at any rate, are different from those which would appear by using a higher opportunity cost rate with no shadow pricing. The point is clearly a version of the second-best theorem, and is somewhat akin to an argument first advanced I think by Maurice Dobb some decades ago in discussing Soviet investment decisions: it might be correct, he argued, to work with a very low discount rate even though investment resources were extremely scarce.

In his paper Flemming explains how Arrow and his associates justify the use of an STP rate, with shadow pricing of investment goods, and other elegant complications introduced by considering a two- or three-sector model. He concludes that the Treasury approach through the test discount rate, though far less elegant, may be the best we can offer. The constraints necessary to justify the unwieldy STP shadow price criteria, he argues, are too special and implausible to be credible.

If I may be permitted a little *esprit d'escalier* (I was too slow witted to think of the point during the Conference), I myself am not convinced that the general public has a social time preference very much below, say, 10 per cent in real terms. It is of course an observed fact that many of us in our private lives save even though the real return on our savings may be very low (and indeed in inflationary times substantially negative). It is also true that in many decisions we show a willingness to abstain from present consumption in the interests of our grandchildren, again with an apparently low rate of return, especially remarkable when we bear in mind that our grandchildren may be richer than us and therefore have a lower marginal utility of income.

But in other aspects of our personal life – as voters, as wage bargainers, and as decision makers in practical matters (like car purchase) I assert that we use or imply very much higher discount rates. How many votes would be received by a party which presented as one of its main planks at the election the view that, because we believe the price of oil was going to rise at 3 per cent a year in real terms for the next two decades, we should refrain from using any oil from the North Sea during the next decade? In my view, very few votes would be cast for such a party, and it would be hard enough to get a majority if the number were pitched at 10 per cent and the same conclusion arrived at.

This is no doubt an argument which will rage still for many years and in many learned works and I would only plead that after readers have studied John Flemming's chapter they should ask themselves and their colleagues whether the elegant papers that he criticises really come to very much: his conclusion, and mine, is that the traditional Treasury stance has a lot to commend it.

Another long standing and desperately difficult problem has been the argument about the extent to which risks should be taken account of in public sector decision making. Again perhaps the simplest reference to the naive commonsense ruling in some parts of the public sector is to my own treatment of the question.[4] It is common ground that 'loading the discount rate' is an inappropriate way to allow for risk; it is equally common ground that because the public sector is a very big operator it is exempt from the St Petersburg paradox and benefits from the law of large numbers; and the most that might be conceded is that, first, a public sector body which has a bad track record of failures should be set a higher standard of performance as some way of 'aiming off' for error, and secondly, some unspecified penalty might attach to really risky projects.

Nevertheless, the question of the degree of risk aversion which it is appropriate for the public sector to have in mind continues to vex many observers, who are not satisfied with the injunction 'merely exhibit to decision makers the true range of possible outcomes, and allow them to make their own judgements about relative riskiness of different options and the absolute degree of risk they are prepared to run'. This injunction, it is felt, passes the buck too openly to the decision makers from the economists – surely it is true that *some* advice can be given!

This is a matter to which Rees refers several times in his more applied paper, and Peston assumes the task of explaining to us clearly and succinctly, and then criticising, a recent contribution by Arrow which purports to solve the problem by proving once and for all that risk aversion is not socially justifiable. Again, readers must ask themselves how far this apparently rigorous proof can be applied in practice, since, for example, the risk that a chosen nuclear technique will ultimately prove to be unworkable is the sort of risk which most of us in our professional activities are just not prepared to discount to zero.

Where risk walks in economics, uncertainty is not far behind, and Heath's paper in particular reminds us of the horrors facing forecasters peering into the unknown. He suggests that this uncertainty may lead decision makers to reconsider and reformulate the whole proposition under anlaysis, thus affecting the whole nature of the decision to be taken.

The literature on public goods, now widely spread throughout the economists' world, should perhaps be able to give us some guidance on two important questions: which goods should be included in the scope of the public sector in any country at any time? and how should resources be distributed among different 'public goods'? Mishan addresses himself to these problems, and arrives at the response that we must rely on politics and commonsense to answer the first question, and that the whole gamut of economic analysis, not just the theory of public goods, is required to answer the second question. The discussion of this paper at the Conference was particularly vigorous, and Mishan has made a number of changes to accommodate the arguments presented by several commentators, particularly James Meade. But I doubt very much whether any individual objector to the original text will be fully satisfied with the amendments, and many readers will themselves wish to question Mishan's classifications and procedures. This is no criticism whatsoever of Mishan's paper, and indeed provides ammunition to support what I take to be a chief conclusion of his analysis – namely that the theory of public goods represents more an intellectual *jeu d'esprit* than a central contribution to the practical problems which we face. But this negative conclusion is itself extremely valuable, since it enables economists to turn their minds to the central issues without the worrying doubt that some important contribution from pure theory has been missed. We have to take the public sector as it is served up to us by politicians, and then try to advise on the solution of public sector problems using such economists' tools as come to hand.

One particular problem of some political moment is that of *charging* for public goods: if we follow some economists' precepts fully, many services which have only accidentally (or for purely political reasons) fallen into the public sector can be effectively 'privatised' by charging for their use. Burrows investigates the logic of some of this argumentation, and suggests that the case for pricing often rests on an unacceptably narrow definition of Government objectives. A wider Governmental 'objective function', he argues, in many cases can provide rationale for interferences with 'efficient pricing'.

Wynne Godley's paper represents a typically careful and subtle attempt to refine another special set of tools – that which attempts to reduce public expenditure flows of many different types to a common measuring rod. Godley sets out to be highly practical, and the refinements in this paper are designed to provide a theoretical underpinning of the practical rules which he is proposing, not as an exploration in pure theory for its own sake. The notion of resource cost and the accompanying realisation that different components of public sector expenditure might have different ratios of resource cost to money cost became fairly current among practitioners in the trade in the late 1960s. But it was not until the Treasury offered evidence to the House of Commons Select Committee on Expenditure when Godley was its specialist adviser in 1972 that numerical estimates of the resource cost content of different components of public expenditure were first made public. Godley now takes this notion very much further, seeking as a common denominator, as I understand it, the change in employment which would be required to provide on a continuing basis £x of expenditure of various different types. Only when we can bring all public expenditure to some satisfactory common measuring rod can we begin to ask, in quantitative and detailed terms about the cost–benefit ratios with which the rest of this book is chiefly concerned.

This book therefore is offered as a contribution to the understanding of the problems, techniques of analysis, and achievements of public sector economics in this country. It is not of course comprehensive, even within the fairly narrow framework which we have set ourselves. It does not attempt to describe, in a comprehensive way, 'The State of the Art', but instead tries to explore the frontiers of the subject.

The object of economic analysis in this field is to draw attention to the implied evaluations of the outcomes of different spending programmes, and to contribute to the discussion of these evaluations by the use of economists' arguments. It is never, in my view, possible for an economist to lay down that, for instance, the riskiness of a particular project should get some specified weight (either zero or something negative); nor that certain environmental considerations must inevitably be equated with some precise financial measure; nor that the valuation of time in transport studies must have some specified relationship to earnings; nor that the expenditure of x per cent of the Arts Council's budget on opera is excessive. What *can* be done is to go a certain way (in practice a very long way) with straightforward arithmetical calculations, and then provide some guidance as to how senior officials, politicians, or the public might proceed past that frontier.

First, some costs and benefits can be brought straightforwardly to the measuring rod of money, and translated straightforwardly (using Godley's techniques or some others) into resource cost. Secondly, other costs, not normally expressed in money terms, can with ingenuity and care be expressed fairly well in money terms. The careful work done for the Roskill Commission in investigating the private evaluation of noise levels, or studies of the expenditure of time and the travelling cost of fishermen seeking suitable recreation waters, goes a long way towards producing a rational framework for decision making about airport location or water board expenditure on recreation access.

But, thirdly, there is another sort of cost or benefit which resists obstinately this sort of approach. In my hypothetical example of child care, no economist or other 'expert' should have the cheek (what is called in other academic disciplines, the *hubris*) to offer a personal evaluation of the additional benefit which a child might receive from having loving foster parents rather than living in a home. (Nor, in defence of economists, is this a field into which the social psychologists can be wheeled to fill the gap which I believe we should leave by our voluntary abdication of the throne of philosopher king. Social psychologists *may* be able to tell us something about the long term consequences of different forms of child care, but they cannot themselves evaluate these consequences.)

What the economist can do is to ask the question – how much in resources is it worth paying for this particular benefit, which we are incapable ourselves of evaluating? And they can go further than this, because they can say: 'According to our calculations, taking account of everything which can easily be brought to our normal measuring rods, if we persisted with method *A* of child care instead of the "cheaper" method *B*, the country would be implicitly evaluating the extra benefit of method *A* at about equivalent to £200 per child. Oh Minister, do you really think the benefit is that high?'

Now of course I do not wish to assert the silly proposition that economists can abstain from judgements, or be entirely value free in their activities. The tone of voice and certainly the context in which questions like this are put very often display the very proper personal opinions of the 'experts', and very often help to sway the ultimate political decision. There is nothing wrong with this, but we should, with a certain fastidiousness, avoid pushing our views too hard or too far, and maintain such a measure of objectivity as is open to us. My reason for this policy recommendation about the behaviour of economists is that only by behaving in this way will we retain the respect and affection of our non-professional colleagues in public life or in the country at large.

NOTES

1 An earlier sketch of this story was offered in my paper printed in Sir Alec Cairncross (ed.), *Britain's Economic Prospects Reconsidered*.

2 The most naive exposition is to be found in Chapter 6 of my book on *Fuel Policy: A Study in Applied Economics*. The far more sophisticated version in John Flemming's Chapter 3 below also leads, through better drawn paths, to similar conclusions.

3 As introduced in the Town and Country Planning (Amendment) Act 1971. The system is described informally in *Structure Plans: The Examination in Public*, obtainable from the Department of the Environment.

4 M. V. Posner, *Fuel Policy, op. cit*, pp. xxx–xxxii.

Theoretical issues in expenditure decisions*

I. C. R. BYATT

Synopsis
This paper is concerned with the role economic analysis could play in providing information for decisions on the allocation of public expenditure. The discussion is not confined to what is done at the moment, but is limited to discussing the possible existing techniques within the limitations resulting from the type of activities undertaken by the public sector and the nature of democratic Government. Inevitably a general discussion covering such a wide area must be somewhat superficial; a lot must be taken for granted and it is impossible to go deeply into any of the theoretical problems which arise.

In order to organise the discussion, the public sector is divided up into 4 categories of activity and the type of economic analysis most relevant to each category is discussed. The categories are:

(i)   Public utilities and other trading or quasi-trading activities (pp. 23–6).
(ii) The public provision of health, education and defence (pp. 26–8).
(iii) Intervention in the economy; support of industry, regional policy, etc. (pp. 28–33).
(iv) Income transfers and social security (pp. 33–4).

It is concluded that although there are a number of common elements in all 4 categories, there are significant differences between the types of analysis appropriate to each of them. The paper suggests ways in which more intensive economic analysis could yield useful results.

Introduction
This paper is not concerned with fundamental theoretical issues. This is only partly because some of these at least are discussed by other con-

---

* The views in this chapter are those of the author; they are not necessarily those of the Treasury.

tributors. It is also because I want to look at some of the ways in which economic analysis could, without major new breakthroughs in the subject, be used in relation to the allocation of public expenditure. That is to say I want to go wider than what happens at the moment and to speculate a little on possible roles for economic analysis. But this does involve adopting a position about some fundamental questions – a position I shall set out without attempting to justify. Broadly it is:

(a) In our pluralist society, the idea of overall social optimising is a will-of-the-wisp; there is no one group whose social valuations are obviously preferred to any other; nor is there any unique mechanism by which we decide which group's (or groups') social valuations should dominate at any one point in time. Thus, in practice, economics will be useful in considering small changes in a particular area, against a historically determined background.

(b) That, in practice, microeconomic analysis is – and should be – confined to consideration of market values of costs and benefits, or with valuations which can be inferred from behaviour in a market or quasi-market. Thus it should go a good deal wider than what is currently included in GNP, not only to include items which national income statisticians do not choose to measure at the moment, like the value of housewives' services, but – where relevant – consumers' and producers' surpluses (Harberger, 1971). Important matters like beauty, amenity, national security, culture, social cohesion, etc. can only enter into such calculations in terms of what people are – or might be – prepared to give up to pay for them in the sense of giving up marketable goods and services. But such a valuation may not cover their full social value.

(c) That where markets are functioning badly, either in the technical sense (lack of information, monopoly, etc.) or because there is a clear view that, as a community, we do not want to rely on market mechanisms, specific shadow prices – which differ from market prices or prices derived from market behaviour – are often appropriate. But it would be unhelpful to try and produce and use a large number of shadow prices.

(d) That the structure of valuations and prices given by the existing distribution of income and wealth should broadly be accepted for analytic purposes. Economists will often wish to display income distribution, and the consequences of changes in public policy on income and wealth distribution. (This typically involves fairly complex pieces of economic analysis.) But they will make little progress by trying to construct ideal distributions, or from inferring income redistribution objectives from government decisions and using the results of such exercises in resource allocation analysis.

Also, if I am to say something about the use of economics, I am obliged to have some view about the state of the subject. Our technical knowledge of the economic effects of government activity is extremely limited; we have to make do with inadequately tested models and bad data in constantly changing conditions. Doubtless this will change; it is reasonable to assume that over a number of years a much improved body of knowledge will be built up along existing lines of development. Much of the paper discusses frameworks within which this knowledge could be used. But although I believe our understanding of relevant economic effects will grow rapidly, it will I think still be the case that the application of a piece of economics to a particular problem will continue to require a high level of ingenuity. Currently, the biggest pay-off from using economics comes from applying basic concepts – often little developed from general concepts like opportunity cost – to a specific problem. The implements in the microeconomist's tool-box may be powerful, but they are usually fairly rudimentary; the main return comes from successfully adapting a general purpose tool in order to use it for a specific problem. Usually this involves careful use of economic theory. But inevitably it carries with it very real dangers of over-simplification. As the existing tools are developed and shaped to deal with particular types of problem, the need for over-simplification will be reduced. But the need to make a judgement on what the main elements of the problem are – and hence about how economic analysis could be applied – will remain. Whatever the state of economic knowledge, it is virtually axiomatic that governments will require advice in less time than it takes to do a reasonably satisfactory piece of analysis.

I do not think that there is any useful definition of what constitutes the public sector, nor that it is worth searching for one. Public expenditure could well be defined differently from what appears in the Public Expenditure White Papers. Where the allocation of public expenditure is concerned, there is often little analytic merit in distinguishing between public expenditure, tax reliefs and compulsory private expenditure – the last including not only compulsory payments like third party motor insurance, but all kinds of costs imposed on the private sector by government regulations, e.g. pollution control and land-use planning. So although for some purposes it is appropriate to consider the determination of total public expenditure and then its allocation to different programmes, this is not the way I propose to proceed in this paper. Rather I shall divide public expenditure (as conventionally defined) into 4 rather different categories and discuss economic techniques which are – or could be – useful in each of these areas. Indeed the classification is very largely in terms of type of analysis which seems to me most appropriate to each category. In addition, I shall also discuss a general approach to cost analysis which is relevant both to comparison of the different kinds of costs in the different categories and to overall consideration of the economic cost of public expenditure.

The field is very big and I cannot attempt more than a Cook's tour through it. The flavour of what I want to say can best be conveyed by example. The use of different examples would present a different picture, and I am conscious that mine are drawn from my area of experience and may thus be somewhat unrepresentative.

Classification of types of activity

In order to show broad orders of magnitude, public expenditure (Cmnd 5519) has been allocated to the four categories, although when regulation and/or taxation are so often employed as alternative policy instruments, there are obvious problems about measuring their importance in programmes in terms of expenditure alone. The categories are:

(A) Activities where the public sector is producing a marketable good or service or one that could be marketed, i.e. where we are concerned with private goods where externalities are either not of major importance or can be allocated reasonably satisfactorily to individuals. Nationalised industry capital expenditure and road building come into this category; so does local authority housing investment. Annual public expenditure in this category (primarily capital investment) is currently around £4½ billion.

(B) Activities where the public sector is the sole or primary provider of services, some of which – like defence – cannot be allocated by any sort of market, and some of which – like health and education – we choose not to allocate in anything like a market way. Where income distribution is an object of policy, it works through the allocation of physical resources. Public expenditure in this category is currently around £13 billion.

(C) The area of expenditure where the Government influences resource allocation by paying subsidies to industry, agriculture and housing. But by contrast with categories (A) and (B), public expenditure is only the instrument of policy. Also in this category there is a considerable amount of intra-marginal expenditure, which affects the distribution of income rather than resource allocation. Public expenditure, without taking account of taxation foregone, is currently about £4 billion.

(D) Income transfer programmes. Social security makes up the bulk of this category. Although the prime purpose of these programmes is income redistribution, the social security system also has some resource allocation effects. Public expenditure is currently £5½ billion, but taxation policies are important.

The reasons for such a classification are:

Public expenditure by categories 1973–74

	£ million (1973 survey prices)	
Category A:		
Nationalised Industry Capital Investment	1,815	
Roads and Transport	1,338	
Water and Sewerage		
(includes current expenditure of £87 m.)	430	
Local Authority Housebuilding (net of sales) and		
House Improvement Expenditure, Housing Administration	932	
		4,515
Category B:		
Defence	3,398	
Environmental Services (other than Water and Sewerage)	995	
Law and Protective Services	948	
Education, Libraries, Science and Arts	4,163	
Health and Personal Social Services	3,286	
		12,790
Category C:		
Agriculture, Fisheries and Forestry	576	
Trade, Industry and Employment	1,574	
Housing Subsidies (and Option Mortgages)	650	
Improvement Grants	148	
Housing Loans	434	
Support to Nationalised Industries	575	
		3,957
Category D:		
Social Security		5,458
Residual*		2,213
Total Public Expenditure Programmes (Cmnd 5519)		£28,933

* Overseas Aid, Administration and Northern Ireland
Source: Cmnd 5519, *Public Expenditure to 1977–78.*

(i) on the demand side there are major differences in our ability to measure benefits; and thus in the appropriate types of approach to output measurement or assessment;

(ii) on the supply side there are major differences in how costs may be handled.

Category (*A*) activities are susceptible to normal demand analysis and its extension into measurement of consumers' surplus. Where goods and services are sold, as in the case of the nationalised industries, market behaviour can be studied, either in order to get 'commercial' estimates of demand at 'appropriate' prices, as is relevant to many nationalised industry operations, or as a means of inferring demand (and consumers' surplus) for a non-marketed good or service, e.g. road space, from behaviour in a comparable market.

On the demand side, category (*B*) activities are in a different position. It is not possible to measure benefits from defence by any known technique, nor is it easy to even begin to see how one might be developed. In the case of education, the only work on the measurement of benefit in monetary terms has been social rate of return analysis (Morris and Ziderman, 1971 and Morris, 1976), which has not sought to look at what people might be prepared to pay for education but at production benefits where these are measured in terms of the net additional (discounted) GNP benefits. Such calculations may be very useful, but quite apart from income distribution complications, they ignore significant benefits that people (parents as well as students) would be prepared to pay for. Quite apart from 'non-economic' returns, the technique is inappropriate for the bulk of educational expenditure, i.e. that on compulsory education. There are also public goods' elements in education. There would also be major difficulties involved in measuring the benefits of health expenditure in monetary terms. The redistributional problem, involving transfers between the sick and the healthy, as well as between the rich and the poor, is particularly complex. The demand which the elderly would make for health services at charges which covered costs, is likely to be very closely related to the income support they receive from the State. Hence estimates of demand from the elderly, on the assumption of some hypothetical level of income support, might tell us little more than we could learn by looking at a hypothetical level of provision in relation to conventional (paternalistic) concepts of need, then merely costing it and relying on political judgement. More generally, economists tend to shy away from the concepts of 'need' applied by those in the social services, preferring instead notions of preference. This has its value on a number of occasions, but one should not assume, as economists sometimes do, that it is the central point to the whole analysis. Also, as with education, GNP benefits to health provision (getting people back to work faster, prevention of infectious disease) can be calculated, and indeed such calculations would be useful; but they are likely to be only a small element in total benefits.

Category (*C*) activities are directed to a whole range of objectives: for example, improved resource allocation (regional policy measures to increase productive potential, agricultural subsidies designed to save imports), a faster rate of economic growth (support of technologically based industries), income redistribution (housing subsidies), achievement of public goods type benefits (a 'better' geographical distribution of population), provision of basic essentials of life (house improvement grants), etc. Because such activities are concerned with affecting the operations of markets and not, as with categories (*A*) and (*B*), with governmental provision, any particular element of public expenditure will both affect the output of particular commodities and transfer income to factors of production. Thus the payment of REP seems both to increase employment in particular parts of the country and to leak into wages. One of these effects may be thought desirable and one undesirable; or both may be desirable, yet to differing extents.

The principal objective of category (*D*) is income redistribution. The desirability of personal income redistribution essentially depends on some social judgement; benefit measurement, in the usual economists' sense, is scarcely relevant. But presentation of redistributive effects is not straightforward. For example, public policy is concerned with redistribution over individuals' life spans and not just with redistribution between persons or generations; estimation of the effects of different social security systems on lifetime incomes would involve complex analysis. Moreover, category (*D*) activities also have resource allocation effects; e.g. changing the earnings' rule for pensions may affect the supply of labour. Hence the distinction between categories (*C*) and (*D*) may largely be one of degree.

On the supply side, the major distinction is between categories (*A*) and (*B*) on the one hand, and (*C*) and (*D*) on the other. In the former, public provision means that public expenditure is closely associated with resource use; in the latter, the relationship is more complex.

The resource costs of activities in categories (*C*) and (*D*) bear no close relationship to public expenditure. Two somewhat different approaches are relevant; one is to value the inputs shifted from one use to another as a result of public expenditure. For example, a subsidy to housing will (*ceteris paribus*) lead to an increase in the volume of resources devoted to housing, the amount of resources shifted to housing depending on the elasticities of supply and demand as well as on the rate of subsidy. The other approach is to estimate the resources which the private sector must give up as a result of switching command over resources to those receiving subsidies. In this case it would be necessary to take account of expenditure by recipients of housing subsidies on non-housing goods and services, and of any additional tax paid by them.

I now turn to discuss the type of economic analysis which seems most relevant to each of the 4 categories (*A*) to (*D*).

Public bodies and trading agencies

Traditional public utility economics and cost–benefit analysis play the major role in category (*A*). But a host of theoretical problems arise when general theory is applied to particular problems. While there is a fairly extensive literature on public utility pricing in general and in electricity

pricing in particular, the specific characteristics of some important industries – for example, gas supply or water supply and waste water disposal
– have not been much studied, at least in this country. For example, the
identification of marginal cost is a difficult technical operation in a system
where collection of water in one place affects the cost of collection elsewhere,
and where the water can be supplied either by collecting rain water or by
purifying waste water. If an adequate cost model of the whole system
existed – which it certainly does not at the moment – then, in principle,
marginal costs could be identified, but the construction of such a model
would be a major operation (Water Resources Board, 1973). It is necessary
to estimate a large number of functional relationships between physical
variables, to show how such flows relate to costs, and to incorporate some
cost minimising procedures. Also it is theoretically necessary to know the
elasticities of demand for water and water disposal before the right price can
be set. Furthermore, it may be necessary to identify and quantify externalities (public health issues). Also, in the construction of tariffs some com-
promise will usually have to be made between theoretical perfection and
practical considerations. Take, for example, water supply and waste water
disposal; a strict application of marginal cost pricing where investment is
lumpy might well require tariffs which fluctuated undesirably sharply. Even
when the microeconomic issues have been, so to speak, settled, there
remains the contention that the holding down of nationalised industries'
prices could slow the rate of inflation. The argument is sufficiently plausible
to deserve to be taken seriously; but the practising microeconomist searches
in vain for enlightenment from his macroeconomic colleagues on the influence which such a policy would have on the rate of inflation and on how
the costs and benefits of small changes in the rate of inflation can be
assessed.

How, one asks, can economics be used in such a situation, bearing in
mind that typically there is also a good deal of mistrust about the
recommendations of economists? Initially, there is little to do but set out
simple points about the role of pricing in resource allocation. But this must
be followed up by empirical demand studies which could range in sophistication from simple market research surveys to econometric estimation of relevant elasticities. But while certain simple demand analyses should present
no difficulty (although they are too infrequently carried out), it is well known
that successful estimation of elasticities is extremely difficult and the results
of any econometric studies must always be used with caution. Economists'
involvement in supply side work is also vital if estimates of marginal costs
are to be available. Marginal cost is not a unique quantity in any situation,
even for the text-books. In practice it is necessary to pose and answer a
whole series of questions before we can arrive at an operational notion of in-

cremental cost. Such work will be a combination of economics and commonsense: what is allocable and what is not? What is a sensible unit of output (a passenger on a train, a railway carriage, a train, a railway service between two towns)? Over what time period are costs to be covered, etc.? Sometimes economists only know that there is no unique answer to such questions; but in the primitive state of knowledge which exists, this is not a negligible contribution. Given the highly generalised state of the theory of production and the development of mathematical programming models, I suspect that economists will make most progress if working closely with OR teams.

In the case of some of the nationalised industries, there is more systematic knowledge of relationships, although such knowledge is, in the sense of tested hypothesis, all too scarce and likely to remain so; but one can see how it will grow in time as quantitative methods are increasingly used in management. Also, the answer to so many problems involves extrapolating outside the limits of existing knowledge. For example, any analysis of the position of nationalised fuel industries at the moment must allow for the fact that what quantified knowledge we have relates to oil price levels which we are unlikely to see again.

Decision rules are more of a problem. I have briefly referred to pricing criteria and the difficulty of identifying marginal cost. As the discount rate is to be discussed in another paper, I shall be even briefer about it. But no one can be happy about the intellectual foundations of a public sector test rate of discount. There are not only profound theoretical problems about the relevance of opportunity cost and time preference, about risk, uncertainty and bias, but the empirical basis for any particular rate is too narrow for comfort. It is arguable that the actual number used is less important than the discipline imposed on the decision maker and the requirement to develop relevant information; but it is by no means a wholly satisfactory position to be in.

Cost—benefit analysis is a very useful tool in category (A) activities, partly because the concern is with private (in the technical economic sense) goods and services and partly because redistributional questions are usually not sufficiently important to render the use of market data and producers' and consumers' surplus measurement inappropriate. The distributional issue in cost—benefit analysis has caused a good deal of concern; but on the whole I am strongly inclined to conclude that this concern is somewhat misplaced. Sometimes it may be useful to display the distribution of benefits (and indeed of costs) − but to do more, i.e. to introduce some decision takers' weights, runs the risk that numbers will be invented to justify a decision taken on other grounds. To be useful, I think cost—benefit analysis, like traditional public utility analysis, must broadly accept the existing distribution of income. Thus the main general conceptual problem in cost–benefit work is the comparison of its results with the results of 'commercial' appraisals. Unfortunately, however, there appears to be no straightforward relationship between commercial and cost–benefit returns (Harrison and Mackie, 1973).

But as cost–benefit analysis is particularly appropriate in transport work, I can leave discussion of specific applications to other contributors.

Public provision of health, education and defence

Category (*B*) activities, where public goods and redistribution problems abound, are not ripe for overall monetary benefit estimation. Progress in this field seems likely to be made by using programme budgeting techniques, where output-oriented accounts are linked to measures of intermediate output and to cost-effective analysis.

A few years ago it seemed possible that output or programme budgeting might eventually replace conventional budgeting for all public expenditure. Some progress has been made; the overall Public Expenditure Survey forward budget is on a broad functional classification. Functional costing has been developed in the Ministry of Defence (e.g. Cmnd 5231), and output budgeting in the Department of Education and Science (DES, 1970). PPB has been developed in relation to the work of the Police (Wasserman, 1974). Work in the Department of Health and Social Security on a programme budget for the health services is described in Chapter 13. In other areas, those attempting to develop this tool have run into major problems. It seems to me that there are two major conditions necessary for the development of a useful programme budget; they are:

(*a*) that the use of national resources by the activity is reasonably well represented by public expenditure:
and
(*b*) that output categories can be developed without raising major cost-allocation problems – which an accounting system concerned with the assembly of a large number of figures from diverse places would find it difficult to cope with.

Condition (*a*) is broadly fulfilled for the Defence, Education and Health programmes, but it is very far from being fulfilled in most other areas. In the case of industrial policy, regulations and controls, the machinery of fair trading and competition policy, location restrictions and taxation policy all interact with financial assistance. In such circumstances, little is gained by displaying public expenditure alone in relation to objectives. Devising a total resource budget would be virtually impossible except as an academic exercise; it could only be based on opportunity cost, which would involve postulating different states of the world in order to compare them with the present situation. This would be hard enough to do in the case of company taxation, where the concept of a par situation is imaginable, if difficult to define convincingly. But in the case of regulations, etc., any number of different states of the world can be postulated, several of which have a good claim to consideration. Similar considerations apply to physical planning, anti-pollution policies, agricultural support, housing policies, etc. This does not mean that resource costs cannot be investigated, but suggests that there is little point in trying to pull them together in an overall budget.

Condition (*b*) imposes a limit on how far cost allocation can go. In the case of education, it has been found relatively easy to allocate costs to client groups (i.e. groups of pupils or students), primarily because teacher costs comprise the bulk of total costs and because many other costs bear a relatively fixed relationship (for each type of educational institution) to the number of teachers. But it is quite impossible to allocate costs to the final objectives of education; to increased productivity, transmission of a common culture, social cohesion, etc. In Defence, the functional costing stops at an earlier point. Expenditure on Nuclear Strategic Forces, European Theatre Ground Forces, and other Army combat forces, comprising a total of only 18 per cent of the Defence Budget, is fairly closely related to specific objectives. Other combat forces, which are much more difficult to allocate even to potential theatres of war, amount to a further 27 per cent of the Defence Budget. Nearly half the Defence Budget consists of support facilities of a general kind which cannot be sensibly allocated on any accounting principles. To go further, a quite different approach becomes necessary; this involves the identification of commitments and the estimation of the marginal cost of the changes in capabilities, including associated support facilities, which would be required to meet changes in commitments or changes in the level of commitments. Such an exercise can scarcely be an accountancy exercise; it should almost certainly stop short of full cost allocation.

Programme budgets may provide some of the material for cost-effectiveness studies; but the extent to which they will has often been exaggerated. A programme budget is extremely useful in structuring the past, and in formulating plans involving the broad-brush allocation of resources to broad objectives of policy. But it will only be used in this way if it is reasonably simple and can be produced quickly; otherwise decisions will be taken on the input budget. In order to conduct specific cost-effectiveness studies, additional cost information will usually be required, either by special abstractions or analyses of the regular statistical information, or by collecting special information. There is little to say in general about such studies; the degree of complexity and sophistication which will be appropriate will vary according to the nature of the problem and the extent of our knowledge of the relevant relationships – and of course the urgency of the need for an answer.

Intervention in the economy

Category (C) activities cover a wide range of activities including expenditure on regional policy, support to high technology industry, compensation to nationalised industries for price restraint, industrial training, housing and agricultural subsidies. The appropriate economic analysis differs entirely from area to area, except that it is desirable to have a comparable measure of cost for macro decision making (Treasury, 1972a). Many of the problems are problems of incidence. It is often of much more interest to public policy to estimate the distribution of benefits to a subsidy than to look at it from a narrow cost–benefit point of view. Housing is a particular case of this; there are major housing policy issues which require better economic analysis; but trying to quantify the non-market benefit of housing would not come high on my list. The following two examples are intended to illustrate this. (They also illustrate the general proposition that while economic analysis provides a simple and helpful way of approaching the problem in a broad way, investigation can rapidly become complex.)

The first example concerns the incidence of low interest rates for house purchase. Theory suggests that the price anyone is prepared to pay for an asset which yields a given utility stream and a terminal sum of cash, will be inversely related to the opportunity cost of the funds required to buy it. Therefore, if the Government lowers the mortgage lending rate, purchasers would be prepared to pay more for a given house. If mortgage funds are available and the supply of housing is completely inelastic, the price will in time rise to a point where – for the first-time purchaser – the rise in price cancels out the reduction in the interest rate and where consequently the gains of the policy accrue to existing owners. Any advantage to first-time purchasers may be very short lived.

This simple piece of economics is, of course, not without value. But it needs expansion and qualification. On the demand side, the picture is greatly complicated by transaction costs, which – if search and disruption costs are included as well as financial costs – can easily be 5–10 per cent of the purchase price, and by expectation of future price changes engendered by price adjustments. On the supply side, higher house prices should induce new building. But the supply of existing assets needs rather different treatment from that of the supply of building resources. Where the supply of existing assets is concerned, expectations about the future market prices may be a critical factor. The supply of existing assets (land for building and existing houses released by dissolution or emigration of households, or by a desire to trade up or down) are clearly functionally related to expected future prices, especially where the past rise in prices has been more rapid than interest rates.

In order to show the quantitative effects of changes in interest rates for house purchase, it would be necessary to construct some kind of policy-simulation model. Putting reasonably researched sets of coefficients into such a model would not be easy. Even fairly straightforward estimates on the housing market turn out to be surprisingly difficult to make. Housing models, which appear to fit one set of data quite well, have the nasty habit of breaking down when used outside the time period for which they are estimated. Thus any attempt to go beyond the very general non-quantitative predictions that the bulk of the benefit of lower interest rates will be capitalised in the hands of existing owners would involve a great deal of work on the way the housing sector works.

Another example showing the difficulties into which the analyst so quickly gets when trying to see how the market works is provided by the issue of the size and incidence of the benefit provided to council tenants as a result of setting rents below the market. Such estimates are obviously important, but surprisingly difficult to make properly. Prima facie, the average subsidy per householder is not a very sensible proxy. Traditional incidence theory shows that the division of the benefit of a subsidy between producers and consumers will be determined by relative elasticities (or slopes) of demand and supply functions. But this is not an appropriate model; local authority housing is not produced to the point where supply and demand are equated at the subsidised price; housing is allocated to those whose place in a waiting list is administratively determined. This – allied to the desire of the public sector to raise housing standards above what people might be prepared to pay and the attempt to achieve various physical planning objectives – means that the cash subsidy can easily exceed the difference between actual rents and notional market rents.

But in a situation of administrative rationing, it is not obvious that the difference between actual rents and notional market rents is a good measure of the benefit accruing from Government operations in the market. The extent to which it is or is not depends on the operations of the administrative allocation scheme.[1] Added to this there is the conceptually rather more straightforward but empirically very tricky problem of making an estimate of market rents where there has been scarcely any free market in rented accommodation for over 50 years.

In this situation, there is often a choice between adopting a readily comprehensible and perhaps generally acceptable – but basically wrong – criterion, i.e. the cash subsidies paid, and adopting ingenious – but not entirely convincing – methods of getting some approximation to the correct number. One attempt at approximation might be to calculate, from owner–occupier data, what tenants with similar characteristics (income, etc.) would be prepared to pay for accommodation of given quality, assuming that their demand functions are the same as those of owner–occupiers, and to compare the rent they actually pay with what they would, on this criterion, be prepared to pay. The differences in price would have to be adjusted to allow for differences in the amount of housing actually consumed, as these differences will affect the amount of disposable income available for consumption of other goods and services. But this calculation involves:

(a) a measure of housing quantity. One can think of candidates, of which rateable value is perhaps the best; but none is entirely satisfactory; and

(b) knowledge of the real interest rate; there are the greatest difficulties about this in the absence of a free market in rented houses, when there is credit rationing in the market for owner-occupied houses.

In the area of industrial and regional policy, the main policy need is ability to trace through consequences of subsidies, etc., injected in a particular way. The method of valuing the ultimate benefit in practice often presents less of a problem than working out the connection between government intervention and changes in output – although if intervention is designed to improve the balance of payments, the valuation of exports and imports becomes conceptually involved. When the exchange rate is clearly over-valued, it may be convenient to use a general shadow price (a Foreign Exchange Premium) in such calculations. But in other circumstances, the issue is far from clear-cut; there are a wide range of policies (tariffs, quotas, export credit, agricultural support, etc.) which affect the terms of trade; but as they also serve other objectives, it is not clear that their existence justifies general preference for devoting resources to the balance of payments.

Often a major economic objective is closely associated with wider social objectives. Regional policy is a good example and illustrates how one might set out a framework for analysis. Some of the benefits are straightforwardly economic ones; regional policies are designed to bring into productive employment resources which would otherwise have remained idle, and this produces a gain in productive potential (i.e. GDP can be increased without raising the pressure of demand). Since capital can, in the medium to long term, be regarded as a mobile factor which is always fully employed, the major source of economic gain is the employment of men and women who would otherwise have been unemployed. This is not the same as the net increase in employment in the region, where an assisted project is located; some of the people now employed in the region would, in any case, have found productive employment by migrating to the prosperous areas, whereas others who have been drawn from existing employment in the region may now be used more productively. On the other hand, many of the benefits of regional policy are general social benefits often associated with views about the appropriate distribution of welfare between people in different parts of the country.

It is convenient in such circumstances to transfer the economic benefit to the cost side of the account, deducting it from other costs to provide a net cost, which — as the other benefits are fairly closely associated with additional employment — can conveniently be expressed as the net cost-per-job created. If this is done for each of a variety of regional instruments, it is possible to make rough comparisons of their cost effectiveness.

There are, however, problems about what constitutes cost. This can be seen from the following figure. The demand for a region's output is shown by D and supply at actual market prices by S_0. Supply at opportunity cost is S^*. (The main divergence between market and opportunity cost supply results from the divergence between the actual wage rate and the opportunity cost of labour. The latter, which it is convenient to call the shadow wage rate, must allow for the extent to which increased employment draws labour from the unemployed or those who would otherwise be employed.) Let us assume a government subsidy which shifts the supply curve to S_1. The increment in productive potential — the output of the additional inputs used at actual market values, minus their opportunity (shadow) costs — is given by the horizontally shaded area. The loss of 'private efficiency' — the disadvantage which private producers see in regional production and which must be overcome by subsidies, is given by the vertically shaded area. The net gain is the difference between the two areas. It can be measured by estimating the difference between the actual and shadow wage bill, minus the subsidy which is required at the margin to induce the production of the extra output.

Figure 1

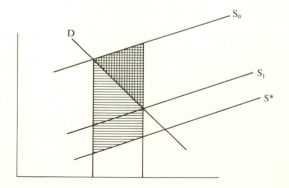

In Figure 1, the subsidy is less than the difference between actual and shadow supply. In Figure 2, the reverse is shown; the optimum subsidy, from the point of view of economic gains and costs, is where $S_1 = S^*$.

But subsidies are rarely only paid at the margin. Intra-marginal subsidies are income transfers, but if the subsidy is paid to all units of a factor (there may be administrative difficulties in paying the subsidy on marginal units only), then income transfers will take place which may not be 'justified' on income distribution grounds. Also, even where such transfers are 'desirable', it may be convenient to estimate the extent to which such subsidies involve a claim by the private sector on the supply of resources. These income transfers can be illustrated by Figure 3. S_1 is set, for convenience, at S^*; the net resource gain is shown by horizontal shading. The transfer to consumers is shown by diagonal left to right shading; transfers to producers are shown by diagonal right to left shading. How much of these cross-shaded areas should be entered as the costs of the policy must be a matter for political judgement; but economic analysis may have useful light to cast on this. Suppose a regional policy becomes necessary because national wage agreements eliminate the regional differentials which may be necessary to ensure full employment, and suppose further that society broadly judges the eliminations of such differentials as 'fair'. Then a labour subsidy designed to lead to full employment would lead to 'undesirable' income transfers if some of it leaked into even higher wages in the region.

Such a 'cost-per-job' approach directs the analysis of instruments of regional policy into two types of operation. The first is the estimation of a shadow wage rate, or rates, which can be applied to the regional employment created by any particular policy instrument. If a standard shadow wage rate could be devised, or perhaps one applicable to a particular type of area, it could be promulgated and used widely by the Government. The second operation is the estimation of the effect of a policy instrument on

Figure 2

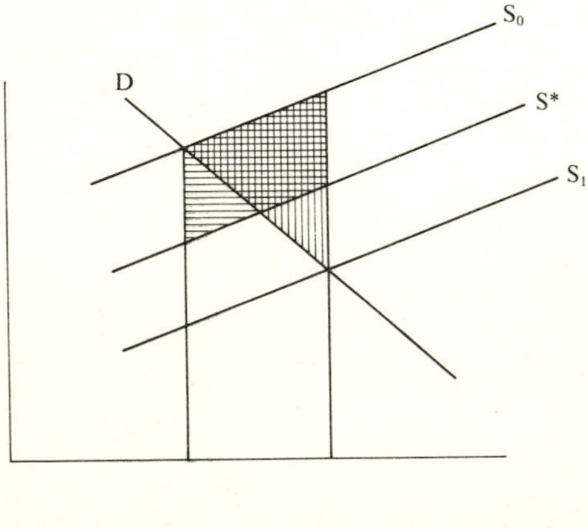

regional employment. There are major problems involved in isolating the employment effects of particular regional policy instruments, partly because of data shortages, partly because of time-lag problems (it is generally recognised that regional policy instruments can only act slowly – often too slowly for the patience of governments), but partly because of a lack of empirically tested theories of production. Many regional incentives operate by subsidising capital, and so the net effect on employment is made up of output and substitution effects. When incentives take the form of expenditure on infrastructure (roads etc.) the analytic problems involved in estimating the effects on firms' operations become insuperable in our present state of knowledge – and are likely to remain so for a considerable time.

The net resource cost-per-job approach is applicable to a fairly wide range of industrial subsidies and assistance, as the employment consequences of giving or withholding assistance are often important. In principle, at least, a number of other economic elements can be readily incorporated. A project which has direct balance of payments' consequences, like support to aircraft or shipbuilding, can be fitted into the framework by applying some foreign exchange premium to the relevant revenue stream in order to adjust the net cost (Treasury, 1972b). But as the aircraft industry example reveals, the net cost will not always be paid to cover the general welfare effects of job creation in a particular area, but for other unmeasurables like additional national prestige. To this extent, the cost effectiveness of various interventions is being inadequately measured. Nevertheless, by applying what are rather sophisticated cost labels, the economist is providing a necessary, if not a sufficient, condition for better decision making.

Income transfers and social security

The issue of the treatment of transfers is perhaps even more important in category (D) activities. Social security payments obviously have

Figure 3

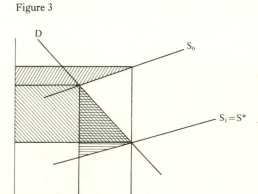

resource effects. Changes in the value of deferred pensions and the earnings' rules for pensioners may change the supply of labour. There are a number of parallels between a change in the earnings' rule and a regional subsidy. A change in the earnings' rule (whereby pensions are abated when earnings rise over a certain amount) will affect some people's willingness to work, but will involve some pure income transfers. As income distribution objectives may already have been met, the change in the rule may involve 'undesirable' transfers. But the main economic impact results from the pure income transfer aspects of social security. There is no objective way of evaluating the overall benefits of such income transfers. The income distribution effects can be displayed for political judgement, although doing so involves a number of problems. For example, there is only limited value to be derived from looking at the distribution of social security payments in relation to current income; they are, in part, designed to compensate for variations in income over a lifetime. But, however one decides to display distributive effects, the economist is concerned with incidence problems, i.e. with the effect of both contributions and payments on wage rates, prices, etc.; with the effect on wage rates of instituting different methods for, or levels of payment for, injuries at work; with the effect of a change from flat rate (employees and employers) contributions to graduated contributions on relative wages; with the effect on prices of relating employers' contributions to the levels of illnesses or accidents which obtain in different types of work. Also, because transfer payments involve calls on incomes earned in the course of production, it is highly desirable to have an overall measure of cost in terms of the use of national resources.

A general approach to the economic cost of public expenditure[2]

Because all transfer payments, like public expenditure on goods and services, involve a call on incomes earned in the productive process, i.e. on GDP, it is necessary to have a general cost calculus which enables transfer payments to be put alongside other public expenditure. Such a calculus also allows many of the different cost elements, discussed in earlier sections of this paper, to be compared with each other. Hence the Treasury has devised a method of measuring the extent to which the public sector is using resources in programmes involving transfer payments, as well as those involving the direct use of goods and services (Treasury, 1972a). The various elements of public expenditure are given demand coefficients which indicate the relationship between changes in a type of expenditure – e.g. on pensions – and changes in the demand on resources. This allows for the fact that the Government automatically recoups some of its expenditure in taxation, either by direct taxes – e.g. income tax on family allowances – or by indirect taxes on expenditure resulting from expenditure by those receiving transfer payments. It also allows for the fact that some of the expenditure will affect saving rather than spending. But the methodology allows only for first round effects; multiplier and accelerator effects are ignored. This is because strategic decisions about public expenditure are usually taken against the background of certain broad objectives of economic policy, e.g. maintaining the internal pressure of demand and the balance of payments. In these circumstances, multiplier and accelerator effects are irrelevant since the implication is that these processes will not in fact be allowed to operate. The relevant question is what has to be done to offset a change in public expenditure if the policy objectives are to be met. For many expenditures this is measured by the 'direct' effect of the expenditure change. If pensions are increased, then other demand has to be cut by the amount of the increase in pensioners' consumption. But expenditures which involve a balance of payments' liability, e.g. expenditure abroad, must be scored in full regardless of their direct impact on the UK economy. (If the balance of payments' objective is to be met, resources must be diverted from the home market and this means that home demand will have to be cut in order to preserve the internal balance.)

Such an analysis can be used either for overall public-expenditure planning within a medium-term macroeconomic assessment (Cmnd 5519), in order to examine the implications of public-expenditure plans for taxation and for privately-financed consumption (i.e. consumption out of earnings and profits), or for consideration of shorter-term increments or decrements in public expenditure. The approach to these two problems would vary. If public expenditure were being used as an instrument of short-term economic management, multiplier and accelerator effects would be relevant. But in such a case it would be appropriate to incorporate public expenditure proposals in the usual short-term model of the economy. The former is a broad-brush exercise, as befits the context. In considering a specific cut or increased package, both the particular demand effects of the package and their timing will be important. But such analysis can also be used in allocation decisions. This requires refinement of some of the coefficients; broad averages can be very misleading in particular circumstances. It is sometimes also desirable to apply demand coefficients to the 'desirable' or 'undesirable' transfers discussed when a cost-per-job approach to regional policy is used.

In many cases, supply side effects can conveniently be incorporated. For example, the effect of the regional employment premium on productive potential would be included in any micro estimate of its claim on the supply of resources. Another example where supply side effects would be important is student grants; an increase might increase the total number of students (or at least affect the amount of vacation work) and hence reduce productive potential. It is not only cash payments which can have these effects; the raising of the school leaving age was associated with a reduction in productive potential, which may have been greater than the public expenditure involved. The amount of refinement which it is sensible to strive for must depend, of course, on the amount of accumulated knowledge of the workings of the relevant markets, as well as on the degree of refinement required for a policy decision. For example, it will be clear from the discussion on housing that quantification of the resource cost (in the sense under discussion now) of housing subsidies would be very hazardous.

Such a calculus is a great advance on looking at expenditure purely in cash terms. Also, as well as incorporating many relevant parts of the tax system, it enables non-expenditure items, e.g. effect on productive potential, to enter into the calculations. But in using the results of such resource-cost calculations, it is of course most important to know who is bearing these costs; typically, these costs are an amalgam of costs to the community as a whole and costs to particular groups. Sometimes the 'group' which bears the cost overlaps the group which benefits. If, for example, the earnings' rule for pensioners were relaxed, the following effects would be likely to take place:

(a) some pensioners would work longer hours;
(b) some people would retire earlier and work part-time instead of full-time;
(c) public expenditure on pensions would rise;
(d) taxation receipts would rise insofar as pensioners' income rose and fall insofar as those retiring earlier earned less.

The monetary gain to the community as a whole (ignoring the value of leisure foregone) is given by the addition to supply resulting from (a) minus (b). Taxpayers would lose insofar as the increment in pensioners' consumption exceeded the increment in pensioners' pre-tax earnings.

Hence although the notion of resource cost enables a number of somewhat different elements to be brought together in a convenient way, it does so at the potential cost of disguising what may be important distinctions. In a sense, these problems arise from the essentially unclear nature of the distinction between the public and the private sector. But some definition of the public sector and thus of public expenditure is inescapable in a world where we have no adequate calculus for measuring the benefits accruing from all the activities of each sector of the economy and a clear notion of the income distribution (in all its dimensions) which society (whatever that is) desires to have, and hence a capability for objectively determining the appropriate level of activity in each sector and the appropriate distribution of all benefits. Such a calculus and such a capability are not only beyond our grasp, but I believe ungraspable.

Conclusions

The following general conclusions can be drawn from the above concerning the directions which economic analysis might usefully take:

(*a*) There is immense scope for work in positive economics directed to getting a better understanding of relevant markets. The housing market is an obvious example, but other examples are the labour market (in relation to education and health policy), and the whole land – and location – market (in relation to regional policy, transport, housing, etc.). Knowledge is scanty, although in some areas it has improved greatly in recent years.

(*b*) There is scope for using the results of market analysis in some areas to impute values to non-traded services (or more strictly to services not always traded). Examples abound in transport; certain environmental factors can be treated in this way. But although some imputation of values is likely to be useful in almost all pieces of analysis, it will not generally be possible to take it to the point where full cost–benefit analysis is possible. This is particularly the case for programmes whose objectives include significant elements of redistribution, as well as for public goods.

(*c*) There is scope for undertaking a fairly wide range of studies designed to establish the incidence of subsidies, etc., where the Government is intervening in a particular market. Such studies would enable costs to be more firmly linked to benefits, and in particular would be a necessary condition for displaying the redistributional consequences of changes in public expenditure.

(*d*) Even where there are significant non-quantifiable benefits, there is considerable scope for developing useful cost analysis. Such analysis will typically involve economic analysis rather than cost accounting. Such costing might take a number of forms:

(i) Estimation of the marginal costs of public utilities. This activity will not become less important if the emphasis in public utility policy shifts away from the 'commercial' approach of Cmnd 3437.

(ii) Allocation of the costs of programmes to objectives, or to client groups (the Programme Budgeting Approach to Health, Education and Defence).

(iii) The estimation of net costs, where measurable economic benefits are treated as negative costs. This technique was illustrated in the regional policy field, but could be very widely used, e.g. the cost of nursery education might be set out net of the production benefits resulting from mothers working, and the cost of health might be estimated net of the production gains resulting from getting people back to work.

(iv) The inclusion of 'undesirable' or 'unintended' transfers in net cost figures where resource allocation policies involve significant intramarginal payments.

(v) The estimation of the full resource effect of changes in transfer payments, such as grants to students.

(e) There is considerable scope for tracing out the economic consequences of administrative procedures for allocating resources. I am indebted to Maurice Peston for suggesting this as a conclusion following from my example of the effect of housing subsidies. But, as he pointed out in discussion on this paper when originally presented, there are a large number of areas where the economic consequences of administrative rules could be traced out.

These conclusions do not suggest a unique theoretical approach to questions of the allocation of public expenditure, nor to the need to develop such an approach. In particular, they show that public expenditure economics goes wider than cost–benefit analysis. This is no accident. Because the paper was designed to discuss ways in which economics could be helpful, it inevitably became concerned with how far economics could take us in a number of rather different areas or activities, some of which have little more in common with each other than that they are all in the public sector. Thus different theoretical approaches are appropriate and an attempt has been made to give examples of them. But the handicap which any author must face is that, so far, so many areas have had so little systematic practical thought directed to their particular problems. The only general moral I would like to draw is the obvious, but unexciting one, that it is – and will be – desirable to approach most specific problems in specific ways. For this, the main need is for much more economics of the kind we already have, where ingenuity is combined with better empirical knowledge of straightforward market concepts like supply and demand.

NOTE

1 The problem can be set up in familiar terms in the following diagram. In a no-subsidy market, a household with the postulated indifference map and a budget constraint *AB* will consume *OD* of housing and *OE* of other goods and services. A housing subsidy changes the budget constraint to *CB*. But the administrative allocation system may prevent the household from switching to housing consumption of *OF* and consumption of other goods and services of *OG*. Within the terms of the model, the household may finish up by consuming any amount of housing between *OH* and *OJ* and of other goods and services between *OK* and *OM*. Thus the subsidy, plus administrative allocation system, can result in more or less consumption of housing than previously. In order to get a solution, it is necessary to specify the workings of the administrative allocation system. Typically, some kind of points system is used and at least some of the points based on household size (points based on factors like length of time on the housing list clearly will not), may bear some relationship to monetary demand. But it is not obvious what the relationship will be; big families need more housing, but they also need more food, clothes, etc. Often they also have low household incomes.

However, it would be necessary to study the dynamics as well as the statics of local authority allocation procedures. Prospective tenants have some choice about council housing; but it is limited. Successive refusals of offers can lead to a household being moved down the housing list.

n.b. The budget constraint is over-simplified in this model. For example, the system of rent rebates under the Housing Finance Act 1972 would produce a budget constraint which is itself a function of housing consumption.

Figure 4

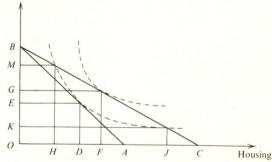

Other goods and services

2 This section reports the approach current in 1974. Since then, Treasury thinking has changed quite significantly. The use of demand effect analysis has become much less relevant. The PSBR, quite correctly ignored in a description of the approach of the early 1970s, has acquired considerable prominence, not only because of its significance in the eyes of the outside world and its relevance to the control of the monetary aggregates, but because in an under-employed economy changes in public expenditure will affect the level of employment and hence of GDP.

BIBLIOGRAPHY

Cmnd 5231, 'Annex B; Functional Analysis of defence expenditure and civilian manpower in 1973', *Statement of the Defence Estimates*, 1973.

Cmnd 5519, *Public Expenditure to 1977–78*, 1973.

Department of Education and Science, *Output Budgeting for the DES*, 1970.

Harberger, A. C. 'Three Basic Postulates for Applied Welfare Economics; An Interpretative Essay', *Journal of Economic Literature*, IX, 3, 1971.

Harrison, A. J. and Mackie, P. J., *The Comparability of Cost Benefit and Financial Rates of Return*, Government Economic Service Occasional Paper No. 5, 1973.

Morris, Vera, 'Investment in Higher Education in England and Wales; a subject analysis', in Baxter, O'Leary and Westoby (eds.), *Economics of Education Policy*, London, 1976.

– Morris, Vera and Ziderman, Adrian, 'The Economic Return on Investment in Higher Education in England and Wales', *Economic Trends*, 211, May 1971.

HM Treasury, Public Expenditure (General) Sub-Committee, 15 February 1972, 'Public Expenditure and Demand on Real Resources', *7th Report from the Expenditure Committee*, 1972a.

– *Forestry in Great Britain*, 1972b.

Wasserman, G. J., 'Applying PPB to Police Expenditure', in W. D. Reekie and N. C. Hunt (eds.), *Management in the Social and Safety Services*, 1974.

Water Resources Board, *The Trent Research Programme*, 1973.

PART II: THEORETICAL ISSUES

3

What discount rate
for public expenditure?

J. S. FLEMMING

Introduction

The recent literature on discount rates for the public sector can conveniently be considered in two parts. The first set of papers construct and elaborate criteria applicable in the public sector when the authorities' rate of discount for consumption benefits[1] diverges from the social marginal product of private investment.[2] This literature might be associated particularly with Marglin (1963*b* and 1967) and Feldstein (1964*a*, *b*, 1974*a*, *b*) but does not originate with them (see e.g. Eckstein (1957) and Steiner (1959)). This approach has been extensively expounded and reviewed in the burgeoning literature of cost–benefit analysis and its applications (e.g. Mishan (1971), Dasgupta and Pearce (1972), Layard (1972), Bates and Fraser (1975). These discussions take the divergence of the social opportunity cost (SOC) and the social rate of time preference (STP) as their starting point; in contrast, the contributions to the second part of the literature develop models with the property that SOC/STP divergence can be shown to characterise the (second-best) social optimum. Of course such divergence does not necessarily imply that the return to investment in the public and private sectors should differ. Where returns are equalised in the two sectors we refer to possible divergence between (unique) social marginal product of capital (SMPC) and STP. However Arrow (1966) and Sandmo and Drèze (1971) have developed different models in which, at the optimum, returns are not equated in the public and private sectors.

The plan of this paper is as follows: section I briefly establishes the second-best criterion appropriate, on certain assumptions, to a given divergence of SOC and STP. Section II reviews the alternative sets of constraints required for the second-best optimum to be characterised by sectoral divergence of return. In particular we will distinguish constraints generating such divergence from those justifying the use in the public sector of a rate different from the STP rate. It will be argued that the former set of constraints are not realistically descriptive of either developed mixed economies or of developing countries. The possibility of savings behaviour generating a second-best situation in which both sectors should use the same rate (not equal to STP) is pursued further in section III. Throughout, the discussion is restricted to closed economies and, for the most part, full employment is assumed.

Since I have indicated that I shall be questioning the relevance of the criteria to be presented in section I it might be useful to deal at once with the predictable response of their defenders since this contributes to establishing the context of the discussion. Feldstein (1974a) justifies a second-best criterion by drawing a distinction between 'ideal' and 'predictive' opportunity costs: the former relate to the best *possible* alternative use, the latter to how resources would *actually* be used. The relevance of this distinction depends on whom one is implicitly advising in one's work. In Britain the public sector is instructed as to the discount rate to use by the Treasury: thus discussion of public sector discount rates is implicit advice for the Treasury. The Treasury is also responsible for overseeing other aspects of the economy and thus neither it, nor a would-be adviser, is entitled to take the difference between the predicted and the ideal for granted – it may be attributable only to Treasury error. It may be that writing with the Army Corps of Engineers in mind, as is the case of much American cost–benefit (water resource) literature,[3] a different approach is appropriate.

I

The first step is to derive an expression for the social value of £1 of private investment when SOC and STP diverge. If p is the social rate of return on private investment (SOC)[4] and r is the authorities' discount rate for consumption benefits (STP) then the social value of a £1 private perpetuity (yielding £p per annum) would be the present value of £p p.a. discounted at r, i.e. p/r, if all the benefits are consumed. Thus in this case the shadow price of private investment

$$V_1 = p/r \gtrless 1 \text{ as } p \gtrless r. \tag{1}$$

If a constant fraction, s, of project output is saved[5] and reinvested at the same rate p, consumption in year t attributable to the original private project is not p but $(1-s)p(1+ps)^{t-1}$. Second year output is $p + sp^2 = p(1+ps)$ since a return p will be earned on the first year's investment of sp, thus second year consumption is $(1-s)p(1+ps)$; hence, discounting the consumption stream at r, the shadow price of a unit of private investment is[6]

$$V_2 = (1-s)p/(r-ps). \tag{2}$$

If there is no divergence between social and financial direct costs and benefits the social present value of a project is now seen to be given by

$$SPV = \sum \frac{N_t}{(1 + r)^t} [V\beta_t + (1 - \beta_t)] \tag{3}$$

where N_t is the net benefit in year t, V is as above (i.e. s, r and p are assumed constant) and β_t is the proportion of N_t diverted from (if $N_t < 0$) or contributing to ($N_t > 0$) private capital formation. On certain assumptions $\beta_t = s$ for all t: more generally it has been suggested that β_t depends on the sign of N_t, being higher when N_t is negative, i.e. when the project requires financial injections (e.g. Bradford (1972)). Furthermore it has been suggested that β_t in this financing phase might vary with the method of financing, typically being assumed higher for debt than tax finance (e.g. Feldstein (1964*a* and 1974*a*), Musgrave (1969)).

Whether or not $\beta_t = s$ for all t a constant value of β makes the sign of SPV at (3) equal to the sign of $\Sigma[N_t/(1 + r)^t]$, i.e. the present value of the project at the STP rate r which can thus be used, it is argued for instance by Kay (1972), and less dogmatically by Bradford (1972), even in the presence of the complications considered. This view is discussed further in section III below.

If we relax the assumption that there is no divergence between social and financial benefits at a particular point in time we have a net social benefit NS_t not necessarily equal to the net financial benefits (cash flow) NF_t: the difference ($NS - NF$) can be defined as the social surplus (SS) of the project. In this way (3) can be generalised as

$$SPV = \sum \frac{SS_t[V\beta_{st} + (1 - \beta_{st})] + NF_t[V\beta_{ft} + (1 - \beta_{ft})]}{(1 + r)^t} \tag{4}$$

where β_s and β_f measure the impact of social surplus and cash flow on private capital formation.

It is interesting to speculate whether social surpluses have any impact on savings behaviour: at one extreme the construction of a neighbourhood playground is unlikely to affect savings positively while taxation to finance its provision would probably do so negatively. On the other hand the surplus arising from the reduction of the cost of a publicly provided private good might lead to an increase in real savings.[7]

II

The authors of such criteria can be criticised for their willingness to prescribe remedies for a disease they have not diagnosed. The failure to account for the STP/SOC divergence means that the criteria proposed involve recommending policies which do not go 'to the heart of the matter' (Bhagwati, *et al.* (1963)). STP/SOC divergence, if it exists, is the symptom of a deeper ill; the response is unappealing[8] to the extent that it will not even alleviate the symptom let alone cure the unspecified disease.

The literature to which this criticism is not applicable is relatively small; in what follows we examine two models which between them incorporate most of the constraints which people seem to have in mind when discussing STP/SOC divergence.

Arrow (1966) (and more rigorously, Arrow and Kurz (1970)) considers the following model:

(*A*.1) There are two types of capital, which are not perfect substitutes in production, one of which is assigned to the public, and one to the private sector.
(*A*.2) Tax revenue can be raised without relevant distortion.
(*A*.3) There is no public debt.
(*A*.4) Private savings depend only on current disposable income.

It is easy to see that the optimal consumption path requires an optimal path for each type of capital but only the time path of tax revenues is available as a policy instrument. The suppression of the time dimension clearly requires rigorous justification, but Arrow has shown that one is, in fact, justified in comparing the number of targets with the available instruments in this case. Assumption (*A*.1) implies that there are two targets, (*A*.2 and 3) that there is only one instrument while (*A*.4) implies that although taxes do not distort, savings decisions do not reflect private, let alone social, optimisation.

Sandmo and Drèze (1971) have a different model:

(*B*.1) is as (*A*.1).
(*B*.2) The only available tax is an income tax with well known intertemporal distortion effects (Baumol, 1968, Kaldor, 1955).[9]
(*B*.3) There is a public debt.
(*B*.4) Consumers' saving is determined as the result of explicit and fully informed private optimisation.

Again a full optimum requires that each capital stock be optimised (Sandmo/Drèze use a two-period model which simplifies the time path). This time there are two instruments but one of them is the distorting tax so that a full optimum is still not attainable.

The constraints in each of these models (*A*.1, 3, 4; *B*.1, 2) are thus just sufficient to generate an *intersectoral* divergence of returns at the (sub-)optimum. The model of section I in asking the question 'what rate is to be used for public projects when SOC ≠ STP?' clearly envisages the possibility that some other rate than the SOC rate should be used; it thus contemplates an intersectoral divergence which could only characterise an optimum if constraints similar to those deployed by Arrow and Sandmo/Drèze are assumed to be operative.

In the following paragraphs I consider the realism of assumptions 1–3 of these models while discussion of different assumptions about savings behaviour (4) is postponed to section III. Since each model has just enough constraints to achieve its purpose my rejection of two in each case (*A*.1 and 3; *B*.1 and 2) is to overkill: it may however provide an opportunity to introduce other objectives such as full employment.

1. Both models assume that output is a function of distinct public and private capital inputs. While the capital stock is obviously heterogeneous, and certain components (houses and furniture on the one hand, dams and tanks on the other) are typically provided by one sector, it is not clear to me that there is a binding constraint here. Public ownership of all means of production is not unknown and even societies that have a political preference for decentralised decision structures could operate without restricting public projects to highways and schools.[10]

2. Arrow's tax does not distort while that of Sandmo/Drèze (and Baumol) does distort private sector intertemporal choice. Since consumption (expenditure) taxes are available I find the Sandmo/Drèze assumption unacceptable as a constraint. While it is true that many countries have income taxes many also have investment incentives and the deductibility of interest for corporation tax is more important than is often realised (Stiglitz, 1973).

3. Public debt exists and Arrow (1966, §VI) explicitly points out that this renders the first best attainable (unless the debt has to become negative in which case we run into difficulties with assumption 1 again). He suggests that introducing a full-employment target means that even if debt is available as an instrument there is a deficiency of instruments; however, if one also rejects assumption 1 this ceases to be true.

Thus despite the formal validity of both the models we have considered, the realism of their postulated constraints, and thus the relevance of criteria such as those developed in section I, is highly suspect. However the sectoral inefficiency associated with different discount rates for public and private investment is not the only second-best feature of possible (sub-)optima. A general savings deficiency may lead to divergence between SMPC and STP and thus between SOC and STP in circumstances in which the public sector should use the SOC rate.

Such a deficiency could arise, even if there were no distorting taxation, if the capital market has features Arrow describes as 'imperfections' but which are almost invariably modelled by savings functions not derived from private optimisation.

III

Arrow and others who make 'imperfect capital market' assumptions typically use a very simple 'Keynesian' consumption function in which disposable income, sometimes lagged,[11] is the only argument. This is clearly not a very adequate representation either of the effects of risk or of the source of the externalities which have bothered Sen (1961 and 1967), and Marglin (1963a). This type of assumption was criticised by Diamond (1968) in a comment on Marglin (1963b).

A vital issue here is the extent to which consumers might anticipate the benefit of public projects and thus offset by reduced private savings any increase in public investment. Since Keynes was working in the short run with given expectations the invocation of his name in defence of the simplest assumption is not persuasive. It may therefore be profitable to explore the more general non-optimising function

$$C = c(Y - T) + dI_g \tag{5}$$

in which, given disposable income, $(Y - T)$, public investment I_g has a positive effect on current consumption. If the investment is tax-financed $T = I_g$ and

$$C = cY - (c - d)I_g. \tag{6}$$

Drèze (1972) has considered a model formally identical to this by introducing debt,[12] and shows that in this case the required rate of return in the public sector is $ar + (1 - a)p$ where a is the fraction financed by debt issue; i.e. the required return is a weighted average of SOC and STP. In our case this condition becomes[13]

$$\frac{c - d}{c} r + \frac{d}{c} p. \tag{7}$$

Drèze points out that his result refutes the conjectures of Feldstein (1965), Kay (1972) and Bradford (1972), who have all suggested that the validity of weighted average criteria is restricted to two-period models. However Drèze does not pursue this result as he is not particularly interested in capital market imperfections other than that introduced by a distorting tax.

The expression (7) indicates that the use of the STP rate r is only appropriate (given the relevant constraints $A.1$–4) if $d = 0$, as is assumed by Arrow, Kay and Bradford. How reasonable is this assumption as a characteristic of consumer behaviour even in the absence of debt?

I believe that $d > 0$ is a more plausible assumption: the principle at stake is similar to that of the effects on personal saving of social security contributions and of corporate retained earnings. On the first it seems eminently likely that taxes to finance higher pensions and more defence respectively would have different impacts on the consumption of a middle-aged consumer. Indeed studies by Feldstein (1972 and 1974*b*) suggest that this effect is substantial and also that shareholders do offset, in part, saving done on their behalf by companies.

Against such a consumption function Kay says that 'it does not seem realistic to visualise current dissaving in anticipation of future benefits of the electricity generation programme'. If one were to ask people 'have you reduced your savings because the government is building so many power stations?' the answer would certainly be negative: but the question does not indicate the relevant choice. If the respondent assumed that what is now planned for power stations would otherwise be spent on gas works his negative response is consistent with Diamond's model. The appropriate question is hypothetical, 'would you reduce your consumption if the government raised taxes to finance extra power stations?' It has to be hypothetical because actual tax changes are dominated by macroeconomic considerations.

Kay also criticises Diamond's assumption from within the framework of his own crude consumption function: if I_g is not explicitly added to disposable income as an argument of the consumption function the hypothesis that tax-financed public investment does not reduce private consumption may be taken to imply $c \approx 0$, and $s = 1 - c \approx 1$; but s near unity raises problems for the boundedness of V_2, the shadow price of displaced private investment, as the consumption stream generated by private investment does not converge if $r < ps$. In (7) the savings effect of public investment is through d which could be made quite large without making s so large as to threaten convergence — s and d are quite independent.

If $c = d$, so that total investment in the initial period is fixed at sY, any change in I_g is fully offset by a fall in private saving (and investment). (7) indicates that the SOC rate is then appropriate even though a part of the benefits is invested. This is because if it returns less than the private investment it displaces public investment and reduces future income and saving. It is possible, however, that the project generates 'surplus' benefits which do not enter into measured income: any such benefits should be discounted at the STP rate, though if, as mentioned above, they also affect private savings an appropriate shadow price must also be applied.

In a similar vein Little and Mirrlees (1969) consider a situation in which a certain proportion of wage income is inevitably consumed: thus the wage content of the income generated by the marginal project adds to consumption. Little and Mirrlees handle this by computing a shadow wage rate that depends on the SMPC/STP divergence and then using the SMPC rate to discount project benefits evaluated at shadow prices. In their model the consumption constraint is assumed to take a form which implies that it will eventually cease to bind; this is also discussed by Dasgupta and Pearce (1972).

IV

The Treasury sometimes appears to base its use of the SOC rate on the assumption (which I question) that public investment must displace private investment, as current consumption (and sometimes even its growth) is 'politically determined.' This might be represented by setting $c = d$ in the model of the previous section and thus indeed imply that the public sector should use the SOC rate. However it is only in the context of Arrow's first model that $c = d$ is a necessary condition for sectoral efficiency to characterise the constrained optimum, and we have already seen that two of the other constraints (A.1 and 3) of that model are implausible. Thus even if one rejects the Treasury's argument one can endorse their conclusion that the same rate should be used in both the public and private sectors.[14]

My reluctance to accept that the first best is beyond the Treasury by virtue of any constraint other than the competence of its official and unofficial advisers, does not imply, in the context of the analysis of section I — where the social return on private investment is taken as a datum — that one should adopt the *given* SOC rate for public sector appraisals. To deny the existence of relevant constraints is not to deny that a practical optimal growth policy requires positive government action and is difficult to design and implement.

Kay suggests that the Treasury Test Discount Rate based on SOC is computationally a 'softer option'[15] than the STP rates he advocates. This might be true for the Nationalised Industry Division if it were told to see that public projects pass the test applied in the private sector (adjusted for taxes etc.): but no government could leave it there; the difficult problem of ascertaining and agreeing the formula[16] for the STP rate would merely be shifted to some other section charged with ensuring SMPC = STP at all times. Only the purest *laissez-faire* assumptions would indicate that this was an easy task: the rejection of several of the constraints considered in section II was not in any way based on the belief that the requirements for *laissez-faire* hold.[17] To suggest, as I do, that policies exist which make the first best attainable in this area (in principle), is not to say that the optimal policy is indistinguishable from no policy.

NOTES

1 Hereafter social time preference, or STP.

2 Hereafter social opportunity cost (of private investment), or SOC.

3 e.g. Eckstein (1958); Krutilla and Eckstein (1958); Hirschleifer, De Haven and Milliman (1960); Hufschmidt, Krutilla, Margolis and Marglin (1961); Maass *et al.* (1962); Arrow (1966).

4 Special assumptions are required if competition in the private sector is to establish a unique social return on marginal private projects.

5 The assumption of non-optimising savings behaviour is central to this approach: see further below.

6 (2) is derived on the assumption that $r > ps$ which is necessary for convergence of $[(1 + ps)(1 + r)]^t$. The consequences of this condition not holding are discussed by Kay (1972).

7 The point is probably not the public/private dichotomy in the sense of Samuelson (1954) but whether the good is sold. Kay (1972) refers to 'pecuniary' and 'non pecuniary' benefits. Probably even more important is whether consumers were previously incurring pecuniary costs to meet the same end as is met by the publicly provided good.

8 Except perhaps as advice to a low level but public-spirited agency in a distorted and decentralised system, see above p. 44.

9 Firms equate the marginal efficiency of capital to the pre-tax interest rate, i, while consumers' marginal rate of intertemporal substitution is related to the net of tax interest rate $i(1 - t)$ so that marginal rates of transformation and substitutution are not equalised.

10 This is the effective burden of criticism by Mishan (1971, p. 218) and Carr (1966) who assume that returns available anywhere in the economy can be captured by a public project. Or do they assume away distorting taxes and savings externalities so that private consumption and investment must always be deemed equally valuable socially?

11 Lags are referred to by Arrow (1966) and analysed explicitly by Kay (1972) who writes, somewhat disingenuously, that they 'incorporate essential features of the life-cycle savings hypothesis' despite their exclusively retrospective nature.

12 If debt D is issued to finance part of the project

$$C = c(Y - T)$$
$$I_g = T + D$$
$$t = aI_g$$
$$C = cY - caI_g$$
i.e.
$$ca = c - d.$$

13 Although in Drèze's case the relative weights on r and p are the tax and debt contribution to the project's financing, on the alternative interpretation (7) the relative weights $c - d : d$ are not proportional to the displacement of consumption $(c - d)$ and savings $(s + d)$.

14 See also Diamond and Mirrlees (1971) for arguments that the absence of lump sum taxes does not justify productive inefficiency.

15 'Easy but irrelevant' versus 'harder but relevant,' *ibid.*, p. 377.
16 A formula because STP depends on expected growth of consumption and population and other things; see Marglin (1963a) and Feldstein (1965): it is not a parameter for macro-planners.
17 To reject the 'imperfect capital market' assumption (*A*.4) would be to move considerably nearer to *laissez-faire* (in the absence of tax-induced distortions): it has not been rejected here. In section II it is argued that it is not sufficient on its own for sectoral inefficiency while in section III we explored a slight generalisation of the usual formulation of non-optimal savings.

REFERENCES

Arrow (1966), 'Discounting and public investment criteria', In *Water Research*, Kneese and Smith (eds.), Baltimore.

Arrow and Kurz (1970), *Public Investment, the Rate of Return and Optimal Fiscal Policy*, Baltimore.

Bates and Fraser (1975), *Investment Decisions in the Nationalised Fuel Industries*, Cambridge.

Baumol (1968), 'On the social rate of discount', *American Economic Review*, vol. 58.

Bhagwati and Ramaswami (1963), 'Domestic distortion . . .', *Journal of Political Economy*, vol. 71.

Bradford (1972), 'Constraints on government investment opportunities and the choice of discount rate', Institute of Advanced Studies, Vienna, Research Mem. 1967.

Carr (1966), 'Social Time Preference vs. Social Opportunity Cost . . .', *Economic Journal*, vol. 76.

Dasgupta and Pearce (1972), *Cost Benefit Analysis*, London.

Diamond (1968), 'The opportunity costs of public investment: comment', *Quarterly Journal of Economics*, vol. 82.

Diamond and Mirrlees (1971), 'Optimal taxation and public production I and II'. *American Economic Review*, vol. 61.

Drèze (1972), 'Discount rates and public investment: post scriptum', Centre for Operations Research and Economics, discussion paper No. 7225.

Eckstein (1957), 'Investment criteria . . .', *Quarterly Journal of Economics*, vol. 71.

– (1958), *Water Resource Development*, Harvard.

Feldstein (1964a), 'Net social benefit calculation . . .', *Oxford Economic Papers*, vol. 16.

– (1964b), 'Social time preference . . .', *Economic Journal*, vol. 74.

– (1965), 'The derivation of social time preference rates', *Kyklos*, vol. 18.

– (1974a), 'Financing in the Evaluation of Public Expenditure', in *Essays in Public Finance and Stabilisation Policy*, ed. W. Smith, Amsterdam.

– (1974b), 'Social security, induced retirement and aggregate capital formation', *Journal of Political Economy*, vol. 82.

Feldstein and Fane (1973), 'Taxes, corporate dividend policy and personal savings', *Review of Economics and Statistics*, vol. 55.

Hirschleifer, De Haven and Milliman (1960), *Water Supply*, Chicago.

Hufschmidt, Krutilla, Margolis and Marglin (1961), unpublished report.

Kay (1972), 'Social discount rates', *Journal of Public Economics*, vol. 1.

Kaldor (1955), *Expenditure Tax*, London.

Krutilla and Eckstein (1958), *Multiple Purpose River Development*, Baltimore.

Layard (1972) (ed.), *Cost Benefit Analysis*, London.

Little and Mirrlees (1969), *Manual of Industrial Project Analysis II*, OECD.

Maass *et al.* (1962), *Design of Water Resource Systems*, London.

Marglin (1963a), 'The social rate of discount', *Quarterly Journal of Economics*, vol. 77.

– (1963b), 'The opportunity costs of public investment', *Quarterly Journal of Economics*, vol. 77.

– (1967), *Public Investment Criteria*, London.

Mishan (1971), *Cost Benefit Analysis*, London.

Musgrave (1969), 'Cost benefit analysis and the theory of public finance', *Journal of Economic Literature*, vol. 7.

Samuelson (1954), 'Pure theory of public expenditure', *Review of Economic Statistics*.

Sandmo and Drèze (1971), 'Discount rates for public investment . . .', *Economica*, vol. 58.

Sen (1961), 'On optimising the rate of saving', *Economic Journal*, vol. 71.

– (1967), 'Isolation, assurance and the social rate of discount', *Quarterly Journal of Economics*, vol. 81.

Steiner (1959), 'Choosing among alternative public investments . . .', *American Economic Review*, vol. 49.

Stiglitz (1973), 'Taxation, corporate financial policy, and the cost of capital', *Journal of Public Economics*, vol. 2.

4

How should we treat risk?*

M. H. PESTON

It is generally accepted that investment decision making in the public sector requires the use of some kind of discount rate. Although controversy continues on whether this should be a weighted average of social time preference and the opportunity cost of capital, or whether it should reflect only social time preference, the opportunity cost aspect being dealt with by a shadow price for capital, it is agreed that the rate should be a riskless one [1]. That being the case, and given that risk is attached to individual investment projects, some other way must be found of taking it into account.

Until recently most students of the subject have treated risk as something to be allowed for, in the sense of a project with larger risk being regarded as inferior, other things being equal, to one with smaller risk [2]). The approach has been to estimate the risk and then deduct something from the present value of the project to allow for it. Alternatively, if such precise calculation were not possible, the decision maker was to be confronted with a description, more or less detailed, of the risks which he could then weigh in judgement against the present value of the project [3].

If it were asked why risk should be allowed for, the answer would be made up of two parts. Firstly, it would be said that the social welfare function, according to which public sector decisions are to be taken, exhibits risk aversion, in the sense of diminishing marginal utility of outcomes. Secondly, it would be said that private sector investment decision making allowed for risk, and preferred less risky projects to more risky ones, *ceteris paribus*. What we have here is, of course, an analogy to the argument about discount rates. Taxpayers are averse to risk, so we must allow for this in public investment. A public sector investment project replacing a private sector one with equal expected discounted present value would lead to a decline in social welfare if it involved more risk.

* I am indebted to a number of participants at the conference for helpful criticism. In particular, this paper has benefited considerably from the contribution of the discussant, Mr Ng.

Now, while this approach appeared unexceptionable, it has been called into question in a remarkably interesting series of articles by Arrow and Lind [4]. In essence their argument is that the risk spread over a sufficiently large number of people becomes negligible so that each project may be considered solely in terms of its expected discounted present value, no allowance being made for risk. An elementary proof of the theorem is as follows.

The government is considering introducing a project, the outcome of which is a random variable Y. A typical individual will then end up with a situation defined by $X + kY$ where X is what he would get in the absence of the project and k is his share of the outcome of the project. For the sake of simplicity we assume that the expected value of Y is zero. (Alternatively, we can follow Arrow and Lind by assuming that the expected value is incorporated in X.)

The individual's expected utility is given by $E[u(X + kY)]$. There exists a certain sum which we will write as $X - P$, the utility of which is equal to this expected utility.

$$E[u(X + kY)] = u(X - P). \tag{1}$$

P may be defined as the risk premium corresponding to this risky prospect.

We may take differentials of (1) to obtain the following expression

$$E[u'(X + kY)Y]dk = -u'(X - P)dP. \tag{2}$$

The expression on the left-hand side may be expanded by Taylor's series to give

$$E\{[u'(X) + kYu''(X)] Y\} \, dk = -u'(X - P) \, dP \tag{3}$$

i.e. $\{E[u'(X)Y] + E[u''(X)kY^2]\} \, dk = -u'(X - P) \, dP.$

The first term on the left-hand side is zero if Y is independent of X and has an expected value of zero.

$$\{E[u''(X) kY^2]\} \, dk = -u'(X - P) \, dP \tag{4}$$

i.e. $\dfrac{dP}{dk} = \dfrac{-E[u''(X) kY^2]}{u'(X - P)}.$

This is positive if $u''(X)$ is negative.

Assume that there are n people incurring the risk equally so that k equals $1/n$. The sum of their risk premiums is given by

$$R = \frac{P}{k} = nP. \tag{5}$$

Consider how R varies as k varies

$$\frac{dR}{dk} = \frac{k\dfrac{dP}{dk} - P}{k^2}. \tag{6}$$

From (4) this may be rewritten as

$$\frac{\dfrac{-E[u''(X)\,k^2 Y^2]}{u'(X-P)} - P}{k^2}$$

$$= \frac{-1}{k^2 u'(X-P)}\{E[u''(X)\,k^2 Y^2] + Pu'(X-P)\}. \tag{7}$$

By Taylor's series this may be expanded to

$$= \frac{-1}{k^2 u'(X-P)}\left\{E[u''(X)\,k^2 Y^2] + Pu'(X) - P^2 u''(X)\right\}. \tag{8}$$

If we expand both sides of equation (1) by Taylor's series we have

$$E[u(X) + u'(X)\,kY + u''(X)\,k^2 Y^2/2]$$
$$= u(X) - u'(X)P + u''(X)P^2/2. \tag{9}$$

The first term on the left-hand side equals the first term on the right-hand side, while the second term on the left-hand side is zero.

It follows that

$$2u'(X)P + (Ek^2 Y^2 - P^2)\,u''(X) = 0 \tag{10}$$

or

$$(Ek^2 Y^2 - P^2)\,u''(X) + u'(X)P = -u'(X)P < 0. \tag{11}$$

In other words, the expression in the curly brackets in equation (8) is negative so that dR/dk is positive. Thus as n increases, R, equal to nP, decreases.

When k is zero, P is zero. In considering what happens to R as n goes to infinity we have zero divided by zero. Applying L'Hopital's rule,

$$\frac{P}{k}\bigg|_{k \to 0} = \frac{\dfrac{dP}{dk}}{1}\bigg|_{k=0}$$

$$= \frac{-E[u''(X)\,kY^2]}{u'(X-P)}\bigg|_{k=0} \tag{12}$$

$$= \frac{0}{u'(X)}\, n$$

$$= 0.$$

Therefore, as the number of people bearing the risk tends to infinity the sum of their risk premiums tends to zero.

Before proceeding it is worth noting that a similar result may be obtained if there is risk preference rather than risk aversion. From (4) dP/dk has the opposite sign to u''. It follows that P is negative if u'' is positive, and k is positive. (Recall that P equals zero when k equals zero.) This means that in equation (11) $-u'(X)P$ is positive, making dR/dk negative. Thus, as n increases R increases to zero.

One additional result may be obtained immediately from equation (10). Since EY is zero, EY^2 is σ_Y^2. We can then see how P varies with σ_Y^2.

$$\frac{dP}{d\sigma_Y^2} = \frac{-k^2 u''(X)}{2[u'(X) - Pu''(X)]}. \tag{13}$$

If $u''(X)$ is negative, i.e. we are dealing with risk aversion, this expression is positive, implying that the risk premium increases with the variance of the outcome.

An alternative and simpler explanation of the theorem may be given in diagrammatic form.

Referring to Figure 1, in the initial situation a single individual bears the whole of the risk. He receives either $0A$ or $0F$ units of income each with probability of one half. This is made up of $0D$ for certain plus DF or minus AD, where DF equals AD. His expected income is $0D$. The utility of expected income is CD. The risk premium measured in units of utility is $CD - \frac{1}{2}(AB + FE)$.

If he gets rid of half the risk, he receives $0D$ plus DF^* with probability $\frac{1}{2}$ or minus A^*D with probability $\frac{1}{2}$. A^*D is half AD and DF^* is half DF. The risk premium is now $CD - \frac{1}{2}A^*B^* + E^*F^*)$.

The risk premium in the first case may be rewritten as $\frac{1}{2}(CD - AB + CD - FE)$. The risk premium for one person in the second case may be rewritten as $\frac{1}{2}(CD - A^*B^* + CD - F^*E^*)$. For two people the total risk premium becomes $(CD - A^*B^* + CD - F^*E^*)$. The difference between the total risk premiums is

$$\frac{1}{2}[(2CD - 2A^*B^*) + (2CD - 2F^*E^*) - (CD - AB) - (CD - FE)].$$

This may be rewritten as

$$\frac{1}{2}[2(CD - A^*B^*) + 2(CD - F^*E^*) - (CD - A^*B^* + A^*B^* - AB) - (CD - D^*F^* + E^*F^* - FE)].$$

In turn this becomes

$$\frac{1}{2}\{[(CD - A^*B^*) - (A^*B^* - AB)] + [(CD - F^*E^*) - (E^*F^* - EF)]\}.$$

Assuming diminishing marginal utility, both differences in square brackets are clearly negative. In other words, twice the risk premiums in the shared situation is less than the whole risk premium in the initial situation.

In an important article discussing the theorem, my colleague, R. Rees, has pointed to some interesting assumptions implicit in it, the general acceptability of which is open to doubt [5]. To begin with, the project is one the total benefit from which does not vary with the number of risk takers involved. It would be, for example, a nationalised industry investment of which the surplus over costs would accrue to the general taxpayer, on whom would also fall any deficit. If, at the other extreme, it were a public good, the benefit or cost to the individual would not wholly depend on the number of

Figure 1

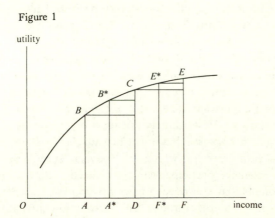

other people participating. The utility function for the typical individual would be $u(X + Y_1 + kY_2)$. If Y_1 itself is a random variable, $u(X + Y_1)$ would be less than $u(X + \bar{Y}_1)$. Thus, in equation (9) the first term on the left-hand side would not equal the first term on the right-hand side, and there would be an additional finite risk premium to be taken into account for each individual. Thus, the risk premium for society would not be zero. Note, of course, that as long as Y_1 and Y_2 were uncorrelated, the risk premium due to Y_2 would still tend to zero. It is also worth noting that the risk premium attributed to Y_1 will depend on the correlation between Y_1 and X.

A second point is that for some projects the relevant benefits and costs may not be spread over the whole population, and the benefits may not accrue to the same group that the costs fall on. If the potential benefiting groups are small, they may not treat the project as equivalent to one with the same expected benefit. They may prefer, for example, the status quo to a change generating a positive expected benefit. Similarly, the potential cost-bearing group may prefer to pay a larger cost for certain than the expected cost of the project. Thus, it could easily happen that the aggregate expected benefit exceeded the aggregate expected cost of the project, but that it did not increase expected social welfare.

Thirdly, an important step in the argument concerns the independence of X and kY, respectively, the individual's initial income and the extra that he gets as a result of the project. In getting from equation (3) to equation (4) these are assumed to be independent. If they are not independent, it is easy to show that the theorem need not hold, and that the sum total of the risk premiums may tend to a positive constant.

These and other points that Rees makes limit the proposition that the public sector should not allow for risk in its investment decision making, at least insofar as it is based on the Arrow–Lind theorem. There is, however, a little more to be said by way of interpretation.

Consider a number of people deciding on a risky project. The value they place on it depends on their attitude to risk, and, assuming risk aversion, this will be less than the expected money value of the project.

If the expected money value does not vary with the number of people involved, the risk premium will vary inversely with the number of participants in the equity. It will be a minimum when that number is a maximum, i.e. when it equals the total population. The effect of the market mechanism is to move the decision criterion closer to maximising expected present values of net money benefits. This suggests that in the private sector all people will participate in all risky projects for which the independence assumption holds. In fact, such extensive participation is not usual. The reasons are many. The obvious one is that the independence assumption may not hold. Another is that there may be organisational and transaction costs involved in increasing the number of participants. There may be disagreements between potential participants on the nature of the risk, and the basic success of the project may depend on secrecy concerning its various outcomes and their likelihoods. Related to this is the problem of moral hazard, and the extent to which the outcome is under the control of some of the shareholders.

Nonetheless firms in the private sector have large numbers of shareholders, and it is well known that people incurring risks can sell part of them to others to their mutual benefit [6]. It might be thought, therefore, that risk premiums in the private sector would not be very high, and that a project taken from the private to the public sector would not, thereby, need to be discounted very much less for risk. Clearly, if there were considerable discounting for risk in the private sector and none in the public sector, *ceteris paribus*, the government would place a higher expected value on any project than its private sector participants did. This means that it would pay all concerned for the government to buy at least a share of the risk. (Essentially they would be doing this to compensate for market failure in the private sector.) They will value the share they take at its expected money value, while the original owners will value it at something less. How much the government takes up depends on this difference and also the method of finance that is used. If the number of participants is very large and the private risk premium very small, the share that the government buys will be small. In other words, government action depends on the extent of market failure.

A further comment must also be made about moral hazard. The outcome of the project may not be independent of whether or not the government finances it. On the one hand, the activities of management may change, possibly for the worse; on the other, the government may be tempted to rig the market situation of the enterprise, granting it special privileges.

A different but related point to bear in mind is that, despite apperances, the risks being discounted in the private sector may not be those borne by the shareholders, but by the management. Even though there may be enough equity owners to justify from their point of view a concentration on expected money values, management may see some risks as falling particularly on themselves. Examples would include the possibility of bankruptcy, and low cash flow. It could happen, therefore, that comparing two investment programmes, the shareholders would be better off with one having a higher expected value (if they knew about it), but management chose one with a lower expected value in order to make their own position safer.

In sum, even if the Arrow–Lind theorem held it would not necessarily imply a great deal about public ownership. It is also worth emphasising that even where public shareholding is indicated, this does not mean that the investment project in question should actually be undertaken by the public sector. The theorem is at least as relevant to the operations of a state investment company as to outright nationalisation.

More generally, if the Arrow–Lind theorem holds and private sector risks are optimally dealt with by the market, there will not be much discounting for risk in either the public or private sectors. If there is market failure and high premiums for risk in the private sector, welfare may be raised by public sector equity participation in private enterprise. It may also be raised by substituting public investment for private investment.

This leads me to my final comment. I would hypothesise that there is much more alleged discounting for risk than can be explained by market failure of the kinds that have been discussed. Firms are sufficiently large, risks sufficiently independent, and markets extensive enough to suggest that objective risks expressible in probability distributions would be largely taken care of in terms of the Arrow–Lind approach and the various theorems concerning the optimal allocation of risk. One is left with the view, therefore, that most so called discounting for risk is an attempt to cope with what is properly to be called uncertainty. This is what Keynes was discussing in his chapter on 'The State of Long-Term Expectation'. To quote him: 'human decisions affecting the future, whether personal or political or economic, cannot depend on strict mathematical expectation, since the basis for making such calculations does not exist' [7]. Now, while it might be thought that Keynes was going too far, in that he comes close to arguing that there is no such thing as risk, it is apparent that the market behaving as well as it can is strictly limited in its capacity to deal with uncertainty. (Again, reverting to a point made earlier, the relevant uncertainty may be that affecting management, as may be the relevant decision criteria.) Moreover, in the public sector spreading uncertainty over a large number of people does not necessarily reduce the extent to which it has to be allowed for.

This is easily shown by an example. Consider a payoff matrix, A, the rows of which correspond to a series of mutually exclusive investment projects and the columns to alternative states of nature. The matrix $(1/n)A$ may be regarded as the payoff to a single person in a population of n individuals. To take the simplest case, corresponding to that discussed by Arrow and Lind, suppose all the people involved have the same utility function and the same decision criterion under uncertainty. Each of them will choose the same project as best, and this will be the same as the choice by the government applying this criterion to the matrix A. Now, if this decision criterion implies uncertainty avoidance (i.e. it is based on maximin or minimax regret), it will do so independent of the number of people affected by the uncertainty.

My conclusion, therefore, is that Arrow and Lind make an extremely important point concerning the public sector treatment of risk. They also remind us of the essentially second-best character of the problem, and the need to examine public policy with respect to the market allocation of private sector risk. Nonetheless, it is probable that the chief problem arising from lack of certainty is uncertainty, and here the Arrow–Lind theorem is less helpful and may be misleading.

REFERENCES

[1] Layard, Richard (ed.), *Cost Benefit Analysis*, Penguin, 1972.

[2] Prest, A. R. and Turvey, R., 'Cost–Benefit Analysis: A Survey', *Economic Journal*, vol. 75, 1965, pp. 685–705.

[3] Merrett, A. J. and Sykes, Allen, *The Finance and Analysis of Capital Projects*, Longmans, 1963.

[4] Arrow, K. J. and Lind, R. C., 'Uncertainty and the Evaluation of Public Investment Decisions', *American Economic Review*, vol. 60. pp. 364–78.

[5] Rees, R., 'A Note on the Arrow–Lind Theorem', unpublished, 1973.

[6] Arrow, K. J., *Essays in the Theory of Risk-bearing*, North-Holland, 1971.

[7] Keynes, J. M., *The General Theory of Employment, Interest, and Money*, ch. XII, Macmillan, 1936.

5

Income distribution and public expenditure decisions*

ALAN WILLIAMS

1   Introduction

Because the title of my remit is potentially misleading, I had better start by indicating which aspects of this vast topic I am going to tackle, so as not to be accused of luring unwitting readers into wasting valuable time on this chapter in the hope of gaining some enlightenment on problems which I have no intention of dealing with.

I start from the observation, in Byatt's contribution to this volume (p. 25), that

> The distributional issue in cost–benefit analysis has caused a great deal of concern; but on the whole I am strongly inclined to conclude that this concern is somewhat misplaced. Sometimes it may be useful to display the distribution of benefits (and indeed of costs) – but to do more, i.e. to introduce some decision takers' weights, runs the risk that numbers will be invented to justify a decision taken on other grounds. To be useful, I think cost–benefit analysis . . . must broadly accept the existing distribution of income.

My purpose in what follows is to discover what, if anything, we as economists can positively contribute to the solution of this problem, and to explore how any such bright ideas might be taken on board within the rubric of cost–benefit analysis. By 'positive' here I mean to indicate that I intend to exclude from this particular paper any contributions we might make to this dialogue in other roles, such as political advisers or philosopher–kings. Our public image notwithstanding, I believe that economists generally are as sensitive as any other group in society to matters of equity or fairness or justice, and have as much right as anyone else to argue for or against the adoption by the community of particular ethical or behavioural or

* This paper is partly based on work done under the auspices of the Public Sector Studies Programme at the Institute of Social and Economic Research at York, financed by the Social Science Research Council.

procedural norms. But while we have as much right to be heard in this kind of debate as anyone else, we have no right to claim special expertise. But when it comes to the economic implications of adopting a particular stance, then we can make such a claim, and it is in this 'consequential' area that I wish to pitch this discussion.

To do this we need to be rather more precise about what the problem actually is, just in case it turns out not to exist or to be rather different from what it seems to be at first sight. We also need to decide whether Byatt is right in believing that concern over it is 'somewhat misplaced'. This is the subject matter of section 2 of this paper. Then, in section 3 I go on to consider various analytical devices which might be imported into the appraisal of public expenditure to satisfy any concern we might nevertheless feel. Then in section 4, I outline a rather different strategy for coping with some of these problems, and suggest that some redirection of effort and ingenuity by economists might lead to more fruitful results than continuing to concentrate on devising suitable sets of weights for use in cost–benefit analysis.

2   **What is the problem (and can we ignore it)?**

If, as in the orthodox view,[1] cost–benefit analysis is seen as the practical application of the 'new welfare economics', operating in a strict Paretian framework, then, put very crudely, what a cost–benefit study is doing is

(a) estimating what is the maximum that the beneficiaries would be prepared to pay for the benefits they will enjoy;

(b) estimating what is the minimum that the maleficiaries would be prepared to accept as compensation for the costs they will suffer;

(c) subtracting costs from benefits to see if the balance is a surplus of benefits over costs or vice versa.

The implication is clearly that any scheme offering a prospective surplus of benefits over costs should be carried out, but not any which offers a prospective surplus of costs over benefits.

This implication follows if and only if

(a) all relevant costs and benefits have been included and properly evaluated;

(b) any divergence between potential and actual compensation is of no consequence; and

(c) the Paretian criterion (at least one person would consider himself better off, and none worse off) adequately takes care of distributional norms.

Let us admit that it is unlikely in practice that all (or indeed any) of these conditions will be fulfilled. In the first place it is not going to be practicable to investigate all ramifications of a scheme *a l'outrance*. There will always be some *de minimis* conventions which determine the level at which repercussions are judged not worth pursuing further, and, more seriously, there will be some items which are regarded as irrelevant by the decision takers but which may assume considerable importance to others. An even more intractable set of problems arises over items which are not readily made commensurable in money terms, and where intuitive judgements consequently play an important role which may be difficult to make explicit. As regards the second condition, compensation mechanisms are not so well developed that we can be confident *either* that all significant losses will be actually compensated *or* that such compensation will be at the expense of potential gainers rather than at the expense of the community at large. The third condition is also suspect, as witness the widespread prevalence of strongly held views about the degree of inequality in society (which means that some 'Pareto-preferred' changes might be ruled out because those better off as a result of the change are the people who are already regarded as 'too well off'), and the recent upsurge of interest in these matters in the literature,[2] stimulated partly by Rawls' advocacy of the rule that only distributional changes favoured by the worst off should be accepted.

What crumbs of comfort are then to be gleaned which would justify continuing to use this simplest cost—benefit format in the face of these apparently damaging admissions? One source of consolation is to be found in adopting the philosophy of the *optimistic pragmatists*,[3] which might be summarised as follows:

Although on any particular occasion a scheme may benefit some at the expense of others, so long as every single scheme passes the *potential* compensation test, and given the fact that thousands of schemes are carried out each year affecting a wide range of activities and locations and with a great variety of purposes, it seems highly probable that any adverse distributional consequence of one scheme will be offset by the favourable distributional consequences of others, so we can afford to ignore the distributional consequences when appraising any particular scheme.

This is obviously a very comforting doctrine, which it is tempting to espouse not only for the reasons stated, but also because to go further into the problems of finding suitable distributional weights is extremely daunting as a technical exercise, and is therefore likely to be extremely costly (and possibly even humiliating!). But the temptation should nevertheless be resisted, because it requires us to accept some propositions which are rather hard to sustain.

The most important of these propositions comes in two variants. The weaker alternative is that the existing distribution of real income is socially acceptable and the cumulative effect of all projects is neutral. This appears to be Byatt's position. The stronger variant is that the existing distribution of real income may not be socially acceptable, but the cumulative effects of all projects is corrective. The chief consideration making this latter position seem even harder to sustain than the former is that, even if the avowed purpose of a significant proportion of all projects were to correct the distribution of income, there is evidence, from the few that have been studied intensively with respect to their distributional effects, suggesting that they probably had distributional consequences opposite to what was intended.[4]

But even the weaker variant, which only entails reliance on a kind of 'random walk' hypothesis, depends on there being no systematic bias (with respect to distributional matters) in the generation and selection of projects. Just suppose it were true (as I suspect it is) that projects are typically 'promoted' for analysis by the better-off professional groups in society (so that even projects with altruistic purposes will be based on the notions of 'deservingness' which that particular group holds) and are likely to be ones where prima facie the *benefits* are pretty 'obvious', i.e. they are readily identifiable immediately and accrue in a fairly concentrated way for particular interest groups (e.g. better roads for motorists) rather than being vague in their nature, remote and diffuse in their incidence (e.g. anti-pollution projects). Conversely, if the *costs* of any projects appear prima facie to be clear and concentrated, then such projects are more likely to be opposed at an early stage in the political arena (or suppressed at the administrative stage for fear of adverse political repercussions) than if such costs are vague and diffuse. Furthermore, if the people bearing these concentrated costs happen to be fairly well off, they can afford to commit resources to political action opposing them which poor people would not be able to spare. So the combined effect of these informal selection filters is that the projects most likely to get put forward for serious analysis and eventually accepted are those which are believed to offer obvious benefits and not-so-obvious costs, unless more obvious costs happen to fall on the relatively defenceless.[5]

This leads directly to the next observation, which is that there is increasing evidence that certain groups in society tend to be persistently 'disadvantaged' despite the vast array of social policy measures ostensibly designed to help the worse off (e.g. rehousing, rent subsidies, free compulsory education, health and welfare services, social security payments, etc.). The growing concern[6] with 'multiple deprivation', and, still worse, with 'transmitted deprivation', suggests that there may be an important flaw somewhere in the empirical foundation of the stance adopted by the 'optimistic pragmatists'.

Finally, a rather heroic act of faith is required to suppose that the cumulative distributional effects of public projects are neutral (or *a fortiori* favourable) when we have not yet analysed a large enough sample of such projects to have any firm basis for such a supposition. Moreover, if we accept it as a working hypothesis we never shall have such a sample,[7] so we shall remain in perpetual ignorance, which may be good for our faith, but is unlikely to be particularly helpful to the more rational conduct of public policy.

So I conclude that there *is* a problem which we cannot ignore and that analysts have got to grapple with it. I will consider the possible responses in two stages: firstly the identification of the incidence of benefits and costs, and, secondly, their evaluation. I shall then suggest another possible escape route, which, if it succeeded, might make optimistic pragmatists of us all!

3   **Measuring and evaluating the incidence of benefits and costs**

Most writers on cost–benefit analysis have come to the conclusion that, for at least some projects, the major distributional consequences must be displayed for consideration by decision makers, since they will almost certainly be interested in them.[8] No evident agreement exists, however, on how far the analyst should go, or how he is expected to solve the incidence problems which have plagued the theory of public finance from time immemorial.

The writer who has consistently adopted the most radical stance on the appropriate nature of the cost–benefit framework with respect to incidence matters is Lichfield (1962, 1971). The essence of his 'planning balance sheet' approach is that 'producers' and 'consumers' of both costs and benefits are separately identified throughout, and the outcome is presented as a matrix of effects, tangible and intangible, which the decision maker has to appraise as best he can (and, Lichfield would doubtless add, as *only* he can!). Thus the appropriate subclassification of the community for incidence purposes enters the process of analysis *ab initio*, which is markedly different from the usual approach in which the 'efficiency' calculus is done first, then, as an optional extra, authors examine the distributional effects almost as an afterthought. I think that 'mainstream' cost–benefit analysts have been suspicious of the 'planning-balance-sheet' approach because of its failure to distinguish 'technological' from 'primary' spillovers (or 'primary' from 'secondary' effects) hence leaving itself vulnerable to the danger of double counting. It seems as if our desire to eradicate the early errors of multiple counting of benefits in an *efficiency* calculus[9] may have led us into a rather purist stance which has made it more difficult for us to respond appropriately to questions about *incidence*. Yet it has never been denied that these 'pecuniary' or 'secondary' effects were relevant for incidence calculations,[10] and these have been central to Lichfield's interests.

Short of this rather radical recasting of approach the more typical response is to attempt to 'display' the distributional effects in the form of supplementary tables after the efficiency calculus has been described and presented. This is consistent with the basic conceptual notion that the distributional considerations constitute a set of 'constraints'[11] bounding the 'feasible' set of solutions, so that any outcome satisfying these conditions will be checked 'OK on distributional grounds' and the efficiency calculus will then be used to select which of the 'OK' projects within this set will be undertaken.

Although this is doubtless a caricature of the situation, it is surely close enough to reality to be recognisable as familiar by experienced practitioners, whose first task then becomes to divine what particular distributional sensitivities their particular decision makers exhibit.[12] As has been pointed out many times by others,[13] these sensitivities may not only relate to 'rich' versus 'poor'. Inter-racial, urban versus rural, 'depressed' versus 'prosperous' areas, inter-industrial, inter-state, inter-national and many other subdivisions of society may equally well be relevant. This all adds up to a big job for the analyst, and one that we are not all that well equipped to undertake if a very high degree of accuracy is called for. Perhaps our chief consolation here lies in the thought that even a modest foray might be extremely useful since it is clear that there is plenty of light to be shed in this murky zone.[14]

Setting aside these qualms, however, we move quickly into the territory in which the basic conceptual stance is one in which both efficiency and equity considerations are integrated into a well-articulated social welfare function. This is the underlying rationale of those[15] who argue for an explicit set of weights to be postulated, or derived by calculation, to enable us to fuse the separate incidence statements into a one-dimensional criterion for choice.

Several different approaches are possible to this problem (leaving on one side the approach of recommending one's own favourite set of weights). The most a priori and agnostic approach consists in postulating a variety of weighting systems, exploring their implications, and seeing how the decision makers react. This has the advantage that it gives analysts plenty of scope for displaying creative imagination and technical virtuosity without overstepping the bounds of positive economics. It has the disadvantage stressed by Kneese (1968) that it offers too much scope for special pleading ('poverty can become every special-mission-oriented agency's hobby-horse'), a view echoed by Lichfield (1971) with respect to the Roskill Commission and by Byatt in the quotation with which I opened.

One way of limiting the range of possible weights to be considered, is to try to infer the system that is implicit in some past discussion. This too generates problems, however, such as (a) whether there is one unique set of weights to be inferred, (*b*) whether the actual consequences from which the weights are inferred were the intended consequences, and (*c*) whether views might have changed in the meantime. Foster (1973) has vividly described the difficulties that are likely to be encountered in trying to unscramble the past in this way.

A variant on this approach is to take some device which the community uses to effect redistribution, and to try to infer from it what society's weights are. The marginal rates of income tax are the favourite candidates for this kind of treatment, but these suffer from the marked disadvantages that they are not determined purely with distributional objectives in mind, and they are only part of the whole tax/transfer system anyway, and to seek implicit weights by analysing the whole system involves an even bigger job than the enormous one we are already trying to tackle. At this stage a philosopher–king usually stands forth to *recommend* particular sets of weights, casting off the shackles of positive economics in order to play the more congenial role of policy adviser.[16]

4   Back to square one?

It is clear that extensive intellectual investment is going to be required (*a*) to develop techniques of analysis to the point at which each new study does *not* have to incorporate a major breakthrough in order to be successful, (*b*) to apply any such techniques over a wide enough range of real-life problems to feel confident that all the possible snags have been encountered, and (*c*) to persuade decision takers that it is now both safe and useful to incorporate the particular distribution weights so derived into the analytical routine. It therefore looks as if we are in for a long haul. Meanwhile, public expenditure decisions with possibly important (but nevertheless obscure) distributional consequences will continue to be made and implemented. What should be our strategy in this situation?

I have come round to the view that we shall have made a small but important immediate gain if we can merely ensure that the major unintended[17] distributional effects of public projects *are* neutralised, by putting renewed emphasis on devising and implementing better compensation arrangements. After all, our initial difficulties over distributional matters stemmed partly from the fact that the efficiency calculus works on *hypothetical* compensation tests, while the distributional calculus works on *actual* compensation arrangements, and there is often considerable divergence between the two. So we should, perhaps, re-examine the scope for improving compensation arrangements so as to narrow this gap, since even small improvements on this front may lead to disproportionately large reductions in people's sense of injustice.[18]

The standard arguments against extending the scope, or increasing the generosity, of compensation schemes are

(*a*) that the legal/administrative costs of the quasi-judicial procedures inevitably entailed are high in relation to the compensation flows;
(*b*) that there are a variety of adverse incentive effects which impose 'excess burdens' of one kind or another on the system;
(*c*) that the financing of such schemes may create additional inequalities or inefficiencies;
(*d*) that the information demands are just as great as for the incidence calculations which I have set aside in the short run as too costly and time consuming.

The force of each of these objections needs therefore to be re-examined.

The extent of legal/administrative costs clearly depends on the complexity of the scheme, the contentiousness of the subject matter, and the litigiousness of the participants. It is certainly true that some mechanisms for the recovery of compensation have been reported as absorbing a large fraction of the sums awarded[19] and if this is true it points to the adoption of cruder, but easily implementable, formulae which can be applied on a discretionary basis in the typical circumstances of particular sorts of public project rather than relying on complex and finely-tuned all-purpose systems which are likely to generate a great deal of precedent-setting disputation.[20] It is clearly possible to devise such all-purpose rough-and-ready systems, as witness the arrangements set up in the 1965 Redundancy Payments Act.[21] Indeed, the latter scheme highlights a fundamental characteristic of the situation which is strongly stressed by Michelman (1967) as well as by many other writers in this field, namely, that in arguing for more widespread and more generous tests of compensatability we are essentially arguing for a more appropriate definition of property rights in society.[22] These ethical issues are of the form: under what conditions does an individual have the 'right' to (or 'legitimate expectation' of) continuance in employment *in a particular job*, or to the enjoyment of the particular characteristics of a particular place of residence? Important though these ethical issues are, I am arguing for more effort to be diverted to finding less costly ways of enforcing the rights we have already agreed people should have (or even *do* have, in principle if not in practice).[23]

The arguments concerning possibly adverse incentive effects from redefinition of these rights certainly have some force, in the sense that one would expect behavioural patterns to change, and not always in a manner consistent with other social objectives.[24] But in a second-best world the existence of such effects is not *per se* fatal to such schemes. We need to weigh, say, the incentives to 'premature' retirement, to temporary (but prolonged) withdrawal from the labour market generated by more generous redundancy compensation arrangements against the avoidance of the hardship, sudden disruption of life style, and precipitate entry into unsuitable alternative employment which the absence of such schemes might entail. Equally, on the financing side, we need to weigh all these considerations against any adjustments generated by high tax or contribution rates (which, again, in a second-best world, may not all be socially adverse).

Whether the information requirements for such piecemeal and ad hoc compensation schemes are greater or less than those required for the major incidence studies which would underpin the 'grand efficiency calculus' is a moot point, which can only be settled when specific compensation proposals are under discussion. One great advantage in favour of the latter, however, is that they give individuals a stronger incentive to reveal their situation in the relevant degree of accurate detail, and to do so directly and privately rather than through political agitation and public posturing, and this fact alone offers far more scope for generating researchable data than does the 'dialogue with decision takers' which is the essence of the alternative approach. The 'dialogue with decision takers' will, of course, still take place, but when it does it will be that much more reliably informed on likely consequences than if one relies exclusively on the statements of 'attitude' or opinion as the basic data on which the political system works.

In arguing for more effort to be put into improving *actual* compensation arrangements I do not wish to imply that these ideas are in any way original[25] or that work is not already going on in the area of endeavour to which I refer. In Britain there have been some promising recent developments, both analytical and practical, in the field of compensation arrangements, in which, at a technical level, lawyers, administrators and economists have all been active, as well as other professional groups (such as planners, social welfare workers and medical personnel). The development of ideas and practice in the field of personal injury was reviewed recently in Lees and Shaw (1974), and developments in the urban planning field are well epitomised in Chapter 19 of the Department of the Environment Report of the Urban Motorways Project Team (1973) and in Davies (1974), both of which indicate the current pressure on 'the social treasury' to go further than hitherto in accepting responsibility for helping the unwitting victims of schemes that are pursued 'for the public good', while at the same time indicating very clearly the obstacles to progress, both conceptual and practical.

It seems to me that economists have a potentially fruitful role to play here, both as critics of existing practices, and, what is rather more difficult and challenging, as members of multidisciplinary research teams and working parties seeking to bring about tangible improvements in compensation mechanisms. Thus when it comes to making better provision in public expenditure decisions for their unintended distributional consequences, I suspect that there will be a greater immediate pay-off for society if economists devoted relatively more time and energy to collaborating with lawyers and administrators in devising improved mechanisms for compensation, than from additional resources devoted at the margin to eliciting 'grand efficiency' weights from politicians and other decision takers. Such a statement can obviously be no more than a personal judgment, conditioned by the circumstances of a particular society at a particular historical stage in the development of its social investments, and so is not promulgated as a general rule applicable to other societies, or indeed as a timeless truth for Britain. Perhaps, less grandiosely, it should simply be seen as a little plea to those professional colleagues who are looking for fresh fields to conquer to give this one more than passing consideration.

NOTES

1 As epitomised particularly in the work of Mishan (1971, esp. chapters 45, 46 and 47) and restated recently with characteristic vigour (1974). A much more circumspect position is adopted by Dasgupta and Pearce (1972, esp. Chapter 3). I personally would be prepared to depart a good bit further than Dasgupta and Pearce from the 'conventional' view, see Williams (1972).

2 See, for instance, Rawls (1971), Sen (1973) and Phelps (1973). Associated material, on the multiplicity of the dimensions involved and on consequent measurement problems, is to be found in Atkinson (1973), Beteille (1969) and Roach and Roach (1972).

3 Among the members of the sect are such well-known pioneers in this field as Eckstein (1958) and Krutilla (1961), though later Eckstein (1961) appeared to have moved to the view that a display of distributional consequences and even an articulation of weights was desirable.

4 See, for instance, Bonnen (1968, 1970) and Downs (1970), which together seem to fulfil Boulding's fears, concerning water projects in particular (quoted in Marglin (1965), p. 21n), that:
'It would be well to be quite sure
Who are the Undeserving Poor
Or else the state-supported ditch
May serve the Undeserving Rich.'

5 If some such mechanism were at work, it would certainly support Pearce (1971) in his observation that 'the cumulative distributional effects of many investments may be significant, even if the effect of one project is slight' (p. 27), which echoes an earlier opinion expressed by Foster (1966) with particular reference to rail closures.

6 On the British scene, see for instance Abel-Smith and Townsend (1965), Douglas (1964), West and Farrington (1973), Wedge and Prosser (1974), Wedderburn

(1974) and Stevenson, A. (1974). At a practical level, the setting up of comprehensive community development projects is one important outcome of these concerns.

7 A point made strongly by Millward (1971) p. 354.

8 This has certainly been my own position, see Walsh and Williams (1969; esp. pp. 17–19). An early exponent of this view was McKean (1958, pp. 206–8 and 240–3); while the considerable technical problems involved even in this 'useful, though modest, step' are well illustrated by Weisbrod (1968) and stressed by Musgrave (1969).

9 Margolis (1957), McKean (1958), Eckstein (1958) are classic examples, and their stance has been emulated and approved by their successors, see, for instance, Prest and Turvey (1965), Dasgupta and Pearce (1972). One recent manual on project evaluation (Harberger (1972)) pursues efficiency questions so single mindedly that no independent distributional objectives are recognised at all.

10 For instance, Dasgupta and Pearce (1972) go on to observe that 'pecuniary effects would, however, be very relevant if the social welfare function used in cost–benefit contained explicit distributional weights' (p. 121n). It is not necessary for such stringent conditions to be applied, however, since all that is necessary is that the decisionmakers be known to be interested in distributional questions; they may or may not have explicit weights to apply. See Walsh and Williams (1969) p. 5.

11 Marglin (1962), for example, has recommended this analytical stance, though he clearly recognises that 'constraints' are but a peculiar version of weights (see, in particular, Marglin (1965) pp. 20 *et seq.*).

12 McKean (1963) has argued that we need to do this for the additional reason that the cost–reward structure is an important element in people's perception of what is a 'feasible' project, which brings us back to the 'informal sifting' problem referred to earlier on p. 68 of this chapter.

13 e.g. Weisbrod (1968) and Millward (1971).

14 A useful collection of relevant studies is to be found in Boulding and Pfaff (1972) and in Boulding, Pfaff and Pfaff (1973).

15 The foremost advocates of the all out assault on the problem are Weisbrod (1968, 1970), McGuire and Garn (1969), and Aaron and McGuire (1970), though the latter's arguments were not directed at the treatment of particular projects, but they might well have been.

16 e.g. Foster (1966). A nicely judicious intermediate position is occupied by Little and Mirrlees (1974), who, in discussing (pp. 234 *et seq.*) how policymakers might determine the numerical values of 'consumption weights', use such phrases as 'We take it that most governments, administrators, and advisers would wish to ...', 'The one adjustment we think worth making is ...', 'It might be thought right to have the weight depend on ...' 'Planners and others concerned with consumption weights should not ignore ...', 'On admittedly extremely inadequate evidence we guess that most people would put n in the size 1–3 ...' [n is the (negative) elasticity of the consumption weight with respect to total consumption] and, most forthright of all, 'For our own part, we would find it hard to select a set of weights which did not support the suggestion ... that the consumption of rich capitalists should normally be given a zero weight in cost–benefit calculations.'

17 The 'unintended' qualification is necessary because some public projects will obviously have as their purpose some redistributive consequence and to the extent

that these are fulfilled by the project it would be ludicrous to try to neutralise them by 'compensation'.

18 This will be the case if Runciman (1966) is correct in concluding (p. 285) that 'Most people's lives are governed more by the resentment of narrow inequalities, the cultivation of modest ambitions and the preservation of small differentials than by attitudes to public policy or the social structure as such' and (p. 286) that 'the relationship between inequality and grievance only intermittently corresponds with either the extent and degree of actual inequality, or the magnitude and frequency of relative deprivation which an appeal to social justice would vindicate.'

19 Lees and Doherty (1973) (Table 2, p. 23) estimate the respective costs as follows:

Ratio of administrative costs to compensation

Tort	74%
Social security*	7%
Industrial injury and disablement*	15%
Life assurance	15%
Personal accident insurance	55%
Sick pay	5%

*includes estimate of costs of collection met by employer

20 This conclusion is reinforced by the sort of considerations underlined by Michelman (1967) when he challenges the 'implicit assumption that the courts offer the only feasible forum and method for administering compensation discipline, that compensability decisions *must* be made indirectly through the promulgation of general rules of decision conforming to judicial requirements of incisiveness, impersonality and precedental consistency. If, however, we can see no reason why political actors might not administer their own fairness discipline on a far less rigorous basis, we shall be unable to accept as fair a failure to compensate based on a settlement cost calculation which assumes inflexibilities applicable only to courts'. (p. 1252)

21 Mackay and Reid (1972) conclude that 'redundancy payments do provide some offset to the costs of redundancy, but it is important to emphasise the roughness of the justice'. (They also observe 'how difficult it is to find a model simple enough for administrative purposes which would accurately identify at the time of redundancy those who will subsequently experience the greatest costs'.) 'Any method which attempts to assess need *ex ante*, as does the Act, is therefore likely to be less effective than one which measures need *ex post*, as does unemployment benefit.' Yet the *Department of Employment and Productivity* study (1970) showed that the typical view of redundancy payments by redundant workers is as compensation for lost earnings, and that the typical payment would have been enough to maintain earnings at their pre-redundancy level for about 60 weeks, and were regarded as free of stigma by recipients who declared that they would not apply for supplementary benefits (which are the epitome of '*ex post* need measurement'). Some other threads in this tangled skein are described in Wiseman and Hartley (1965), Hauser and Burrows (1969) and Daniel (1970).

22 This has been recognised most explicitly in the field of environmental pollution, see, for instance, such writers as Dales (1968), especially his Chapter V, and

Mishan (1967 and 1971). The whole field was recently reviewed by Furubotn and Pejovich (1974).

23 My own tiny private crusade (and sense of injustice) in this respect is concerned with the frustrations inherent in trying to 'enjoy' public rights of way in those rural areas where the landowners and farmers flagrantly disregard their statutory obligations, obstructing footpaths by ploughing and fencing, with liberal use of barbed wire on gates and stiles, with local authorities and the magistrates taking no effective action to uphold the undoubted legal rights of individuals to use the footpaths. An economical solution here might lie in automatic penalty clauses in eligibility tests for agricultural support programmes!

24 This is a problem which crops up with any kind of 'insurance' scheme, and some idea of the possible ramifications can be gained from Calabresi (1970) esp. Part IV, and from the 'moral hazard' literature, e.g. Arrow (1968) and references cited therein, as well as from the more standard references on the incentive/disincentive effects of tax subsidy schemes.

25 Indeed my present views have been strongly influenced by Downs (1970), Michelman (1967) and the controversy surrounding the amenity losses imposed by road traffic and airports.

REFERENCES

Aaron, H. and McGuire, M. (1970), 'Public Goods and Income Distribution', *Econometrica*, vol. 38, 907–920.

Abel-Smith, B. and Townsend, P. (1965), *The Poor and the Poorest*, Bell, London.

Arrow, K. (1968), 'The economics of moral hazard: further comment', *American Economic Review*, vol. 58, 537–9.

Atkinson, A. B. (1973), *Wealth, Income and Inequality*, Penguin Modern Economics Readings, Harmondsworth, Middlesex.

Beteille, A. (1969), *Social Inequality*, Penguin Modern Sociology Readings, Harmondsworth, Middlesex.

Bonnen, J. T. (1968), 'The Distribution of Benefits from Cotton Price Supports', in S. B. Chase (ed.), *Problems in Public Expenditure Analysis*, Brookings Institution, Washington DC.

– (1970), 'The Absence of Knowledge of Distributional Impacts: An Obstacle to Effective Policy Analysis and Decisions', in Haverman and Margolis (ed.), *Public Expenditure and Policy Analysis*, Markham, Chicago.

Boulding, K. and Pfaff, M. (1972), *Redistribution to the Rich and Poor*, Wadsworth, Belmont, California.

Boulding, K., Pfaff, M. and Pfaff, A. (1973), *Transfers in an Urbanised Economy*, Wadsworth, Belmont, California.

Calabresi, G. (1970), *The Costs of Accidents*, Yale University Press.

Daniel, W. W. (1970), *Strategies for Displaced Employees*, PEP Broadsheet 517, London.

Dales, J. H. (1968), *Pollution, Property and Prices*, University of Toronto Press.

Dasgupta, A. K. and Pearce, D. W. (1972), *Cost–Benefit Analysis: Theory and Practice*, London, Macmillan.

Davies, K. (1974), ' "Injurious Affection" and the Land Compensation Act 1973', *Law Quarterly Review*, vol. 90, 361–77.

Department of the Environment (1973), *Report of the Urban Motorways Project Team to the Urban Motorways Committee*, HMSO, London.

Department of Employment and Productivity (1970), *Ryhope: A Pit Closes*, HMSO, London.

Douglas, W. J. B. (1964), *The Home and the School*, MacGibbon and Partner, London. (New impression, Panther, 1969).

Downs, A. (1970), Uncompensated Nonconstruction Costs which Urban Highways and Urban Renewal Impose upon Residential Households', in J. Margolis (ed.), *The Analysis of Public Output*, NBER, Columbia University Press, New York.

Eckstein, O. (1958), *Water Resource Development*, Cambridge, Mass.

– (1961), 'A Survey of the Theory of Public Expenditure Criteria', in J. M. Buchanan (ed.), *Public Finances: Needs, Sources and Utilization*, NBER Special Conference Series No. 12, Princeton University Press.

Flynn, M., Flynn, P. and Mellor, N. (1972), 'Social Malaise Research: A Study in Liverpool', *Social Trends* no. 3, 42–52, HMSO, London.

Foster, C. D. (1966), 'Social Welfare Functions in Cost Benefit Analysis' in J. Lawrence (ed.), *Operational Research and The Social Sciences*, Tavistock Publishing, London.

– (1973), 'Policy Review as the Verification of Predictions' in *Government and Programme Budgeting* IMTA (now CIPFA), 1 Buckingham Gate, London SW1.

Furubotn, E. and Pejovich, S. (1974), 'Property Rights and Economic Theory: A Survey of Recent Literature', *Journal of Economic Literature*, vol X, 1137–62.

Harberger, A. C. (1972), *Project Evaluation*, Macmillan, London.

Hauser, M and Burrows, P. (1969), *The Economics of Unemployment Insurance*, Allen and Unwin, London.

Kneese, A. V. (1968) 'Comments' (on a paper by McKean), in S. B. Chase (ed.), *Problems in Public Expenditure Analysis*, Brookings Institution, Washington DC.

Krutilla, J. (1961), 'Welfare Aspects of Cost–Benefit Analysis', *Journal of Political Economy*, vol. 69, 226–35.

Lees, D. S. and Doherty, N. (1973), 'Compensation for Personal Injury', *Lloyds Bank Review*, no. 108 (April), 18–32.

Lees, D. S. and Shaw, Stella (1974), *Impairment, Disability and Handicap: A Multidisciplinary View*, Heinemann, London.

Lichfield, N. (1962), *Cost–Benefit Analysis in Urban Redevelopment*, Real Estate Research Program Report, University of California, Berkeley.

– (1971) 'Cost–Benefit Analysis in Planning: A Critique of the Roskill Commission' *Regional Studies*, vol. 5, 157–83.

Little, I. M. D. and Mirrlees, J. A. (1974), *Project Appraisal and Planning for Developing Countries,* Heinemann, London.

Mackay, D. I. and Reid, G. L. (1972), 'Redundancy, Unemployment and Manpower Policy', *Economic Journal*, vol. 82, 1256–72.

Maass, A. (1962), 'Objectives of Water Resource Development: A General Statement', in A. Maass (ed.), *Design of Water Resource Systems*, Harvard University Press, Cambridge, Mass.

Marglin, S. A. (1965), *Public Investment Criteria*, MIT Press, Cambridge, Mass.

Margolis, J. (1957), 'Secondary Benefits, external economies, and the justification of public investment', *Review of Economics and Statistics*, vol. 39, 284–91.

McGuire, M. and Garn, H. (1969), 'The Integration of Equity and Efficiency Criteria in Public Project Selection', *Economic Journal*, 882–93.

McKean, R. N. (1958), *Efficiency in Government through Systems Analysis*, Wiley, New York.

– (1963) 'Costs and Benefits from Different Viewpoints', in H. G. Schaller (ed.), *Public Expenditure Decisions in the Urban Community*, Resources for the Future, Washington DC.

Mera, K. (1969), 'Experimental Determination of Relative Marginal Utilities', *Quarterly Journal of Economics*, vol. 83, 464–77.

Michelman, F. I. (1967), 'Property, Utility and Fairness: Comments on the Ethical Foundations of "Just Compensation" Law', *Harvard Law Review*, vol. 80, 1165–1258.

Millward, R. (1971), *Public Expenditure Economics*, McGraw Hill, London.

Mishan, E. J. (1967), *The Costs of Economic Growth*, Staples, London.

– (1971), *Cost–Benefit Analysis*, London, Allen and Unwin.

– (1974), 'Flexibility and Consistency in Project Evaluation', *Economica*, vol. 41, 81–96.

Musgrave, R. A. (1969), 'Cost–Benefit Analysis and the Theory of Public Finance', *Journal of Economic Literature*, vol. 7, 797–806.

Pearce, D. W. (1971), *Cost–Benefit Analysis*, Macmillan, London.

Phelps, E. S. (1973) (ed.), *Economic Justice*, Penguin Modern Economics Readings, Harmondsworth, Middlesex.

Prest, A. R. and Turvey, R. (1965), 'Cost Benefit Analysis: A Survey', *Economic Journal*, vol. 75, 683–735.

Rawls, J. (1971), *A Theory of Justice*, Harvard, Cambridge, Mass.

Roach, J. L. and Roach, J. K. (1972), *Poverty*, Penguin Modern Sociology Readings, Harmondsworth Middlesex.

Runciman, W. G. (1966), *Relative Deprivation and Social Justice*, Routledge and Kegan Paul, London.

Sen, A. K. (1973), *On Economic Inequality*, Clarendon Press, Oxford.

Stevenson, A. (1974), 'Research on Transmitted Deprivation', *SSRC Newsletter 23*, 10–11, London.

Walsh, H. G. and Williams, Alan (1969), 'Current Issues in Cost–Benefit Analysis', *CAS Occasional Paper No. 11*, HMSO, London.

Wedderburn, D. (1974), *Poverty, Inequality and Class Structure*, Cambridge University Press.

Wedge, P. and Prosser, H. (1974), *Born to Fail*, National Childrens Bureau, Arrow Books.

Weisbrod, B. A. (1968), 'Income Redistribution Effects and Benefit–Cost Analysis', in S. B. Chase (ed.), *Problems in Public Expenditure Analysis*, Brookings Institution, Washington DC.

– (1970), 'Collective Action and the Distribution of Income: A Conceptual Approach', in Haverman and Margolis (eds.), *Public Expenditure and Policy Analysis*, Markham, Chicago.

West, D. J. and Farrington, D. P. (1973), *Who Becomes Delinquent?*, Cambridge Studies in Criminology, Heinemann Educational.

Williams, Alan (1972), review of E. J. Mishan, *Cost–Benefit Analysis, Journal of Public Economics*, vol. I, No. 3/4, 398–400.

Wiseman, J. and Hartley, K. (1965), 'Redundancy and Public Policy', *Moorgate and Wall Street Review*, Spring.

6

'Efficient' pricing and government interference*

PAUL BURROWS

1   **Introduction**

Much has been written, by economists of a particular philosophical bent, on the merits of pricing as a means of allocating scarce resources in both the public and private sectors.[1] The free market, based on the rational behavioural expression of individual preferences and an ideal distribution of income, is seen as providing a benchmark by which government intervention in the pricing system must be judged. The classical conservative and liberal views coincide at this point in favour of a freely operating market system with only marginal incursions by the government to guarantee law and order and to provide the more extreme types of public good.[2]

The pro-pricing case relies on the general efficiency argument that if an ideal income distribution is achieved then prices equal to marginal (opportunity) cost maximise social welfare. The recommendation of marginal cost pricing is based on the two assumptions that the income distribution *is* ideal and that social welfare is merely the aggregation of individuals' welfare. However, it will be the central argument of this paper that the pursuit of objectives other than efficiency in the narrow sense common in welfare economics, may lead the government to interfere with 'efficient' pricing in both the private and public sectors. There remains the second major objection to the operation of the price mechanism in the real world (not to be considered in this paper), which is the failure of prices to display the optimal characteristics of purely competitive pricing due to the existence of widespread market imperfections.

Our first task is to enumerate the circumstances in which the provision of goods and services at less-than-cost[3] may better achieve society's objectives than the free market would (or the simulation of a market distribution in the

* I would like to thank delegates to The Royal Economic Society Conference for their comments. While several of their suggestions have been incorporated into the paper any remaining errors are, of course, my responsibility.

public sector). A number of arguments, found in fragmented form in the
economics literature, are drawn together in section 2 to provide a case for
less-than-cost provision. In section 3 an attempt will be made to trace some
of the consequences of less-than-cost provision compared with a free market
solution to the allocation problem. And section 4 will consider the possible
superiority of the government over the individual in the market place as a
decision taker.

2   Reasons for less-than-cost provision

There appear to be four main groups of argument in favour of
modifying markets by making goods and services available to consumers at
less than the market price.[4] These are concerned with income redistribution
in kind, consumption targets for particular (merit) goods, public good
problems, and the information requirements of pricing.

2.1   *Income redistribution.* The distribution of goods to members of
society can be altered by money transfers or by the provision of goods at
less-than-cost, that is, redistribution in kind. The conventional (liberal)
welfare argument is that money transfers are a more efficient distributive
instrument than transfers in kind because the recipient can reach a higher
indifference curve with an income subsidy than he can with the choice-
constraining receipt of goods of equal cost.[5] However, redistribution in kind
may have certain merits even if the government is not trying to raise the
level of consumption of a particular good (considered in section 2.2), that is,
as a means of redistributing purchasing power. Consider first the implications of the recent debate on redistribution in kind.[6]

Foldes suggests that, in pursuing its distribution objective, the government is concerned to bring about a particular configuration of the (real) distribution of all goods, including the numeraire good, rather than solely a particular distribution of the numeraire, that is of general purchasing power. He
proceeds to demonstrate that there are circumstances in which government
redistribution of purchasing power alone will fail to bring about the target
real distribution. Briefly the circumstances are first, boundary situations in
which there is no unique price line through the target optimum to determine
the pre-trade position which will lead to this optimum and which could be
reached through money transfers alone. Second, where there is uncertainty
as to the location of the contract curve, and therefore of the target optimum,
a particular initial set of endowments of money *and* of other goods may be
the only way of guaranteeing the achievement of the desired post-trade
optimum.

Buchanan replies to the first case, boundary situations, by postulating an
iterative procedure by which a sequence of money transfers and subsequent
trades eventually leads to the desired real distribution, but Foldes rightly

points to the severe requirements (such as the absence of speculation and the availability of considerable information) of such a procedure. Buchanan does not really propose a solution to the second problem, uncertainty, but does suggest a more general criticism of Foldes' position. This is that, contrary to Foldes' assumption, the social welfare function might include the redistribution of purchasing power as the objective, leaving the consequent real distribution to subsequent trade to determine. Foldes' response is that laying down distributive criteria in money terms implies that society is indifferent between different real distributions. This assertion is substantiated by the two causes of ambiguity concerning the consequences of money transfers for the real distribution of goods. But a rebuttal of Buchanan's argument requires an explanation, missing from Foldes' analysis, of why society may *not* be indifferent between two alternative real distributions of goods derivable from a given distribution of money. Why should society care how redistributed income is spent? It seems that Foldes' case for redistribution in kind must be based on the presumption, discussed in section 2.2 below, that certain goods either are inherently meritorious or yield external benefits in consumption.

The debate does not therefore yield a case for using less-than-cost provision as a purely redistributive mechanism. However, other arguments can be offered to support the use of redistribution in kind to this end. These derive from certain problems associated with the money transfer instrument. In the first place one of the most severe difficulties in anti-poverty policy is that of identifying the needy and (in some cases) persuading them to accept a means-tested money transfer. It may be easier to ensure that there is effective redistribution to the poor if (as part of the policy approach) essentials are offered at less-than-cost in the knowledge that these comprise a higher proportion of the expenditure of low income earners than of the rich. Subsidies to the prices of essentials could of course be made selective, limited to the needy, but the implied means-tested receipt is likely to be self-negating in that one of the objectives is to avoid the means-test search for the needy implied by money transfers. It is arguable that flat rate money transfers are preferable to the (equal cost) subsidisation of any product, unless the product has a negative income elasticity, in that the poor gain relatively more with the transfers. However, the problem remains that rate income transfers require the identification of families who do not enter the tax system and who may not be on electoral rolls.

In the second place, it may be an objective of government policy to protect particular members of the family from the domination of expenditure decisions by the income recipient. While less-than-cost provision may be a rather blunt instrument in this context it may nevertheless be one of the few feasible means of mitigating the effects of such domination.

A third problem is the likelihood of political constraints on a pure money transfer approach to poverty. A diverse set of redistributive instruments may be more feasible politically and the probability of this being the case is increased if society (the tax payer) is more generous with redistribution which is offered, like tied aid, with strings attached. But the strings which can be expected are the purchase of certain types of good, which brings us back to merit goods and consumption externalities.

2.2   *Consumption targets.* Less-than-cost provision can be used to pursue two consumption objectives:

(*a*) to raise the level of consumption of a good above the free-market level, and
(*b*) to alter the distribution of consumption of the good, i.e. usually to raise the consumption level of the poor relative to that of the rich. This objective can be achieved via (*a*), but is not necessarily implied by (*a*) since it is imaginable that for some goods the government's intention may be to raise the average consumption level without concern over the distribution (e.g. the encouragement of the arts).

Let us consider possible rationales for the pursuit of objective (*a*). In contrast to the theory of public goods, the theory of merit goods does not start from the assumption that optimality is determined in terms of individuals' private preference maps. Rather there is inherent in the merit good concept a belief that social welfare may be maximised by over-riding, in certain circumstances, the individual's view of the merits of a particular good. Private preferences are viewed as 'distorted' when compared with some socially-determined norm; in particular it is thought that individuals undervalue the merit good as a means of increasing their *own* welfare. There are several circumstances in which such undervaluation may occur: when choices are made with poor information about present and future alternatives; when the consumer is myopic; when he is irrational (in the sense of making non-transitive choices).[7] For any of these reasons the consumer may find it difficult to evaluate the benefits (present and future) to be derived from a product and/or to derive rational choice implications once an evaluation of the benefits has been made. These difficulties may make him choose less of the good than he would choose if he were operating on a preference set which conformed with the social norm.

What are the implications of the concept of merit goods defined in terms of preference distortion? One implication is that criteria for the allocation decision cannot be derived from Paretian analysis since one of the fundamental value judgements required by that analysis is over-ruled; namely that private preferences should determine all decisions.[8] Clearly a degree of social judgement is required in determining the level of provision of merit goods, and it should not be surprising therefore that the success of such provision can be tested *ex post* only in terms of judgements about the desirability of the consequences made by society as a whole as well as by the individual recipient. *Ex post* tests based solely on the individual's own *ex post* preferences are therefore necessarily inadequate.[9] For example, in trying to judge the desirability of compulsory education provided at less-than-cost it is not sufficient to ask those leaving school (then or later) whether they felt it to be worthwhile. Society may decide that there is such a thing as expert opinion which is better able to judge the consequences of education than the individual can judge for himself.

The final implication of merit goods is that provision at less-than-cost may be a necessary but not sufficient condition for the achievement of the socially-desired consumption level. If the freely chosen level *after* the subsidy is introduced is expected to fall below the desired level then there is a case for compulsion (coercion) in the form of minimum regulated consumption levels (such as schooling from 5 to 16 years of age).

An alternative to the preference distortion and merit goods approach as a rationalisation of objective (*a*) is to hypothesise the existence of external benefits accruing to other members of society. Society does not judge that the individual is incapable of making decisions in his own interest, but it does decide that decisions which maximise private welfare do not maximise social welfare. The externality argument is much closer to the hearts of honest, God-fearing Paretians than are merit goods. It does not require the belief, as the merit goods concept does, that the rest of society may express a view about an individual's consumption of a good without there being any (external) benefit from that consumption accruing to the rest of society. Consequently we find Paretians arguing either that merit goods exist only if consumption externalities occur,[10] or that redistribution in kind can be justified only in terms of the suffering experienced by the rich as they observe the plight of the poor.[11]

The implications of the externality argument for pricing in the public sector can be briefly summarised. The externality prevents individuals consuming the optimal amount of the good: their own benefits understate the benefits to society. Consequently society is justified in subsidising provision to an extent equal to the external benefit. The result is Pareto-optimal redistribution in kind and it is important to notice that the redistribution must be tied to the consumption of the externality-generating good.

Let us turn to objective (*b*), the pursuit of which implies, as Foldes has argued, that distribution policy is concerned with the distribution of goods rather than of purchasing power. Once this is admitted the case for less-than-cost provision is strengthened by Foldes-type objections to money transfers for redistribution. However, it is doubtful whether Foldes' assumption of the marketability of the subsidised good (or vouchers) is realistic. If the desired real distribution of goods, including merit or externality-generating goods, is known then *non-marketable* transfers in kind can achieve it. On the other hand if the rich are prepared to buy a subsidised good from the poor, unrestricted (marketable) transfers in kind suffer from the same weaknesses as money transfers as a means of achieving a particular distribution of the consumption of various goods.

2.3   *Public goods and bads.* In the case of public goods the costs of identifying beneficiaries of supply and of enforcing payment are high. It is not then possible to devise a financing method consisting of benefit taxation which parallels full cost pricing. In the polar case of a Samuelsonian public good a case exists for *free* provision to beneficiaries if *any* provision is justified. Tax payers accept their share of the cost, as long as other tax payers do likewise voluntarily or through coercion, so that society can reap the collective return. But there is no guarantee either that all beneficiaries pay taxes, that all tax payers are beneficiaries, or that those tax payers who are beneficiaries make a tax contribution in any way related to the benefit they receive. In other words no public sector simulation of a market pricing method is feasible.

Similarly with public bads, such as pollution which affects a large group of people, the pricing of the negative product with compensation being paid to the sufferers is not possible.[12]

2.4   *Information requirements of pricing negative goods.* The difficulties involved in establishing markets in external costs, which may be viewed as negative goods, are well known. Various iterative tax systems have been proposed as means of simulating market internalisation of the externality in the public sector.[13] These systems typically take as given some target level of pollution reduction and involve a sequence of pollution tax levels in an attempt to discover the level which leads to the desired pollution-reduction response by firms. However, this tax analogy to the pricing of the pollution must be compared with an alternative non-pricing instrument which is the establishment of regulated maximum pollution levels. There are two general grounds on which they can be compared: first, the information and enforcement costs which each involves. It has been argued elsewhere[14] that a case can be made for expecting these costs to be lower for regulation than for pricing (taxing). Second, we can compare the responses of firms to the two instruments. It will be suggested in section 3.2 that the impact of regulation may in some respects be preferable to that of pricing.

In general, therefore, when we look at government participation in the correction of market misallocations due to external costs, it is not at all clear that a public sector analogy to idealised market pricing for internalisation is the instrument to be preferred.

3 **Some implications of modifications to full cost pricing**
The previous section has argued that there are various circumstances in which society may wish to modify the price mechanism in order to pursue objectives which are best attained by provision at less-than-cost, whether the provision consists of subsidised market supply or subsidised public supply. The task of this section is first to consider the impact on recipients and tax paying non-recipients of provision at less-than-cost, and second to summarise the predicted impacts on firms of pricing and non-pricing (regulation) instruments to reduce pollution.

3.1 *Impact of less-than-cost provision of goods.* Let us assume that a typical consumer has to choose between two goods, X and Y, while the latter is judged by society to be meritorious. Assume further that the government is determined to raise the consumption of Y above the level which the consumer would choose freely if the good were priced in the market. There are two possible methods of achieving the target consumption level: either to let the good be priced in the market and legislate a minimum consumption level, or to provide the good free of direct charge and finance the provision from a lump sum tax paid by recipients and/or non-recipient tax payers.[15] Which of these alternatives would be preferred by the individual consumer and by society?

In figure 1 the indifference curves I_1, I_2 etc. represent the ('distorted') preference orderings of the individual. With full cost pricing of good Y and a free choice of consumption level the individual chooses the X, Y combination represented by E_1 on I_2. Society, however, takes a different view of the ordering of combinations of X, Y consumption by the individual. The resulting social indifference curves SI_1, SI_2 etc. are steeper than the individual's indifference curves because society is more reluctant than the individual to substitute good X for the meritorious good, Y. The individual's free choice of E_1 places society on SI_1.

Imagine now that the government chooses as the target Y consumption the level which the individual would choose if Y were zero priced.[16] Retaining market pricing the government legislates OT as the minimum consumption level so that given his budget $OA = ON$ the individual is constrained to combinations in the area TPN. The constrained choice leads the consumers to the equilibrium position E_2 (at point P) on I_1 which is inferior to E_1 as far as the individual is concerned in terms of his own preference pattern, but is preferred by society to E_1 since $SI_2 > SI_1$.

If, instead, free provision of Y is introduced the consumer is faced with a horizontal budget line at the level *OA* as long as the cost of provision is borne by others. The chosen level of *Y* consumption at E_3 satisfies the target *OT* as long as the income effect is zero or positive (zero in the diagram) for the good *Y*, and the *X, Y* combination at E_3 is preferred by both the individual and by society, if no account is taken of the costs of provision, to either E_1 or E_2. But how is the situation viewed when the individual is obliged to pay part or all of the costs as a lump-sum tax? The cost of providing *OT* at zero price is *AB* in terms of good *X*.[17] If the individual has to pay the full cost as a lump sum he is constrained to the budget line *CP* and chooses E_2. Given the target consumption level *OT*, user-financed non-priced provision is equally preferred to the constrained choice with pricing at E_2. But the consumer prefers the non-priced provision if there is *any* degree of subsidy to push the budget line above *CP*. And if the subsidy is sufficient for the individual to rise above I_2, the subsidised non-priced provision is preferred to the free choice with market pricing (E_1). Notice that any degree of subsidisation takes society above SI_2 so that society necessarily judges the *individual's* consumption pattern under subsidy to be preferable to the pattern under full cost pricing with or without a constraint on the purchase of *Y*.

But what of the financing of the subsidy? Clearly the comparison of the positions E_1 and E_2 is unambiguous: society prefers E_2 and there are no costs to non-users to affect the decision. But with zero-price budget lines above *OC* the final decision on the *net* benefit to society of less-than-cost

Figure 1

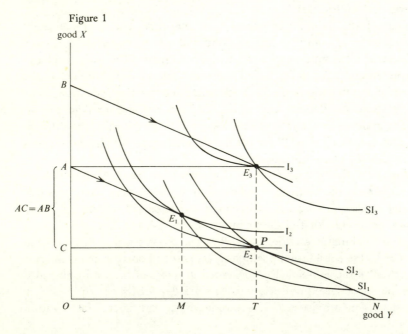

provision is unambiguous only if the implied redistribution from tax-paying non-users to non-tax-paying users is itself judged to be desirable. In this case a position such as E_3 is socially preferred to E_2 (or E_1) both on grounds of the alteration of the individual's choice between the two goods and on grounds of his total consumption level relative to other members of society. If the judgement on redistribution is that it is not desirable, then the cost to tax-paying non-users enters as a cost in the cost–benefit evaluation of the pursuit of target increases in the consumption of the merit good Y.

3.2 *Pricing and regulation to reduce pollution.* The predilection of liberals and conservatives for the pricing of goods has been carried over in the externality literature to the advocacy of pricing (or tax simulation of pricing) of external costs, as mentioned in section 2.4. The case for pricing here rests on the unexceptional argument that, in a world of costless information and transactions, setting a price equal to the value of the externality leads to an optimal level of pollution prevention by each firm. As a result pollution reduction is achieved at the least cost to society.

However, once we leave this perfect world and optimal pollution levels are unknown we must compare the effects of pricing and regulation as alternative means of achieving some pre-determined (probably non-optimal) pollution reduction target. It can be shown,[18] using a positive comparative static analysis, that regulation *may* have consequences (for a given level of pollution reduction) such as higher output and employment levels which society would find preferable to the impact of pricing. The possible higher output under regulation results from the fact that, with regulation, pollution below the target level is not priced so that the firm's marginal costs are lower than under pricing. There is not space in this paper to pursue the argument in detail; I wish only to point out that the attractiveness of pricing in terms of welfare criteria *may* disguise desirable consequences of regulation in the real world.

4 Preference distortion: can governments do better?

It was argued in section 2.2 that the merit good concept is based on a distinction between a private and a social ordering of choices made by the individual. But can it reasonably be assumed that society's (and *a fortiori* the government's) expressed preferences are the 'true' preferences? Are they not equally distorted by irrationality and uncertainty? The following discussion, which inevitably is speculative and reflects my own optimism on the efficiency of government decisions,[19] considers in turn irrationality and uncertainty in government decision taking.

In considering the likelihood of democratic governments pursuing (rationally) social welfare maximising policies, I shall not consider the traditional liberalist fear of concentrations of power in any form, though there is some doubt as to the internal consistency of a philosophy which combines an emphasis on the law and order role of the government (which requires powerful government) and the fear of power itself. A distinction can be made between situations in which the preferences of a small group in society are distorted and those in which many members of society express preferences which deviate from a set of 'true' preferences. Clearly, if 'true' preferences can only be revealed and accepted as the social norm by majority voting then the large numbers case ceases to be of interest: the majority behaviour becomes the norm. But this denies the role of leadership and expert opinion in a democracy. And it denies that people as voters may be willing to support policies which conflict with their freely made choices as consumers. In practice voters are often prepared, in a somewhat schizophrenic fashion, to accept leadership and follow expert opinion in voting for legislation which effectively restricts their own, and other consumers', freedom of choice (for example the freedom to keep children out of school and the freedom to drive without a safety belt or under the influence of alcohol). Such schizophrenia is not irrational. It could reflect the fact that individuals may have two sets of preferences concerning an activity, a 'higher' and a 'lower' ordering. The higher ordering relates to the individual in an objective, detached frame of mind. The lower ordering relates to the individual faced with temptation (such as in the pub before driving home). The individual as a voter may act upon the higher ordering in an effort to protect himself from his own possible actions on the lower ordering. Thus he votes for the blood-alcohol test as an incentive to himself to ignore the lower ordering. Differences between the two levels of ordering may alternatively reflect the (objective, detached) recognition by the voter that as a consumer he is ill-informed about the consequences of certain consumption behaviour.

It is difficult to see why any vote-maximising government should fail to offer such leadership and expert opinion if voters are prepared to behave in this way. The only problem arises when there is no immediate majority of voters in favour of correcting the distortion. The government's pursuit of the correcting policy must then rely on either the expectation of long-run votes in *ex post* recognition of the merits of the policy or on the abandonment of the vote maximising behaviour in favour of leadership as an end in itself. Surely the fact that many policies which are adopted do not have obvious vote-catching (or vote-losing) characteristics suggests that governments do have views of the pursuit of social ends which are not immediately derived from the individual preferences of consumers.

Without being able to offer a theory of government decision taking it is still possible to believe that a combination of vote maximisation and leadership qualities can lead governments to adopt social welfare maximising policies even where a large number of consumers display 'distorted' preferences. The argument seems to apply *a fortiori* when the distortions are displayed only by a small minority.

Turning to uncertainty we may ask whether even if governments *wish* to maximise social welfare by making decisions which are 'better' than free market decisions, the existence of uncertainty about peoples' preferences and about the effects of policies may not prevent welfare maximising policies being adopted.

The answer surely lies in the *degrees* of uncertainty associated with private and public decisions. The government may be in a stronger position than the individual to collect information, which may itself have public good characteristics, to reduce uncertainty. For example, individuals cannot hope to judge the impact of the use of some products, such as medicines and insecticides, on the user and on the environment. The government therefore has a clear role to police markets to rule out dangerous products. But this policing role is tantamount to the provision of merit goods. If the government judges a good to be too risky to allow people a choice of buying or not buying it, it is effectively saying that the absence of the good is a merit good. Little extension is required to take the government from a justified policing role to one of providing merit goods at less-than-cost because of the *relative* certainty with which collective (better informed) decisions can be made. It is worth suggesting, to critics of centralised decision taking, that evidence that governments do make decisions on the basis of poor information is not a sufficient case against intervention. Such a case requires the stronger evidence that private decisions would have been based on better information.

It is arguable that the state can, due to its access to expert evaluations of products and the consequences of their consumption, reduce the uncertainty associated with consumption. Its judgements can therefore reduce this source of divergence between private and 'true' preferences. The government does, however, suffer from being worse informed about individuals' preferences than the individuals are themselves. Consequently we can agree that where irrationality or uncertainty in private decision taking is not in evidence, and there are no distributional or public good elements to justify less-than-cost provision, the price mechanism provides an efficient allocative device. But the area of unconstrained pricing may prove to be the exception rather than the rule, a view which contrasts vividly with the conservative/liberalist belief in pricing as the norm with intervention being the rarely acceptable exception to the rule.

NOTES

1 See for example the Institute of Economic Affairs Hobart Papers and Occasional Papers.
2 A summary of the 'liberalist' viewpoint can be found in Peacock and Rowley (1972).
3 Less-than-cost will be used as shorthand for less than market price including profit.
4 Less-than-cost provision may or may not be accompanied by public production. The question of the relative efficiencies of public and private *production* is not considered in this paper.
5 See, for example, Peacock and Rowley (1972) p. 485.
6 Foldes (1967) and (1968) and Buchanan (1968) are particularly relevant to the following discussion.
7 See Head (1966) pp. 4–6 for an elaboration of these circumstances.
8 But only a dogged commitment to Pareto would lead one to judge, as does Culyer (1971) p. 561, that decisions falling outside the Paretian framework are 'in limbo'.
9 Cf. Culyer (1971) p. 565.
10 Culyer (1971) p. 550.
11 Buchanan (1968) pp. 189–90.
12 A general comparison of pricing and regulation as instruments for the reduction of pollution can be found in Burrows (1974a).
13 See for example Baumol (1972).
14 Burrows (1974b).
15 Clearly there are intermediate alternatives such as charging a price less-than-cost but greater than zero, but we shall limit attention to the polar cases.
16 We could with little change in the analysis assume a target equal to the level chosen under less-than-cost provision but not *zero* pricing.
17 i.e. if good Y were priced at full cost the budget line at B parallel to AN would be necessary for E_3 to be reached, and this would require an increase in income of AB.
18 See Burrows (1974a).
19 An anti-government view can be found in Head (1966), section 6.

REFERENCES

Baumol, W. J., 'On Taxation and the Control of Externalities', *American Economic Review*, June 1972.
Buchanan, J. M., 'What Kind of Redistribution do we Want?' *Economica*, May 1968.
Burrows, P., 'Protecting the Environment in a World of Variable Production Processes' (mimeo, 1974a).
– 'Pricing Versus Regulation for Environmental Protection', in A. J. Culyer (ed.), *York Economic Essays in Social Policy*, Martin Robertson, 1974b.
Culyer, A. J., 'Merit Goods and the Welfare Economics of Coercion', *Public Finance*, no. 4, 1971.

Foldes, L., 'Income Redistribution in Money and in Kind', *Economica*, February 1967.
− 'Redistribution: A Reply', *Economica*, May 1968.
Head, J. G., 'On Merit Goods', *Finanzarchiv*, 1966.
Peacock, A. T. and Rowley, C. K., 'Pareto Optimality, and the Political Economy of Liberalism', *Journal of Political Economy*, May/June 1972.

7

Welfare economics and public expenditure*

E. J. MISHAN

There is no logical affinity between the economist's conception of a 'public good' and the goods used in the public sector of the economy. The economist's 'public good' arises not from a political or sectoral distinction but from a functional one turning on the notion of a benefit simultaneously conferred on a number of people. What, in contrast, may be called a private good is therefore one that, at any moment of time, offers its benefits to the user alone. Thus, bearing in mind that such 'public goods' could be included in the outputs of an imaginary economy having no public sector, and also that the public sector of some other economy could consist only of private goods, misleading connotations may be avoided by referring from now on *to collective goods* rather than to 'public goods'.

Principles of economic efficiency alone cannot determine in advance some ideal size for the public sector of the economy. In general, allocative efficiency is compatible wholly with private ownership and/or private operation or, instead, wholly with public ownership and/or public operation. Nevertheless, in the existing circumstances and with regard to particular institutions, economists may be able to argue the advantages of transferring some economic activities from the public to the private sector, and vice versa.

Accepting, provisionally, the existing distribution of income and wealth, it is in principle possible to determine the number and variety of collective goods in the economy.[1] But there is no economic theory that can allocate particular collective goods or, for that matter, particular private goods as between the public sector and the private sector of the economy.

The statement above, that it is possible, in principle, to determine the number and variety of collective goods in the economy, does not imply that

* I am indebted to Professor James Meade for criticisms of a first draft of this paper.

there are no problems to be faced. There would be fewer if we could assume that the supplies of factors and enterprise were unresponsive to the usual order of changes in relative prices. But if this condition is not met, then any tax finance of a collective good that otherwise meets the allocative criterion does pose a familiar problem. For the tax structure that lays down the rules for ascertaining each person's contribution to the finance of goods in the public sector necessarily entails allocative 'waste' — unless, of course, all taxes are lump-sum taxes — in the sense that it infringes optimal factor-use conditions. Since the economist may have to accept the existing tax structure as a constraint, he will have suggestions for improving allocative efficiency by tampering with the system at other points.

However, the boundary of my enquiry will not extend itself to encompass the public finance of collective goods but only the concept and allocative implications of collective goods. It excludes also, therefore, the practical problem of the actual measurement of the benefits of a collective good, a problem that arises simply because the price mechanism cannot easily be invoked as an allocative device for such goods as it can for private goods.

The repeated emphasis, however, by economists on the difficulties of measuring the benefits of a collective good would seem to suggest that the concept, at least, was quite clear. But until very recently, at least, this has not been the case. Ambiguity about the relevant concept was reflected in the dissatisfaction with the definitions proposed by Samuelson (and here I use the past tense guardedly in consequence of my efforts in 1969 and 1971[2] to sort out the issues). Yet despite the confusion, there is little room for doubt that economists interested in the controversy would have soon agreed on the proper economic treatment of any particular case.

If this belief is accepted, it may be thought that although agreement on the definition and concept has some taxonomic merit it has little 'operational value'. Narrowly interpreted, this may be true. But even if we were wholly convinced of its lack of 'operational value', it is unlikely that we should acquiesce in the ambiguity for long. Apart from aesthetic or metaphysical compulsions there is always the possibility that clarification of a concept, or attempts at clarification at least, will turn our thoughts to considerations that do have significant implications. Accordingly we re-examine this controversy on the definition of a collective good.

Samuelson's original definition (1954), which held a good to be collective if person one's consumption of it did not interfere with person two's consumption, is suggestive but suffers from a number of deficiencies. First, it was unclear about the amounts consumed by each of the beneficiaries. Secondly, and as Margolis (1955) pointed out, it is not generally true that one person's use of a collective good does not affect the enjoyment by other persons of that collective good. Thirdly, the optimal equations proposed by Samuelson to distinguish collective goods from private ones are not unambiguous. Fourthly, and most important of all, the relationship between collective goods and external effects was not cleared up.[3]

A word on each of these deficiencies:

(1) Conceiving a collective good as the service of a capital good,[4] the question is whether each person consumes the same amount of the collective good or a different amount, and also whether each person chooses freely the amount to consume or is constrained to consume some given amount. Classification into *optional* and *non-optional* collective goods is useful here.[5] An optional collective good is one of which a person may take all he wishes at the going price which, of course, may be zero (equal to its marginal resource cost) in contradistinction to a non-optional collective good which bestows some amount on the beneficiary that cannot be altered without in the process incurring costs. With respect to the non-optional collective good, a person's welfare can be affected by the total amount of the collective good (the services provided by external defence, for example) or else by some portion of it particular to him (as, for example, the rain that falls on the land of a particular farmer from 'seeding' the clouds).

(2) In the enjoyment of a collective good, external diseconomies might well be generated by an increase in numbers, or an increase in activity of the given numbers, so that, contrary to Samuelson's definition, a person's enjoyment of the collective good can indeed interfere with that of another. Since the introduction of such external diseconomies can never be ruled out, it is obviously convenient to adopt a definition of collective goods that applies in the absence of externalities.

(3) Samuelson formalised the distinction between private and collective goods by means of their respective necessary conditions for optimal outputs. For private goods the equation was $v^1 = v^2 = c \ldots$ (i) For collective goods it was $v^1 + v^2 = c \ldots$ (ii), where v^1 and v^2 are, respectively, the marginal valuations of persons one and two, and c is the marginal resource cost. This is suggestive but not sufficient. For if the marginal cost of the collective good is zero, which is not an uncommon assumption, equation (i) will also be met by the collective good. On the other hand, if the marginal cost of the private good is constant in the region of optimal output then equation (ii) will also apply if c is interpreted as the increment of cost of producing marginal goods for persons one and two.

(4) The formal connection between external effects and collective goods was not made by Samuelson in 1954 and, in my opinion, it was badly fudged in 1969[6] when he hazarded a new definition that would conceive of a

collective good as one that enters into more than one persons' utility function. It would follow that every good, from cigarettes to motor-boats, which involve an element of consumer externalities could now also be included in this category of collective goods. Indeed, since any person's consumption can, in general, affect the welfare of others, no good – as Dorfman pointed out[7] – could be excluded from the category of collective goods on this definition.

Now it is a fact that there is a close relationship between any satisfactory concept of a collective good, on the one hand, and that of a consumption externality on the other. indeed, from a formal expression alone of the necessary optimal conditions for each, they are indistinguishable.

Thus the equation:

$$\sum_{i=1}^{m} v^{1i} = \sum_{i=1}^{n} v^{2i} = \sum_{i=1}^{q} v^{3i} = \ldots = c$$

can be interpreted (a) in terms of a situation in which the consumption of persons one, two, and three, of a uniform private good confers benefits respectively on another $(m-1)$, $(n-1)$, and $(q-1)$ persons. In that case v^{1i} is taken to be the marginal benefit enjoyed by the ith person from person one's consumption of a private good, and similarly for v^{2i} and v^{3i}, while c is the marginal resource cost of the private good. The equation then expresses the requirement of a (partial) optimal output: that the amounts of the private good consumed by each of the persons be adjusted so that the marginal unit consumed by each confers aggregate social benefits equal to the marginal resource cost.

Alternatively, the same equation can be interpreted (*b*) in terms of a situation in which 1, 2, and 3, are distinct communities comprising, respectively, m, n, and q, persons, all enjoying a uniform collective good. Here v^{1i} is the marginal benefit derived by the ith person from the amount of the collective good used in the first community, and similarly for v^{2i} and v^{3i} for the second and third communities respectively, with c being the marginal resource cost of the collective good. The same equation now expresses the requirement that the amounts of the collective good used in each of these three communities be so adjusted that the marginal unit of the collective good confers aggregate benefits equal to the marginal resource cost.[8]

Thus, whether we interpret the equation in terms of (*a*) or (*b*), the unit resource cost cannot be attributed to any one person, since in general the good confers benefits (and/or disbenefits) simultaneously on a number of people. In both cases, then, the marginal valuations, positive or negative, of the members of the community have to be added algebraically.

What then is the difference, if any, between a collective good and a good producing positive external benefits? Clearly there is no formal difference in so far as necessary and sufficient optimality conditions are involved. But there are two possible distinguishing characteristics that are worth considering briefly. The first and minor characteristic is neither necessary nor sufficient for a collective good: it is that, in contrast to the usual sort of external economy, in which it is more common for the good experienced incidentally by others to differ from the good offered by the activity in question, the side effect of the activity is identical with the primary or intended effect. This characteristic, however, is (as indicated) not necessary. It is quite possible to introduce a collective good that offers benefits that are different for each of a group of people; for example, a reservoir that provides boating for person A, fishing for person B, and swimming for person C. Nor is the characteristic sufficient as it is entirely possible for the side effects of some activity to be identical with those enjoyed by the initiator of the activity; for example, the flowers I grow give the same sort of pleasure to my neighbours as I myself enjoy; or, to take another example, the private guard employed by one family increases the security of the neighbouring households.

The second characteristic is more substantial: following the development of the externality concept, the term external economy or diseconomy had reference to the positive or negative effects that were *incidental* to the activity in question, whether of production or consumption. The smoke produced by the factory is incidental to its purpose, say the production of air-conditioners. The blossom produced by apple-growers on which the neighbouring honey-bees feed is incidental to the production of apples. In contrast, the effects produced by a collective good are, in the first instance at least,[9] wholly intentional.[10] Thus, the concept of a collective good, as distinct from an external economy, already implies the 'internalisation' of its benefits into the economy. The notion of internalising a side effect, or externality, is, admittedly, more commonly associated with the attribution of a market price or an accounting price to a good or 'bad' hitherto left out of the pricing system. But the notion is clearly extendable to the internalising of an effect via the political process wherever such a process explicitly sanctions the introduction of a specific collective good. The economist may, if he wishes, derive from such a political decision some set of implied or virtual prices which he may then proceed to appraise by reference to an economic criterion. But the notion of internalising an effect into the economic system does not carry the requirement that the market, accounting, or virtual price also be an optimal one (even within a partial context). All that may be said is that, guided by economic lights, the closer that such a price is to its optimal value, the more perfectly is the effect in question internalized into the economic system.

Thus we arrive at a definition of a collective good; one designed to confer simultaneous benefits on a number of people. Since this implies that the costs of production cannot be attributed to any one of the beneficiaries but rather to all of them jointly, the necessary total and marginal conditions for optimality require that valuations, total and marginal, of all people affected be algebraically summed. Since all persons benefit simultaneously from a collective good, it follows that the marginal cost of the collective benefit *with respect to variations in number of people* is zero (always excluding the external diseconomies which may arise as numbers increase), and will remain zero even though the marginal resource cost *with respect to variations in capacity* of the collective (capital) good is positive – as it will be for any period but the shortest, this shortest period being defined as a period during which the capacity cannot in fact be altered.[11]

Attention to symmetry would require that we define a collective 'bad' as a purposely designed disservice to be inflicted simultaneously on a number of people, such as those arising out of acts of war or sabotage. A simultaneously suffered disservice that was purely incidental to producing something of market value would then fall into the category of an external diseconomy.

The next logical step in the analysis should properly be that of interpreting the optimal equation for short and long periods so as better to appreciate the adjustment process. But it is as well before taking that step to clear up three small matters that bear on the evaluation of the benefits of a collective good.

The first concerns the effect of the distribution of income on the valuation of goods. In general, the value placed on a collective good will vary with the distribution of income among the potential beneficiaries. It is possible, therefore, that although the total conditions (requiring excess social benefit) for admitting a particular collective good cannot be met with the existing distribution of income, it can be met with hypothetical distributions. The reverse, of course, is also possible: a project that meets the total conditions with the existing distribution of income may be unable to meet them with some other distributions.

If it is believed that there are aspirations toward a more equitable distribution of income – which is commonly assumed to be a more equal distribution – the economist may be tempted to put more weight on the result if the evaluation of a collective good corresponded to that which would arise under a hypothetical and more equitable distribution than if, instead, the evaluation was that which corresponded to the existing distribution.[12]

Three considerations tell against yielding to this temptation:

(*a*) If aspirations toward a more equitable distribution do in fact prevail in the community then it will perhaps be realised in time by the political process. But it is also possible that each member of the community defers in principle to the idea of a more equitable distribution, notwithstanding which few are willing to vote for additional income transfers to the poor and otherwise underprivileged. The economist would be ill-advised to regard his (possibly correct) interpretation of the distributional ethics of society as a mandate from society to base the valuation of prospective benefits on the fiction that a more ethically satisfactory distribution has been or can be implemented by political means.

(*b*) If we base the evaluation of projects on a hypothetical income distribution we shall to that extent be departing from the pattern of allocative efficiency (based on the prevailing income distribution) that guides the rest of the economy. A case could be made for pursuing an efficient allocation that corresponds to some ideal distribution for the economy as a whole, but not for only a part of the economy, say for collective goods.

(*c*) The final consideration is that, on equity grounds alone, the proposed device would be insufficient. Since satisfaction of the total conditions necessary for the introduction of a project entails no more than a *potential* Pareto improvement, it is not ethically compelling. The introduction of any collective good that meets this criterion does not make everybody better off. Generally, it will make some people worse off, including some of the poor. And this is no less true if the evaluation of the collective good is calculated by reference, not merely to the existing income distribution, but to any other conceivable and possibly preferable income distribution.

If economists agree that an acceptable decision criterion should not overlook any discernible distributional consequences of the introduction of a project, provision for this can be made only by explicit recognition of such consequences. For many projects, the distributional effects may be slight and uncertain, in which case they can be ignored. But if the effects are markedly regressive, recourse to evaluations based on hypothetical distributions, or the use of distributional weights,[13] cannot of themselves guard against the possibility that a project that meets a cost–benefit criterion is also one that makes the poor worse off.

The second matter we touch on is the theory of second best. Though a number of papers have been written to allay our uneasiness, economists are still haunted by the spectre of second best. A convention has grown that the economist should at least tip his hat in the direction of the spectre before getting on with the job, in the hope that the spectre won't pay much attention to him.

We need not follow that convention here since the problem posed by the theory of second best is that of revising the allocative rules for the remainder of the economy whenever the 'first best' allocative rules are unredeemably infringed by one or more sectors to start with. The theory has no restrictive implications when the question the economist faces is simply that of transferring factors from some sectors of the economy, or from the economy at large, to a particular project. Regardless of the initial imperfections in the existing allocation of resources, traditional economic criteria will sanction a transfer of any factor or group of factors if — in total and at the margin — their social value in the project under consideration exceeds their opportunity cost, this being calculated as equal to the social value of the benefits that will be lost if they are removed from their existing uses.

The third matter that bears on the evaluation of the benefits of a project is the attitude of the law toward collective goods that affect environmental amenity.

A problem arises because there are two principles on which a consistent calculation of the relevant gains and losses can be done. The more conventional one entails the algebraic sum of compensating variations (CV) of all persons affected by the project. The other entails the algebraic sum of their equivalent variations (EV). A positive algebraic sum of the CVs tells us that the introduction of the project can (granted costless transfers) make everyone better off then he would be without. A negative algebraic sum of the EVs, on the other hand, tells us that by *not* introducing the project everyone can be made worse off than he would be with the project.

Assuming positive or 'normal' welfare effects, a project that yields a positive sum for the CVs will *a fortiori* yield a negative sum for the EVs. On the other hand, if the sum of the EVs is positive then *a fortiori* the sum of the CVs is negative.

Should the CVs be negative, however, which would reject the project on efficiency grounds, then it is entirely possible that the EVs could be negative which, on efficiency grounds, would admit the project.

As Meade has correctly remarked, there is no morally binding reason why the more conventional CV calculation alone should be used in cost–benefit analysis. The EV calculation has as much significance. And if ever these alternative calculations lead to opposite conclusions — if, for example, the CV sum was negative and the EV sum was negative — the outcome of the cost–benefit analysis could properly be held to be inconclusive.

If, therefore, the collective good in question is one that causes some incidental but significant environmental disruption, the conventional cost–benefit calculation based on CVs requires the evaluation of this 'diswelfare' to be an estimate of the minimum sum necessary to compensate the losers — a procedure favourable to the environmental interest. If, on the other hand, the introduction of the collective good is one expected to improve the environment, or if its sole purpose is to enhance the environment, the conventional cost–benefit analysis requires the evaluation of the welfare effects of the environmental improvement to be an estimate of the maximum sum the beneficiaries are willing to pay – which (for 'normal' welfare effects) is less favourable to the environmental interest. For this latter case, then, a cost–benefit analysis based on the sum of EVs would be more favourable to the environmental amenity inasmuch as the welfare it confers is to be calculated as the minimum sum the beneficiaries would agree to accept rather than go without the potential benefits.

However, it may not be necessary to invoke this dual test in cases of possible ambiguity if the law were to sanction a presumption in favour of environmental amenity through recognition of citizens' amenity rights. For then, not only would citizens have to be compensated for losses of environmental amenities, but any environmental improvement – say, the planting of a wood or the cleaning up of a stretch of coast line – would be interpreted as a restoring to people what they should in any case have been enjoying by right. The worth of any collective environmental good that is consonant with this attitude would then be the minimum sum that people would require in order to reconcile them to the loss of its potential benefits. And, as indicated, this minimum sum exceeds in normal circumstances the maximum sum they are prepared to pay for it. Moreover, the greater the impact on social welfare the greater is the difference between these two measures of it, and the more likely it becomes that a collective environmental good that is rejected by the conventional cost–benefit analysis under existing laws would be accepted under a law that recognised environmental amenity rights.

In view of society's deepening concern about the environment, at least in the more highly industrialised countries, and of the likelihood that environmental goods will become increasingly valued over time, the question of which measure to use in evaluating its welfare impact on society is far from academic. The possibility that the law, reflecting the state of public opinion, may determine which measure to use has been discussed in the preceding paragraph. Yet in the absence of such a law the economist is still at liberty to do his calculation both ways – and should, indeed, do so wherever the CV measure of introducing an environmental good is negative – and present the results to the public.

Accepting as data the dispersion of population, the income of each family, and the costs of connecting with the collective goods in question, the demand curve for any particular collective goods, or set of collective goods, is better conceived as a schedule of marginal valuations. Thinking in terms of a long period, and in the absence of any external diseconomies arising from the use of the collective goods, the maximum sum each person, or family, in the community is willing to pay – net of all costs it has to pay in order to connect with, or move to, the collective good in question – for the smallest possible unit of the collective good of a given standard (bearing in mind each family's expected use of the good over some period of time) has to be aggregated to obtain the collective valuation of the first unit of it. By increasing the size of this collective good by minimal amounts we obtain the corresponding collective valuations. The *differences* in these collective valuations as we extend the capacity of the collective (capital) good are the increments of aggregate value that correspond to successive increments of the collective good in the long period. Assuming divisibility, the resulting schedule or curve is one of marginal (aggregate) valuation; and intersection of this curve by the long-period marginal resource cost determines the optimal size of the collective good, always provided that the total conditions are also met.

This optimum development with respect to size or capacity, *ceteris paribus*, is, of course, only one aspect of a multi-dimensional optimum. Variation of each feature that is capable of variation will, in general, produce variations in total value and costs. If the marginal valuation curves, and the cost curves also, were separable for each variable feature of the collective good, a multi-dimensional optimum could be reached by realising successively and in any order the optimum corresponding to each feature of the good. In general, we cannot count on separability of this sort, and a convergent approach to a multi-dimensional optimum is required. Once attained, it implies that no further alteration in any of the variable features of the collective good can add to the excess social benefit. However, for simplicity of exposition we shall restrict ourselves from now on to variations in the size of the collective good, all other features remaining unchanged.

If, now, the distinguishing characteristic of a collective good with respect to optimal conditions is that its marginal cost of production cannot be attributed other than jointly to all the beneficiaries, a service that is collective in the long period may not be so in the short period. For example, an extension of the telephone system – a long period adjustment – even if it is so minute as to bring in one additional family confers to that extent benefits also on all existing subscribers, which benefits have to be aggregated in comparing them with the marginal resource costs incurred. In contrast, during a short period over which no extension of the telephone system can (by definition) take place, so long as each additional telephone call incurs some perceptible cost it can be attributed to a particular caller. On our definition then, the telephone system would be a private good in the short period. Similar arguments apply to a highway, an extension of which benefits all users in varying degrees but over which, at any stage of construction, each vehicle might well impose some perceptible maintenance cost.

The reverse is also possible. A good may be a *collective* good in a short period but not in a longer period. For example, the service offered by a given type of bus or ship already in operation will be a collective good if the operational cost with respect to additional passengers is zero or negligible. But in a longer period, in which capacity can be increased, the construction costs that are incurred so as to accommodate one or more additional passengers are indeed positive. In other words the marginal cost of making provision for an additional beneficiary or additional beneficaries can now be attributed to these beneficiaries – a fact which, on this definition, makes the asset itself, the bus or ship, a private good. Thus a good that is intentionally produced becomes collective in any situation in which, for allocative purposes, the marginal valuations of the beneficiaries have to be added together.

The more common *optional* collective goods that spring to mind – television transmission, the services of parks, bridges, light-houses, street-lighting, museums, theatres, galleries – all have zero marginal resource costs in a short period, or rather in the shortest period over which the existing capacity cannot be altered, although additional people may come to share the existing service. Provided no external diseconomies are generated, marginal social cost remains zero and optimal use requires that the service be freely available to all, which rule also realises optimal exchange efficiency inasmuch as everyone pays the same zero price for the marginal service.

However, as the number of would-be beneficiaries increase there comes a point after which the enjoyment of some will be reduced, and reduced more the larger the increase in numbers. The consequent reductions in the benefit to some or all of the beneficiaries of the collective good as their number increases are a form of external diseconomies that are *internal* to the activity in question. Such 'disbenefits' are to be subtracted from the gross aggregate benefits in determining an optimal short-period output of the collective good, which optimal requires that aggregate marginal net benefit equals marginal resource cost (which can equal zero). It comes to the same thing, of course, if the aggregate 'disbenefits' are counted as 'congestion costs' and added to resource costs proper, the necessary optimal equation now being expressed as requiring an output for which aggregate (gross) benefits are equal to marginal *social* cost, this being equal to marginal resource cost plus marginal congestion costs.

The growth of congestion costs resulting from the increase in use of the collective good, however, provides an incentive to extend the long-period capacity of the collective (capital) good. Any warranted extension of this capacity implies that economies can be effected by substituting long-period resource costs for short-period congestion costs. This process would appear more familiar if there were a competitive market in the provision of collective (capital) goods. According as short-period limitations on the competitive production of such goods generate quasi-rents that are above long-period supply-price, there is an incentive to expand long-period output.

For *nonoptional* collective goods, the amount of services enjoyed by each individual in a short period cannot be individually determined – at least, not without the individual's incurring expenses. In general the provision of non-optional collective goods entails positive marginal resource costs. Thus the optimal number of times during a season that the clouds are seeded, and the optimal amount of rain in any single operation, are attained when the marginal aggregate valuations are equal to the marginal resource cost. But since the amount of rain falling on any one farm cannot be varied (without the incurring of expenditures that might be prohibitive[14]) the marginal valuation of the rain received by some of the farms can be positive, zero, or negative, which would imply that the necessary condition for an exchange optimum is not met. No allocative inefficiency is indicated, however, if it is assumed that rainwater cannot be transferred economically: for advantageous exchange of rain water to the point at which its marginal valuation is the same for all farms is not feasible.

Finally, the optimal long-period output of a collective good is larger, the greater is the decline in long-period marginal cost, the lower is the cost of connecting or moving to it, and the greater is the population density and per capita income.

Are there any economic reasons for expecting to find collective goods predominantly in the public sector?

As Hicks (1944) has pointed out, the production of a good may be economically warranted inasmuch as its production yields a 'social surplus', yet it will not be undertaken by private enterprise unless the goods can be priced so as to cover the inclusive costs. Moreover, if average costs are falling, then, although output can indeed be priced so as to cover, or more than cover, average inclusive costs, the private enterprise will be producing an output at which the corresponding demand price is above marginal cost and therefore, on a partial analysis, a suboptimal output.

Dupuit's bridge is an example. In private hands the service will be priced so that revenues make an adequate contribution to capital costs. If the demand curve is known to the bridge owners, and the price of the service is set so as to maximise profit, the resulting traffic is that for which marginal revenue is equal to marginal cost, and not, as it should be, that for which price is equal to marginal cost – which marginal cost may be taken to be zero in the absence of congestion. Of course, if the numbers using the bridge at any one time increase, congestion costs will occur, and equating price to marginal *social* cost may then make it possible to cover total resource costs.

But this arrangement, if adhered to, can also become uneconomic if an extension of the capacity of the bridge would entail smaller costs for given benefits than the existing congestion costs.

A two-part tariff, say a fixed annual charge plus a unit charge equal to marginal cost, is a familiar solution, one proposed in connection with a decreasing average-cost industry compared with which a collective good with an average variable cost of zero can be thought of as a special case. Thus, a fixed annual charge, in order to make full use of public transport or of a national park or a museum, might appear feasible enough. But not all economically viable collective goods can depend upon such a device. There may be no *uniform* annual charge that would make a project financially sound even though it were economically viable. And though a perfectly discriminating monopolist could, by definition, always cover the full costs of an economically viable project, the concept abstracts from the costs of gathering data about each potential beneficiary and also ignores the political difficulties of charging different prices to different people.

Even if it were otherwise, continuous marginal cost pricing of some collective goods, say theatres or public transport, may be uneconomic for other reasons. As numbers increase, costs would have to be incurred in measuring congestion costs and in administering the corresponding prices. Thus the apparent allocative loss from charging a uniform price for a service, one that is not always equal to marginal cost, may be smaller than the expenses that have to be incurred in gathering the information necessary for, and in administering, a marginal-cost-priced service. To the costs of providing a continuing marginal-cost-priced service, we could also add the costs to the public of possible uncertainties about future prices and their dislike of the apparent inequities involved.[15]

Those collective goods that cannot, by any practical system of pricing, be made financially self-supporting are obvious candidates for the public sector. When placed in the public sector, moreover, such collective goods can be operated so as to meet optimal conditions. True, the raising of income or excise taxes in order to meet the costs of these public sector collective goods will in general, effect some infringement of the factor-use optimal condition. But there have been no reliable estimates made of the order of welfare loss involved in marginal taxation. In the meantime one cannot help hoping that some enterprising economist will produce strong evidence to show that the welfare losses so involved are modest.

In deciding whether to place an economically viable collective good in the public sector regard must also be had to the inefficiencies conventionally associated with bureaucratic management, although of course the risks will vary with each particular case. Against this disadvantage, however, has to be set a factor that militates against the private ownership of a collective good, especially those that are not likely to operate under congestion conditions such as light-houses, museums, galleries, television broadcasting, firework displays, etc. That factor is the need of private enterprise to introduce physical means of exclusion in order to exact payment. Thus, not only is the volume of a privately produced collective good below optimal, its price being above marginal cost, but additional resources have to be incurred in providing effective 'excludability'.

These exclusion costs by themselves may not always be onerous. Facilities for exacting charges for entry into art galleries and museums are not in themselves very costly. The infringement of optimal conditions is likely to be much more important – in that such excludability costs are small compared with the loss in social welfare arising from large reductions in the number of short visits. On the other hand, it would be much costlier to build excludability into a light-house, which could, for example, take the form of constructing a light-house to emit infra-red waves that can be detected only by ships that have bought the necessary apparatus from the private light-house company. Cable television, or the system of 'scrambling' television signals that can be 'unscrambled' only by operating a special device, are familiar examples of incurring significant excludability costs so as to enable private enterprise to charge consumers directly.

The notion of building excludability into a service is thus of some interest. It suggests a closer examination of the role it plays, and the 'unnecessary' costs incurred, in the extension and operation of some sectors of private enterprise.

In conclusion economics can offer us an operative concept of a collective good and indicate its relation to that of external economies, a relationship close enough to render the formal optimality condition for the 'ideal' output applicable to both. Such analysis, though it imparts perspective and clarity, does not offer much guidance to the size or composition of the public sector. What it does is to make it plain that the introduction of collective goods, whether into the private or the public sector, poses problems simply because the market cannot provide the information necessary to determine whether they are economically viable.

Apart from the costs of obtaining information about people's willingness to pay, the *private* production of collective goods suffers from two disadvantages: because of the difficulties of marginal cost pricing (especially where relevant marginal costs are zero), outputs would tend to be suboptimal, and because of the need to build in excludability devices, production would be costlier. Therefore, although public sector finance entails additional taxes which may infringe allocative norms, there may be a number of economically viable collective goods that would not come into existence under private enterprise and some that would be more economical if operated in the public sector than in the private.

No more, perhaps, can be expected of economic analysis than that it should suggest areas of empirical enquiry.

NOTES

1 This is in principle possible even if one admits the complication that the benefit enjoyed by each person from a collective good depends upon his knowledge of the n other people sharing it – inasmuch as the critical concept of excess marginal social benefit of the collective good is still manageable.

2 See bibliography, which includes the comments of other writers in the JPE 1971 responding to my 1969 paper. To some extent this present paper also draws upon, amends, and elaborates, a number of the ideas put forward in my 1969 and 1971 papers.

3 Margolis (1955) also observed that Samuelson's definition of a 'public good' did not fit well with the common examples of public goods, such as hospitals, education, courts of law, etc. But this is a semantic confusion that can be avoided, as indicated above, by using the term collective good to denote the functional distinction being sought.

4 Marglin, in his comments on Samuelson's paper of 1969 (Margolis and Guitton) was of the opinion that the definition of a collective good should be related to the problems of capital theory which has something to do with indivisibilities and increasing returns. It is advisable, therefore, to separate the production aspects of a collective good, which may involve these features, from the collective good proper which is to be conceived as a service unless the text indicates otherwise.

5 This distinction was introduced in my 1969 paper.

6 See Samuelson's paper in Margolis and Guitton.

7 In his remarks on Samuelson's paper in Margolis and Guitton.

8 Though not shown by the equation, the collective good meets – or at least does not infringe – the requirements of an exchange optimum. For, if the marginal valuation of each of the beneficiaries is zero, the formal requirement is met. If, on the other hand, the marginal valuation of the collective good differs from one person to another, either in a short or a long period, so long as the good cannot (as in the telephone example) be transferred or (as in the artificial rain example) is too costly to transfer, there are no gains from an actual change from any existing distribution of the amounts of the good.

9 The proviso, 'in the first instance at least', has to be made in consideration of possible external diseconomies which can occur as the numbers wishing to share the collective good increase. The introduction of external diseconomies accompanying the use of a collective good does not, however, alter the necessary optimal condition, which remains as above – it being understood that disbenefits are now also included in the summations.

10 The aerial from my television set offers potential external economies to any of my

close neighbours who may avail himself of the opportunity surreptitiously to attach a wire to it – the net value to him being a saving equal to the cost of installing
his own aerial *less* the expense and trouble he incurs in attaching his set to my
aerial. Other neighbours may follow his bright example, the maximum number
being limited by the increasing cost of making the connection as the distance
increases.

If my consent to their enterprise were obtained, however, so that their net
benefits came explicitly into the reckoning, my television aerial is then to be
regarded as a collective good – or, perhaps, since only several persons make use of
it, a *shared* good. This sense of shared, however, is more restricted than that implied in Buchanan's 1965 paper, in which any good can almost be shared *over time*
between two or more persons, each taking turns at using it. My use of the word
shared, in contrast, refers to simultaneous use or enjoyment by each of the persons
of the good in question.

11 The reader should notice that the definition states that a collective good is 'one
designed to confer simultaneous benefits . . .' Whether in fact the benefits from the
collective good are enjoyed by a number of people simultaneously or, instead, by a
number of people at different times is irrelevant. What matters is that the benefits
could be enjoyed simultaneously by two or more people.

I might emphasise also that the functional definition of a collective good adopted
in this paper is not modified according to the number of beneficiaries. Two
beneficiaries suffice to identify a collective good – though language usage may
suggest that for small numbers a 'shared' good might be a more appropriate term.
(See note 10 above).

Thus, a motor car that is able to accommodate two or more people can be a
collective good over the short term. Like a bus or an aircraft, the benefit of the service it offers can be shared simultaneously among a number of people: the
operating cost, that is, cannot be attributed to any one of the total number of
beneficiaries, or allocated among them on any economic principle.

Moreover, in some cases the definition will apply to only one component of a
project. If a neighbourhood is beautified by an architect then the extra cost incurred cannot be attributed to any one of the beneficiaries. This component of the
housing scheme becomes a collective good on my definition.

Finally, I confine myself for expositional purposes to benefits experienced directly by individuals from the services of some product or asset. But the concept could
be extended to intermediate goods that can provide a service simultaneously to a
number of industrial processes to none of which, therefore, can the marginal cost
of this service be attributed.

12 It may, of course, be very difficult in practice to discover what the valuations
would be under a distribution of income different from the existing one, since it is
difficult enough to estimate benefits under the existing distribution. But we are
dealing only with concepts in this paper, and though we find ourselves balked time
and again in trying to apply our concepts to the real world, this is all the more
reason for clarifying them thoroughly prior to application.

13 It is sometimes asserted that distributional weights cannot in fact be dispensed
with; that the economist who conducts his calulations in money terms, say in un-
weighted dollars, is implicitly attributing a weight of unity to a dollar gained or

lost by the rich or by the poor. This inference would be valid if the economic criterion adopted were one that turns on the algebraic sum of 'utils' or util-weighted dollars. It is not valid, however, for a *potential* Pareto criterion, one that is explicitly based on the notion of hypothetical compensation, as suggested by the New Welfare Economics.

No defence of the New Welfare Economics is implied by this conclusion, however. But it makes clear that economists who adopt this criterion cannot be charged with unwittingly using an implicit system of uniform weights.

14 Where such expenditures are not prohibitive, however, the relevant (marginal) valuations, in determining optimal outputs, must be *net* of any expenditures incurred by individuals.

15 As Vickrey points out (1948) marginal cost of public transport is highest at peak traffic hours during which most travellers are workers. Those in more comfortable circumstances making use of public transport tend to choose less crowded hours.

REFERENCES

Buchanan, J. M., 'An Economic Theory of Clubs', *Economica*, Feb. 1965.

Davis, O. A. and Whinston, A., 'Piecemeal Policy in the Theory of Second Best', *Review of Economic Studies*, July 1967.

— 'On the Distinction between Public and Private Goods', *American Economic Review*, May 1967.

Dolbear, F. T., Jr., 'On the Theory of Optimal Externality', *American Economic Review*, March 1967.

Evans, A. W., 'Private Goods, Externalities, Public Goods', *Scottish Journal of Political Economy*, Feb. 1970.

Hicks, J. R., 'Rehabilitation of Consumers' Surplus', *Review of Economic Studies*, 1943

— 'The Four Consumers' Surpluses', *Review of Economic Studies*, 1944.

Lipsey, R. G. and Lancaster, K., 'The General Theory of Second Best', *Review of Economic Studies*, 1957.

Margolis, J., 'A Comment on the Pure Theory of Public Expenditure', *Review of Economics and Statistics*, Nov. 1955.

Margolis, J. and Guitton, H. (eds.), *Public Economics*, London 1969.

McGuire, M. C., and Aaron H., 'Efficiency and Equity in the Optimal Supply of a Public Good', *Review of Economics and Statistics*, Feb. 1969.

Mishan, E. J., 'Second Thoughts on Second Best', *Oxford Economic Papers*, Oct. 1962.

— 'Pareto Optimality and the Law', *Oxford Economic Papers,* Nov. 1967.

— 'The Relationship between Joint Products, Collective Goods, and External Effects', *Journal of Political Economy*, May 1969.

Mishan, E. J., and others, Symposium on Externalities and Public Goods, *Journal of Political Economy*, September 1971.

Musgrave, R. A., 'Cost–Benefit Analysis and the Theory of Public Finance', *Journal of Economic Literature*, September 1969.

Olson, M., *The Logic of Collective Action*, Harvard 1965.

Samuelson, P. A., 'The Pure Theory of Public Expenditure', *Review of Economics and Statistics*, Nov. 1954.

– 'Aspects of Public Expenditure Theories', *Review of Economics and Statistics*, Nov. 1958.

– 'Contrast between Welfare Conditions for Joint Supply and for Public Goods', *Review of Economics and Statistics*, Feb. 1969.

Vickrey, W., 'Some Objections to Marginal Cost Pricing', *Journal of Political Economy*, September 1948.

Williams, A. 'The Optimal Provision of Public Goods in a System of Local Government', *Journal of Political Economy*, Jan. 1966.

8

Measuring the effect
of public expenditure*

WYNNE GODLEY and CHRISTOPHER TAYLOR

Real GDP as a concept

Ever since National Income Accounts have been compiled the real GDP – the total of goods and services produced at home measured at the prices of a base year – has been used as the best single indicator of the rate of physical economic activity and also (when expressed on a per head basis) of changes in material living standards through time, though it has for long been realised that the accuracy and meaningfulness of the latter process is dubious.

But the predominant, and by far the most important, official use for statistics of real GDP has, in practice, been for short-term economic management, analysis and prediction, and for medium-term planning, particularly of public expenditure.

To be more precise, in most (if not all?) formal short-term models and less formally in the minds of conjuncture specialists of all kinds, it is the movement of aggregate real GDP which governs the movement of employment and unemployment, and which governs also many predominantly cyclical relationships such as the share of profits in total factor income.

So far as the planning of public expenditure is concerned it has, at least in the UK, become customary for the Treasury to draw up five year projections of the real GDP, deduct 'prior claims' for industrial investment and the balance of trade, and then try to reach a decision about how the remainder should be allocated between competing claims – first a division of spoils between private and public sectors, then a division between the various programmes which make up total public expenditure.

* The authors would like to acknowledge the important early work done by Bernard Stafford and the contributions by Ken Coutts on problems of measurement and analysis. They are also grateful for the generosity of the Social Science Research Council in financing the programme of work from which this paper stems.

It is easy to show that total GDP as conventionally measured has properties which make it seriously vulnerable in these two main uses to which it is put. Take first the relationship beween aggregate GDP and employment. It being the case that value added (GDP at current prices) per unit of labour input differs very much in *levels* between sectors, particularly between the public and private sectors, there is a strong presumption that for this reason alone the amount of employment generated by a change in real GDP will differ according to the structure of demand which underlies it. For instance, a 1 per cent increase in real GDP generated by an addition to expenditure on army manpower will cause a larger increase in employment than a 1 per cent addition to GDP brought about by an increase in expenditure on electricity.

Furthermore, labour productivity *grows* at very different rates in different sectors. Since real GDP is measured at the prices of a base year (i.e., in terms of the physical volume of output produced), a given recurring percentage addition generated by expansion of a demand sector with slow productivity growth will cause employment to rise by an *increasingly* larger amount than would result from the same addition to GDP caused by a demand sector with fast productivity growth.

Identical objections may be raised to the use of aggregate GDP for medium-term planning. If only because productivity levels and growth rates differ between sectors, the growth of productive potential (full-employment output) is not invariant to the structure of demand as operational medium-term models tend to assume. And for the same reasons GDP is an inappropriate numeraire for the measurement of opportunity cost in macroeconomic planning. If the Government wants to spend £100 more, whether at current or constant prices, on army manpower, private expenditure (at least in a closed economy) will have to be reduced by more than £100 if total employment is to be unchanged. The ratio of private expenditure foregone to a given addition to public expenditure would be even larger if both were measured at the prices of some previous year; the longer ago the base year, the larger will be the ratio.

A second set of reasons why aggregate GDP is vulnerable as a measure of opportunity cost in the context of macroeconomic planning is associated with the fact that different sectors of demand have different import contents. The higher the import content of total final expenditure, the worse will be the terms of trade at which the Government can achieve simultaneously a given level of employment and a given target for its balance of payments. Thus, assuming target external balance to be achieved, since a change in the structure of demand can make real full employment national *income* fall in relation to real full employment national *output*, the latter concept becomes an inappropriate numeraire for measuring opportunity cost. Moreover, quite apart from this effect via the terms of trade, but still assuming that target external balance is achieved, the labour content of real total final expenditure, and of real GDP, will vary according to the distribution of expenditure between sectors with high and low import contents if final expenditure per unit of labour in exports differs from that elsewhere in the economy. Since that is likely to be the case, there is yet another reason why GDP is likely to be defective as a measure of overall activity and a means of arriving at opportunity costs.

A possible simple answer

This paper suggests a new numeraire to replace real GDP for its two most important functions (those referred to in paragraph 2 above). It is suggested that other than for the dubious business of attempting to gauge welfare growth and making international league tables, the concept of real GDP may be altogether dispensed with. The new concept will provide a measure of productive potential which is not susceptible to variations in the pattern of demand; it will enable inferences to be drawn about the familiar variables and relationships without the same dangers of error through inappropriate aggregation.

The problem addressed is one which in theory can be solved by the use of input–output techniques. Input–output models tend, however, to be so complex and to require the accumulation of so much data that it has proved difficult to make them operational. It is suggested that by making a few not unreasonable, and eventually testable, assumptions, the aggregates can be adjusted by a series of very simple manipulations so as to make them far less vulnerable than at present while keeping the system very easy to handle.

The essential idea is to correct all estimates of real expenditure (as conventionally compiled) so as to bring them approximately into equivalence with one another with respect to their use of labour. So far as domestic activity is concerned, this will be a matter of correcting real expenditures for differences between them in the level and rate of change of labour productivity. For imports a comparable manoeuvre is suggested; the labour cost of additional imports will be the labour content of the additional exports which will be necessary to pay for them.

To bring the problem into focus we give a numerical example which demonstrates in a very simple case how misleading the concept of real GDP will be if the structure of demand changes and how our proposed new concept should help matters. In the following exposition a closed economy will be assumed with unequal productivity levels and growth rates in the various sectors. Later we give a generalised formulation and remove the assumption of a closed economy.

A closed economy with unequal sector productivities

We assume an economy in which there are only two demand sectors, 'private consumption' (C) and 'public consumption' (G). Labour productivity (value added per unit of labour at base year prices) is twice as high in the base year in the industries serving C as those serving G; and labour productivity in C grows at 10 per cent per annum while in G it does not grow at all. Now consider the conventional measurement of such an economy on alternative assumptions about the evolution of the structure of real demand. Starting from a given position in the base year (0) we consider the real demand and output counterparts (with constant *total* employment) of employment in G on the one hand (1A) remaining constant and on the other (1B) falling 50 per cent. (See Table 1).

In this example, the share of labour costs in value added is 50 per cent in C and 100 per cent in G, implying average earnings of 1.00 in each sector. 'Labour shares' are assumed constant, but this is not essential to the argument; it is, however, essential that labour shares in different sectors should change at the same rate, if they do change.

TABLE 1   *Conventional GDP*

Year	0	1A	1B	Symbol
Employment (numbers)				e_t
1 C	75	75	125	
2 G	100	100	50	
3 Total	175	175	175	
Productivity (output ÷ employment at year 0 prices)				$p_0 q_t / e_t$
4 C	2.00	2.20	2.20	
5 G	1.00	1.00	1.00	
Real expenditure (at year 0 prices)				$p_0 q_t$
6 C	150	165	275	
7 G	100	100	50	
(= REAL GDP)				
8 Total	250	265	325	

The example shows how because of alternative structures of demand in year 1, a given quantity of labour produces completely different amounts of real GDP. Very wrong answers would be obtained if in forecasting such an economy it was assumed that the cost of adding 50 to G is equal to 50 of C foregone, or (what amounts to the same thing) that productive potential is invariant to the structure of demand.

Our suggestion is that a new numeraire, which we call 'ells',[1] may quite easily be inferred from conventional concepts which brings all components of demand into equivalence, at least approximately, with one another with respect to the labour they pre-empt. The principle is to attempt to measure *only* the labour content of each demand sector. In the base year this is simply a question of correcting for differences in productivity levels; for subsequent years there has to be a correction for differences in productivity growth rates. In practice one may correct for productivity levels by using a summary input–output table for the UK which expresses final demands by sector in terms of primary inputs; under this method, the reciprocal of the share (for each demand sector) of income from employment in value added is used as a base-year benchmark for productivity in that sector. The correction for productivity growth rates may be readily inferred from relative price movements if it can be assumed that

(a) Average money earnings (corrected for overtime etc.) increase uniformly across the board.

(b) Trend productivity growth rates *by sector* are invariant to the structure of demand.

(c) The price of output is systematically related to the movement of normal unit labour costs.

In Table 2 the example in Table 1 is extended to show the additional information and arithmetical manipulations necessary to derive ells.

The steps taken are

(a) Obtain an aggregate deflator that is invariant to the structure of demand, termed 'par deflator' for short. We have taken for this purpose the harmonic mean of price relatives weighted by base-year expenditure. Thus, for year 1 the deflator is

$$\frac{250}{(150 \times 1/1.091) + (100 \times 1/1.200)}.$$

(b) Next in lines 15 and 16 we deflate each component of demand at current prices by the (single) par deflator, thus correcting simultaneously for the general rate of inflation and for differing productivity growth rates.

(c) Finally, to obtain 'ells' we weight lines 15 and 16 by the respective base

TABLE 2   *Derivation of ells*

Year	1	2A	2B	Symbol
Price indices*				p_t/p_o
9 C	1.000	1.091	1.091	
10 G	1.000	1.200	1.200	
Expenditure at current prices				$p_t q_t$
11 C	150	180.0	300.0	
12 G	100	120.0	60.0	
13 Total	250	300.0	360.0	
14 'Par deflator'	1.0	1.132	1.132	PD_t
Expenditure at constant prices including relative price effect				$p_t q_t / PD_t$
15 C	150	159.0	265.0	
16 G	100	106.0	53.0	
Ells				L_t
17 C	75	79.5	132.5	
18 G	100	106.0	53.0	
19 Total	175	185.5	185.5	

* Note that the price indices taken in conjunction with productivity growth rates in the first part of Table 1 imply an increase of 20% in average earnings.

year shares of labour in value added (reciprocals of lines 4 and 5, year 0), thereby correcting for differences in productivity levels.

The point of course is that the supply of ells is invariant to the structure of demand and is therefore a better concept for measuring productive potential than conventional GDP. Ells may readily be translated back into conventional measures, enabling a 'rate of exchange' between the demand sectors to be inferred. Thus, ells per £1 of expenditure at base year prices are 1.06 in G and 0.482 in C, giving an exchange rate in terms of labour content of £2.2 C to £1 of G; lines 6 and 7 show that if in year 1 G is cut by £50 measured at year 0 prices then C can be increased by £110 measured in the same way.

Note that only line 3 and lines 6–13 inclusive appear in published statistics. The key lines 1 and 2, representing the labour directly and indirectly required for each demand sector, would normally only be obtained by an elaborate input–output exercise. The main purpose of the present exercise is to show that input–output analysis can be bypassed and labour use in final demand sectors inferred simply from the usual National Income accounts so long as the assumptions listed on p. 117 are valid. Their validity is seemingly plausible though we have so far only carried out a partial and preliminary verification.

The formal derivation of ells[2]

Relative prices

Under certain conditions, the unit labour requirements of a sector or industry will be exactly reflected in its index of unit factor costs. Expenditure on a sector at factor cost (i.e. final expenditure at market prices *less* indirect taxes net of subsidies and imports) is related to employment by the following identity:

$$p_{it} q_{it} \equiv \frac{1}{k_{it}} w_{it} e_{it} \tag{1}$$

where $p_{it} q_{it}$ is net value added at current prices in sector 'i' at time 't', w_{it} is average money earnings, e_{it} is employment (including all indirect as well as direct labour required for final output in that sector) and k_{it} is the share of wages in value added. Unit value added may then be written:

$$p_{it} = \frac{w_{it}}{k_{it}} u_{it} \tag{2}$$

where u_{it} indicates employment per unit of output (e_{it}/q_{it}) in i. Then given w_{it} and k_{it}, p_{it} is directly proportional to u_{it}.[3]

An index of unit value added at t compared with base period 0 can be written:

$$\frac{p_{it}}{p_{i0}} = \frac{k_{i0}}{k_{it}} \frac{w_{it}}{w_{i0}} \frac{u_{it}}{u_{i0}}. \tag{3}$$

If relative earnings in different sectors i, j, do not change through time,

$$\text{i.e.} \quad \frac{w_{it}}{w_{i0}} = \frac{w_{jt}}{w_{j0}} \text{ (all } i, j\text{)}, \tag{4}$$

shares of wages in value added in different sectors either remain constant or move at the same rate through time, i.e.

$$\frac{k_{it}}{k_{i0}} = \frac{k_{jt}}{k_{j0}} \text{ (all } i, j\text{)} \tag{5}$$

$$\text{hence} \quad \frac{p_{it}}{p_{i0}} \bigg/ \frac{p_{jt}}{p_{j0}} = \frac{u_{it}}{u_{i0}} \bigg/ \frac{u_{jt}}{u_{j0}} \tag{6}$$

Thus, under these conditions, an index of *relative prices* (or more strictly, relative unit value added) for any two sectors will indicate relative unit labour requirements of those sectors.[4]

The par deflator

Under the conditions described above (namely, constant relative wages and labour shares in value added), a general price index will reflect unit labour requirements for output as a whole in a manner similar to that for an individual sector ((3) above). This may be illustrated by the example of the GDP deflator. The latter, being an arithmetic Paasche index may also be thought of as a current-weighted (Paasche) harmonic mean of price (or, more strictly, unit value added) relatives which may be depicted as follows:

$$GDPD_t = \frac{\Sigma p_{it}\, q_{it}}{\Sigma p_{it}\, q_{it}\, \dfrac{p_{i0}}{p_{it}}} = \frac{\Sigma p_{it}\, q_{it}}{\Sigma p_{it}\, q_{it}\, \dfrac{k_{it}}{k_{i0}}\, \dfrac{w_{i0}}{w_{it}}\, \dfrac{u_{i0}}{u_{it}}} \quad \text{from (3).} \tag{7}$$

Using (4) and (5) above, this may be written as

$$GDPD_t = \frac{k_0\, w_t}{k_t\, w_0}\left(\frac{\Sigma p_{it}\, q_{it}}{\Sigma p_{it}\, q_{it}\, \dfrac{u_{i0}}{u_{it}}} \right) \tag{8}$$

where w_t/w_0 is a general index of average earnings ($= w_{it}/w_{i0} = w_{jt}/w_{j0}$ etc.) and k_t/k_0 is a general index of labour shares in value added ($= k_{it}/k_{i0} = k_{jt}/k_{j0}$ etc.).

Thus the GDP deflator is equivalent, under the stated conditions, to a general index of wages deflated by a general index of the share of wages in output and multiplied by a harmonic mean of unit labour requirements. It should be noted that the latter mean is weighted by the *current* pattern of final expenditure (minus indirect taxes and imports) by sector in GDP. This formulation suffers from the drawback that the GDP deflator is a current-weighted index, and therefore susceptible to changes in the composition of demand. Ideally what is needed is an index of unit labour requirements for output in general that is independent of changes in the pattern of demand, in the sense that it relates to a unique pattern. (Otherwise variations in the share of public expenditure in GDP will affect the measurement of relative price, which is clearly undesirable). Consequently the ells system utilises a general deflator framed in terms of the pattern of demand in the base period:

$$PD_t = \frac{\Sigma p_{i0}\, q_{i0}}{\Sigma p_{i0}\, q_{i0}\, (p_{i0}/p_{it})} = \frac{k_0\, w_t}{k_t\, w_0}\left(\frac{\Sigma p_{i0}\, q_{i0}}{\Sigma p_{i0}\, q_{i0}\, (u_{i0}/u_{it})} \right) \tag{9}$$

using (3), (4) and (5) above.

Thus the par deflator is equivalent to a general wage index deflated by a general index of labour shares, multiplied by a base-weighted (or 'par') harmonic mean of unit labour requirements.

It should be noted that, by virtue of (3), (4), (5), and (9), for any sector:

$$\frac{p_{it}}{p_{i0}} \bigg/ PD_t = \frac{u_{it}}{u_{i0}} \bigg/ U_t \tag{10}$$

$$\text{where } U_t = \frac{\Sigma p_{i0}\, q_{i0}}{\Sigma p_{i0}\, q_{i0}\, (u_{i0}/u_{it})}.$$

That is, in the conditions described, the 'relative price' of sector i with respect to the price of output in general corresponds to the differential movement between sector i's unit labour requirements and those of output in general.

Index of productive capacity

The productive capacity of the economy at time t is expressed as follows:

$$L_t = \Sigma(k_{i0}\, p_{it}\, q_{it}/PD_t)$$
$$= (\Sigma w_{i0}\, e_{it})/U_t \text{ (from (1) and (9)).} \tag{11}$$

Thus, total capacity is equal to total employment (or, more accurately, the total of sector employments weighted by base-year wages) divided by the 'par' index of unit labour requirements. In index form:

$$L_{t/0} = \frac{\Sigma k_{i0}\, p_{it}\, q_{it}}{\Sigma k_{i0}\, p_{i0}\, q_{i0}} \bigg/ PD_t = \frac{\Sigma w_{i0}\, e_{it}}{\Sigma w_{i0}\, e_{i0}} \bigg/ U_t \tag{12}$$

where $L_{t/0}$ signifies L_t/L_0.

It must be noted that this measure is not *completely* invariant to the pattern of demand, since $w_{i0}\, e_{it}$ will be affected by the distribution of e_{it}. Only if $w_{it} = w_{jt}$ (all i, j) will perfect invariance hold. The modification:

$$L_{t/0} = \frac{\Sigma(k_{i0}/w_{i0})\, p_{it}\, q_{it}}{\Sigma(k_{i0}/w_{i0})\, p_{i0}\, q_{i0}} \bigg/ PD_t$$

completely satisfies the invariance requirement, but requires base-year estimates of direct and indirect *numbers* employed by sector, whereas $w_{it}\, e_{it}$ can be derived from published national income data.

Opportunity costs

Requirements of ells per unit of output by any sector are determined by the share of labour in its value added and by the differential movement between its unit labour requirements and the average for output as a whole:

$$\frac{L_{it}}{p_{i0}\,q_{it}} = \frac{k_{i0}\,p_{it}\,q_{it}/PD_t}{p_{it}\,q_{it} \Big/ \dfrac{p_{it}}{p_{i0}}}$$

$$= k_{i0}\frac{p_{it}}{p_{i0}} \Big/ PD_t = k_{i0}\frac{u_{it}}{u_{i0}} \Big/ U_t, \text{ from (10).} \tag{13}$$

Furthermore, unit opportunity costs as between any two sectors (reflecting relative ells requirements) are determined by their respective shares of labour in value added and by their relative productivity movements. Using (13):

$$\frac{L_{it}}{p_{i0}\,q_{it}} \Big/ \frac{L_{jt}}{p_{j0}\,q_{jt}} = \frac{k_{i0}}{k_{j0}}\frac{p_{it}/p_{i0}}{[p_{jt}/p_{j0}]} = \frac{k_{i0}}{k_{j0}}\frac{u_{it}/u_{i0}}{[u_{jt}/u_{j0}]}. \tag{14}$$

The measurement of the resource cost of public expenditure in the ells system is thus seen to be extremely straightforward. Any public expenditure programme, or group of programmes, for which a 'relative price effect' can be estimated can be expressed in ells using the simple formula:

$$L_{gt} = k_{g0}\,G_t\!\left(\frac{p_{gt}}{p_{g0}} \Big/ PD_t\right) \tag{15}$$

where G_t is programme expenditure in year t *minus* imports and indirect taxes, valued in prices of the base year, and the term in brackets is the relative price effect for the appropriate part of public expenditure (index of unit value added divided by par deflator). The opportunity cost of G in terms of other output, for example private consumption, is then

$$C_t = \frac{1}{k_{c0}}\,L_{gt}\!\left(PD_t\Big/\frac{p_{ct}}{p_{c0}}\right)$$

$$= \frac{k_{g0}}{k_{c0}}\!\left(\frac{p_{gt}}{p_{g0}}\frac{p_{ct}}{p_{c0}}\right)G_t, \text{ from (14) and (15)} \tag{16}$$

where C_t is the value added component of consumption foregone, valued at base year prices.

The resources available for other outputs are given by $L_t - L_{gt}$, and permissible levels of output in other sectors can be found by expressing any chosen distribution of expenditure in terms of relative ells requirements, and reconverting the implied permissible levels of ells per sector into output, using the transforms described above.

The treatment of imports

This section contains a formal account of how the balance of payments problem is dealt with in our system, but the reader is warned that the algebra is rather heavy going bearing in mind the essentially simple manoeuvre which is being carried out. The authors provided a worked arithmetic example which was discussed at the Conference. Copies of the relevant tables can be obtained from the authors on request.

The simple system so far set out assumes that labour is the only strategic constraint on the supply of resources for domestic use. Since in reality the balance of payments is an equally important constraint, any system for measuring resource costs by sector should include the costs of producing exports needed to pay for imports generated by individual sectors.[5] Such a step is particularly appropriate for purposes of public-expenditure planning because the import content of most public consumption is appreciably lower than that of other major expenditure sectors. A relative expansion of the former is therefore likely to reduce total imports and to that extent benefit the balance of trade at given output.

The problem is dealt with in the ells system by distributing the total of direct and indirect manpower needed for exports, adjusted so that the total of value added at current prices in exports equals total imports (minus the import content of exports), between other sectors in proportion to their share of imports. The 'imports–inclusive' ells requirements ('*LM*'s) of any sector of domestic expenditure, LM_{it}, *where 'i' now indicates any sector other than exports*, are as follows:

$$LM_{it} = (w_{i0}\, e_{it} + w_{x0}\, e_{xit})\, PD_t \tag{17}$$

where the suffix x denotes exports and where e_{xit} is direct and indirect employment in exports when the latter are equal in value to the import content of sector i at time t.

Thus,

$$LM_{it} = (k_{i0}\, p_{it}\, q_{it} + k_{x0}\, p_{xt}\, q_{xit})/PD_t \tag{18}$$

where $p_{xt}\, q_{xit} = p_{mt}\, q_{mit}$, m denoting imports and $p_{mt}\, q_{mit}$ being the import content of i.[6]

Then import-inclusive resource requirements in sector i can be stated:

$$LM_{it} = (k_{i0}\, p_{it}\, q_{it} + k_{x0}\, p_{mt}\, q_{mit})/PD_t \tag{19}$$

and requirements per unit of output are:

$$\frac{LM_{it}}{p_{i0}\, q_{it}} = \left(k_{i0}\, \frac{p_{it} q_{it}}{p_{i0} q_{it}} + k_{x0}\, m_{it}\, \frac{p_{mt}}{p_{m0}} \right)\Big/ PD_t \tag{20}$$

where m_{it} is the ratio of imports to output in sector i (i.e., $p_{mi0} \, q_{mit}/pq_{it}$), assumed exogenous and constant.

It then follows that

$$\frac{LM_{it}}{p_{i0} \, q_{it}} = k_{i0} \, \frac{p_{it}}{p_{i0}} \Bigg/ PD_t$$

$$+ k_{x0} \, m_{it} \left(\frac{p_{mt}}{p_{m0}} \Bigg/ \frac{p_{xt}}{p_{x0}} \right) \frac{p_{xt}}{p_{x0}} \Bigg/ PD_t \tag{21}$$

and, from (13)

$$= k_{i0} \frac{u_{it}}{u_{i0}} \Bigg/ U_t + k_{x0} \, m_{it} \left(\frac{p_{mt}}{p_{xt}} \Bigg/ \frac{p_{m0}}{p_{x0}} \right) \frac{u_{xt}}{u_{x0}} \Bigg/ U_t. \tag{22}$$

That is to say, domestic resources needed to pay for imports per unit of output in sector i are determined, as might be expected, by the import propensity of the sector, m_{it}, the share of labour in valued added of exports, k_{x0}, the differential movement of unit labour requirements in exports compared with general output, $u_{xt}/u_{x0}(U_t)^{-1}$, and the terms of trade (expressed as an index of its value in the base year).[7] Considered on its own, an improvement in terms of trade from time 0 to t implies an inversely proportional reduction in import resource costs of all sectors.

Import-inclusive resource requirements for all domestic expenditure sectors combined are as follows:

$$\Sigma LM_{it} = \Sigma[(k_{i0} \, p_{it} \, q_{it} + k_{x0} \, p_{mt} \, q_{mit})/PD_t] \tag{23}$$

and since $\Sigma p_{mt} \, q_{mit} = p_{xt} \, q_{xt}^*$, where the asterisk denotes exports adjusted to achieve the trade target of zero:

$$\Sigma LM_{it} = (\Sigma L_{it}) + L_{xt}^* = L_t \tag{24}$$

(since full employment is also assumed).

Adjustment of the terms of trade

The preceding formulation ignores the problem that, under full employment and with price relativities determined in the manner described earlier, variation in the distribution of expenditure between sectors is likely to produce variation in the overall ratio of imports to total expenditure; if achievement of the target balance of trade involves adjustment of the terms of trade (through changes in the exchange rate or other means) in response to variations in the overall import/expenditure ratio, the 'target-adjusted' terms of trade[8] (and therefore, from (22) above, import-inclusive unit resource costs) are not independent of the pattern of expenditure adopted.

The basic idea is that the volume of exports (measured at base year prices) required to pay for a given volume of imports at any point of time depends in a stable and consistent way on the difference between that volume of imports and the volume implied by the overall import/expenditure ratio of the base year. More specifically:

$$\text{when} \quad p_{xt}^* \, q_{xt}^* = \Sigma p_{mt}^* \, q_{mit},$$
$$p_{x0} \, q_{xt}^* = fm_0 \, PDFE_t + \phi(\Sigma p_{m0} \, q_{mit} - fm_0 \, PDFE_t) \quad (25)$$

where the asterisks are used to denote target-adjusted values, where fm_0 is the overall percentage import content of domestic final expenditure in year 0, where $PDFE_t$ is 'par' domestic final expenditure in year t, i.e. domestic final expenditure at base year prices when the sectoral shares in expenditure are as in the base year,[9] and where ϕ is some stable positive function with a value greater than unity.

Then

$$\frac{p_{x0} q_{xt}^*}{\Sigma p_{m0} q_{mit}} = \frac{fm_0 PDFE_t}{\Sigma p_{m0} q_{mit}} + \phi\left(1 - \frac{fm_0 PDFE_t}{\Sigma p_{m0} q_{mit}}\right) \quad (26)$$

and since $p_{xt}^* \, q_{xt}^* = (p_{xt}^*/p_{x0}) \, p_{x0} \, q_{xt}^*$ and $\Sigma p_{mt}^* \, q_{mit} = (p_{mt}^*/p_{m0}) \, \Sigma p_{m0} \, q_{mit}$,

$$\left(\frac{p_{mt}}{p_{xt}} \bigg/ \frac{p_{m0}}{p_{x0}}\right)^* = \frac{fm_0 PDFE_t}{\Sigma p_{m0} q_{mit}} + \phi\left(1 - \frac{fm_0 PDFE_t}{\Sigma p_{m0} \, q_{mit}}\right) \quad (27)$$

using (25) and (26).

That is to say, if ϕ is known and the import/expenditure ratio associated with any contemplated pattern of domestic expenditure is also known, the target-adjusted import resource costs of any sector i can be calculated. Restating (21) above:

$$\frac{LM_{it}}{p_{i0} \, q_{it}} = k_{i0} \frac{p_{it}}{p_{i0}} \bigg/ PD_t$$
$$+ k_{x0}^* \, m_{it} \left(\frac{p_{mt}}{p_{xt}} \bigg/ \frac{p_{m0}}{p_{x0}}\right)^* \frac{p_{xt}^*}{p_{x0}} \bigg/ PD_t \quad (28)$$

where $k_{xo}^* = k_{xo} \, p_{xt}/p_{xt}^*$

This may be written alternatively

$$\frac{LM_{it}}{p_{i0} \, q_{it}} = k_{i0} \frac{p_{it}}{p_{i0}} \bigg/ PD_t$$
$$+ k_{x0} \, m_{it} \left(\frac{p_{mt}}{p_{xt}} \bigg/ \frac{p_{m0}}{p_{x0}}\right)^* \frac{p_{xt}}{p_{x0}} \bigg/ PD_t \quad (29)$$
$$= k_{i0} \frac{u_{it}}{u_{i0}} \bigg/ U_t + k_{x0} \, m_{it} \left(\frac{p_{mt}}{p_{xt}} \bigg/ \frac{p_{m0}}{p_{x0}}\right)^* \frac{u_{xt}}{u_{x0}} \bigg/ U_t \quad (30)$$

using (13).

Thus the import-inclusive resource costs of sector i are determined as in (21) and (22), except that target-adjusted terms of trade should be substituted for their 'actual' (unadjusted) counterpart.

Validity of assumptions

It is hardly necessary to say that the usefulness of the foregoing 'model' system as a tool for measuring the resource costs and thence the opportunity costs of public expenditure rests on the validity of its key assumptions — namely those relating to the distribution of income (i.e. constant relative wages and consistent movement of labour shares in value added across all demand sectors). Only in so far as these hold reasonably well can movements in 'relative prices' be taken to reflect movements in labour requirements, though there is a strong presumption that the system will be superior to one which ignores differences in productivity and import contents.

A partial test of the validity of our key assumption has given favourable results. Thus computations done at the Department of Applied Economics for quarterly data from 1955 to 1971 show, for example, that the relative price of public authorities' current expenditure (unit value added[10]/par deflator) rose in an extremely regular way at 1.95 per cent per annum, over this period, with very little deviation from this trend. This is exactly what one would expect if productivity in the output of public services grows steadily and consistently more slowly than the national average and if wages in the public sector move consistently in line with the national average.

Existing procedures used by the Treasury

In its annual White Papers the Treasury presents estimates of the 'demand on output' to be generated by public expenditure and also estimates of expenditure at constant prices including the relative price effect ('in cost terms').

The different versions represent different approximations to some concept of opportunity cost. No rationale has ever yet been provided which would justify or explain precisely the properties of the various measures and, in particular, it has never been explained whether, and if so, how, these measures can be incorporated into a framework involving the economy as a whole. We end by briefly discussing the relationship between 'demand on output' and 'expenditure in cost terms' to ells and LMs.

The use of the concept 'demand on output' recognises that the various economic categories of real expenditure as conventionally measured do not pre-empt equal quantities of real resources pound for pound. The idea is to measure cost in terms of private expenditure foregone, given always that the Government, when it authorises expenditure, simultaneously manipulates fiscal and trade policies in an appropriately offsetting way. It follows that public expenditure on goods, services, transfer payments, imports and existing assets like land and houses each may, for a given amount of cash appropriated, cause different amounts of private expenditure to be foregone.

In reaching numerical estimates of 'demand on output' the Treasury counts expenditure on goods, services and imports as all being in equivalence. Estimates of expenditure 'in cost terms' are to be found in the White Paper tables which show annual projections of public expenditure programmes (in total, and individually) at constant prices but including the 'relative price effect' (RPE) defined as a sum of money equal to the excess of the rise in the average 'price' of goods and services purchased by the Government over the rise in the average price of all goods and services produced in the economy.

Figures showing expenditure 'in cost terms' are logically equivalent to projections at current prices divided by the future movement of the GDP deflator, from which it follows that projected expenditures 'in cost terms' will bear the same ratio of GDP at constant prices as future expenditures to GDP both measured at current prices. It also follows that the ratios of individual programmes to one another 'in cost terms' will be the same as the ratios at current prices.

How does the procedure for measuring the resource cost of public expenditure in the White Paper compare with the model described above? Under the White Paper procedure, the 'relative price effect' is applied to programme expenditure valued at 'survey' (base year) prices, so that the resource cost of year t's expenditure valued at base year prices is as follows:

$$R_{gt} = (p'_{g0}\, q_{pt} + p_{m0}\, q_{mgt}) \frac{p''_{gt}}{p''_{g0}} \Big/ GDPD_t. \tag{31}$$

In (31) p'_{g0} represents the domestic unit cost of public expenditure in the base year *inclusive* of indirect taxes, and the term in brackets represents public expenditure at constant market prices as conventionally recorded. p''_{gt}/p''_{g0} represents a price index of public expenditure, *excluding* the indirect taxes but *including* imports. If, as we assume, the real import content of public expenditure is constant, so that $p_{m0}\, q_{mgt}/p'_{g0'}\, q_{gt} = m'_{gt} = m'_{g0}$ (all t), equation (31) may be rewritten:

$$R_{gt} = (p'_{g0}\, q_{gt}) \frac{p_{gt}}{p_{g0}} \Big/ GDPD_t$$

$$+ (p_{m0}\, q_{mgt}) \frac{p_{mt}}{p_{m0}} \Big/ GDPD_t \tag{32}$$

and resource costs per unit of expenditure are:

$$\frac{R_{gt}}{p'_{g0} q_{gt}} = \frac{p_{gt}}{p_{g0}} \bigg/ GDPD_t + m'_{gt} \frac{p_{mt}}{p_{m0}} \bigg/ GDPD_t \tag{33}$$

$$= \frac{p_{gt}}{p_{g0}} \bigg/ GDPD_t + m'_{gt} \left(\frac{p_{mt}}{p_{m0}} \bigg/ \frac{p_{xt}}{p_{x0}}\right) \frac{p_{xt}}{p_{x0}} \bigg/ GDPD_t. \tag{34}$$

This may be compared with the corresponding formula given by the model system (from (29) above):

$$\frac{LM_{gt}}{p_{g0} q_{gt}} = k_{g0} \frac{p_{gt}}{p_{gt}} \bigg/ PD_t$$

$$+ k_{x0} m_{gt} \left(\frac{p_{mt}}{p_{m0}} \bigg/ \frac{p_{xt}}{p_{x0}}\right)^{*} \frac{p_{xt}}{p_{x0}} \bigg/ PD_t. \tag{35}$$

The similarity of these two alternative measures is clear. The only material differences are the following:

(i) LM_{gt} is based on the respective 'labour shares' of the relative price effects applicable to value added and import content, whereas R_{gt} is the weighted sum of the whole of these effects.

(ii) The denominator for 'relative price effects' under the ells system is the par deflator, whereas the White Paper procedure employs the GDP deflator.

(iii) The White Paper procedure makes no allowance for variation between the actual and the target-adjusted terms of trade in calculating the resource cost of the import content of public expenditure, whereas our approach uses the adjusted terms of trade.

NOTES

1 'Ells' because L stands for labour.

2 This section is based on the framework developed by K. J. Coutts and C. T. Taylor in a Department of Applied Economics working paper *Productive Potential in the UK Economy and the Pattern of Demand* (March 1973).

3 It should be noted that throughout this exercise sectoral productivities, u_i, are taken to be exogenous and independent of the level of sectoral output at any point of time.

4 This result holds regardless of whether output and labour are measured in 'physical' units (e.g., tons and employees respectively) or at constant prices and wages respectively.

5 Assuming that a target of zero is set for the balance of trade. However, similar arguments apply to any trade target adopted, provided one is adopted. In what follows, it is assumed that the trade target, measured in current ('t') prices, is zero.

6 In order to simplify the exposition, the argument immediately following omits some complications associated with import and export prices which will be returned to later (see pp. 124–6 below). It can be assumed temporarily that import prices are given, that export prices are determined solely by domestic labour costs plus a constant profit margin, and that achievement of the target balance of trade with full employment involves no change in the terms of trade thus established.

7 It should be noted that the reciprocal of $(p_{mt}/p_{xt})/(p_{m0}/p_{x0})$ is not the conventional terms of trade, since p_{xt}/p_{x0} is an index of unit value added in exports, not the conventional export price index.

8 This description is preferred to 'par' terms of trade because 'par' implies some balanced, normal, or long-run pattern of domestic expenditure, whereas no such connotation is intended here.

9 i.e., when

$$\frac{p_{l0}q_{lt} + p_{m0}q_{mlt}}{\Sigma(p_{l0}q_{lt} + p_{m0}q_{mlt})} = \frac{p_{l0}q_{l0} + p_{m0}q_{ml0}}{\Sigma(p_{l0}q_{l0} + p_{m0}q_{ml0})}, \text{ all } i.$$

10 The computations were much trickier than they may sound. To obtain unit value added by expenditure sector, imports and indirect taxes had to be deducted from each category of expenditure measured at both current and constant prices, using an intricate process of apportionment.

PART III: PRACTICAL PROBLEMS

9

Decisions in the transport sector*

A. J. HARRISON

Introduction: purpose and scope of paper

This paper is concerned with problems which arise in applying techniques of economic appraisal to day-to-day decision taking in the transport sector. Transport, like other fields of application, throws up a large number of technical and conceptual issues, but these will not be pursued in this paper, except in so far as they have implications for the role which economic appraisal may reasonably play in public sector decision-taking. The issues which will mainly concern us stem from the interplay between (economic) analysis on the one hand, and administrative and political processes on the other. A great deal of literature has appeared recently, arising largely from the US experience with PPBS, which has tried to show that the implicit political assumptions of analysis in general, such as those of consistency and rationality, were politically naive, ignoring the facts of power, the needs of politicians for support, the logic of the pork-barrel etc. This literature has also tended to stress the gap between the ambitions and achievements of analysis. Another important, and relatively recent, theme centres round participation and consultation, reaction against unresponsive bureaucracies heedless of what people really want. All three factors tend to diminish the role of analysis.

The main focus of the paper, however, is not on the political process but on the planning and administrative processes which underly it. These obviously interact with the political process in various ways according to the political system of which they form part and the rules under which they are set up and conduct their business but, for well known reasons, administrative processes do possess some autonomy. The paper is written on the basis of experience in the application of economic techniques to day-to-day problems within the former Ministry of Transport and the present

* Any opinions expressed in this paper are the sole responsibility of the author: they must not be taken to represent the views of the Department of the Environment.

Department of the Environment. Perhaps of all UK government departments, these two have been most associated with the practical use of cost–benefit analysis, but this association is not based on a large amount of published material. With some exceptions, the results of economic appraisal have remained within the government machine. Not that there has been any deliberate policy of concealment of the methods being used: indifference to publication on behalf of practitioners is perhaps the most important factor explaining this situation. Whatever the reason the result has been that discussion of the role of cost–benefit analysis in decision taking has tended to be founded on a small number of set pieces, which are not typical of the bulk (in numerical terms) of what is done and, perhaps for this reason, the issues which tend to concern practitioners most are neglected, because their day-to-day importance is ignored and others given unique emphasis.

The paper is in the following sections:

Section 1 considers the development of cost–benefit in the transport sector, identifies some of its successes and outstanding technical problems.

Section 2 outlines some of the features of the planning and administrative features within which economic appraisal may be used, with a view to defining the various roles which it might play, and

Section 3 considers a small number of specific issues.

Section 4 sums up and attempts to define what the appropriate role for economic appraisal is.

1   The development and current state of cost–benefit analysis in the transport sector

Cost–benefit analysis has a long history, comparatively, in the transport sector. Its beginnings have been traced to the 1930s and even before, but substantially it was established, at least in the UK, in the 1960s by the classic studies of the Victoria Line (Beesley and Foster, 1965; Foster and Beesley, 1963) and the London to Birmingham motorway (Coburn, Beesley and Reynolds, 1960). Although these studies are often taken to have been used to justify, ex ante, the construction of these projects, they were in fact exploratory studies, done ex post facto, which aimed mainly to identify the main items of cost and benefit and to have a shot either at estimating their order of magnitude, where items with a directly or indirectly available price tag were concerned, or instead using arbitrary values to test for importance where prices were not available. When these studies were carried out very little by way of methodology or empirical evidence on reasonable values for such items as time savings, was available. This was true not only of evaluation procedures, but also of forecasting processes.

Students of the readily available literature – as opposed to the total available – might be forgiven for thinking that very little had happened since then. In the field of roads, there are only Quarmby's paper (Quarmby, 1970) on the Morecambe Bay barrage and the piece by Pearce and Nash (Pearce and Nash, 1973) which discuss the economics of individual schemes and which have been published in journals economists might read. The civil engineering journals have provided a more important platform than the economic: in particular, early work on the evaluation of inter-urban and urban roads was published in this way. In the case of rail studies, the official Cambrian Coast study (Ministry of Transport, 1969) has been followed by some private ventures, including a reworking of the original figures and technical discussion of some of the component items (Sugden, 1972; Thomas, 1971), but by no more published studies by government departments. Central government has not published a major study of the economics of an individual road or rail scheme, except the Heathrow Link study (Ministry of Transport, 1970) – scarcely a typical investment. The literature on the major benefit items at first sight is scarcely more extensive. A recent flurry of technical academic debate has centred round the theory of the value of time (De Serpa, 1971; Donnea, 1972) and to a lesser degree round the value of life or accident saving (Mishan, 1971). But these papers have not provided, nor have they sought to, specific values which a practitioner might use. More than one has been written in apparent ignorance of previous and obscurely located work in the field.

This shortage of conventional literature hides, however, a very large effort, dispersed through government organisations and those working for them in the private sector and mainly carried out in the course of particular planning operations, which has used cost–benefit techniques or been aimed at extending and improving them. This has centred not only round the major items of benefit, such as the value of time, on which the literature is now voluminous if elusive, but has led to the development of a conceptual – or at least classificatory apparatus – for the discussion and analysis of transport problems, both of appraisal and forecasting. Systems for demand modelling have developed in parallel to the basic economic studies and an agreed, or largely agreed, terminology has been adopted within which economists and others may discuss transport issues in mutually intelligible terms. For example, early work tended to distinguish existing traffic and generated traffic. These two categories are now part of a more comprehensive classification of the way in which trips may respond to changes in transport costs which includes changes of route, mode and destination as well as the decision to travel or not travel.

Within the DOE and hence much of the UK, a number of conventions have come into use for the estimation of the major benefit items. As a result the actual details of the London to Birmingham or the Victoria Line study would not now be repeated if the studies were redone (which it is hoped in the latter case to do) even if the basic conceptual framework remains un-altered. This in itself is of course a modest achievement, but it does reflect a number of important advances. These might be mundane if clearly useful improvements such as those made possible by combining the results of National Travel Surveys and national earnings statistics to obtain better in-come information for those making trips in working time by road; or theoretical progress allied to practical applications which has led to much better understanding of the nature of transport benefits. We consider briefly a number of instances of the latter kind.

Very important advances were made, for example during the course of the London Transportation Study, in developing the concept of consumers' surplus in a situation where there were both shifts along and shifts of de-mand curves, as a result of a transport improvement. The precise solution offered in the early LTS is still debated, but the important point this work established, if refined since, is that extra trip-making will normally denote extra benefit and not extra costs. That this is not an obvious point can be demonstrated by the large numbers of studies which came to precisely the opposite conclusion and the prevalence, even in current discussions of 'good' transport systems, of the assumption that the least cost is best.

This mistake, which perhaps is made easily by engineers and planners naked of the concept of a demand curve, and its avoidance, is a good exam-ple of the contribution which economic analysis may make at a conceptual level of people's ability to think about transport problems and the nature of the benefits to be derived from transport. The primary concept of benefit employed by economists is that of accessibility. Not only does this allow a meaningful interpretation of extra trip-making, but it sets in perspective such common indicators of transport performance as travel speeds or total vehicle miles, changes in which may or may not be correlated with changes in accessibility but which are sometimes proposed as performance measures for transport systems.

There have been other important advances of a similar kind. For example, the insight of Becker (1965), that goods and services had a time price, has been embodied in the notion, used widely in transportation analysis, of *generalised* cost. This defines the cost of travel so as to include money, time and, in principle, any other psychic costs such as consciousness of risk. Whatever view is taken of the ability of economists or others to derive a specific value for time, this concept has been important, not only in facilitating general discussion of transport problems (at least between professionals) but also in contexts such as forecasting the effects of parking policies where both time and money elements must feature. (For many transport problems, time is so correlated with cost that its use alone can be justified for forecasting purposes.)

Allied to the notion of generalised cost are the distinctions between perceived, 'actual' and resource costs. These refer to the way the individual perceives the cost to him, the actual cost to him and the resource cost to society at large. These are important distinctions for both forecasting and evaluation if, as is widely believed, the typical traveller is unaware of the true costs of private vehicle operation to himself and if the actual cost to him has a significant tax component. The precise numerical relationship between the categories of cost is of course difficult to establish, and evidence is conflicting, but again the concepts have an important clarificatory role.

A final example is the value of saving travel time. Early confusions centred on the relationship between savings in non-working time and the wage rate on the one hand and the nature of the time saved, e.g. through a change from a faster to a slower mode. The now fairly extensive theoretical literature has tended to confirm the implicit practitioner's assumption with regard to the first problem, that no necessary connection exists. In relation to the second, it has again elucidated a distinction which most practitioners had probably formulated, if less clearly, between the opportunity cost content of time value and its activity-specific content. The importance of the latter is that the concept of a single value of travel time savings, even for a given individual, is ruled out.

In addition to these very basic ideas, important clarification has been achieved of a number of elements common in transport appraisal such as the treatment of taxation (which is not, as most texts have it, to ignore it), vehicle depreciation and capital savings and a number of other similar items. Similar clarifications have been made of the nature of the benefits from new modes or from changes between existing modes. The convention has become established that both transport costs and benefits are likely to change in real terms through time. And underlying the economic approach, larger quantities of data on trip patterns and the characteristics of trip-makers, mundane but essential facts for any appraisal, are available; some readily.

At this stage one general point can be made; that while the progress briefly recorded here has, as probably all involved would agree, improved thinking about transport problems at the micro, or project level, it has not made the day-to-day application of economic appraisal techniques easier. If anything it has had the reverse effect, since it has opened up technical pitfalls where none were known to exist before and made full understanding of the analysis underlying practical procedures difficult if not impossible for most of those using the procedures to follow. In the case of urban studies in particular, these tendencies have been paralleled in the forecasting/modelling field, in which the operating systems have become increasingly complex and less easy to understand intuitively. We shall return to this point later on.

While progress has been considerable it cannot be claimed that all problems have been solved! A list of outstanding problems would inevitably outstretch the successes. Again we shall be selective, aiming only at indicating the diversity of problems involved and the differing kinds of judgement required in dealing with them. A continuing central problem is the value of (leisure) time. A large amount of empirical work has been done on this, most of it worthless (through faulty specification or bad luck). Attempts to extend the scope of behavioural studies away from the commuting trip (for reasons such as repetition and choice availability much the easiest to study) have been largely, though not entirely, unsuccessful and no serious empirical attempts have been made to tackle directly the small time savings problem, which many people find difficult. The difficulties of these studies have been described elsewhere; here we would only note that operational evaluation procedures must rely on very general (even if to most economists plausible) assumptions about flexibility of time allocation, and a mixture of value and empirical judgement in extending the results of empirical work from the areas where it has been done, to the areas where it has not; e.g. extending the value of the earners' travel time savings to non-earners and children.

But these do not meet the point that the value of time savings will vary with the circumstances of the trip. Empirical work has established that this is not simply a theoretical point. Walking and waiting time, for example, are constantly found to have greater weight in generalised cost functions than 'in-vehicle' time. No successful empirical work using behavioural trade-off analysis has been done on vehicle comfort, despite its early identification in the Victoria Line study, as a benefit item. Thus for this particular situation – similarly for others such as the relationship between income and time value – research has not provided an 'off-the-peg' value to be plugged into any particular study. It has, rather, provided a body of evidence to which resort may be made in any given situation. In some it may be felt to be a reliable guide; in others not. The possibility remains open of doing ad hoc work to meet the particular circumstances of each case. This will never be easy, may sometimes be technically impossible (when no choices exist, preferences will not be behaviourally revealed) and will always be time-consuming and expensive.

The value of time is a well-known problem, but it is doubtful whether it would be picked out by most practising transport economists as the main obstacle to practical evaluation. Views on this will vary, for reasons which we will indicate below, but before doing so it may be useful to explore a small number of problems not frequently discussed but central to the effective use of economic evaluation. They are not problems which have attracted academic attention – the 'in principle' solutions are clear. But their practical solution is usually extremely difficult.

The first is the definition of the do-nothing or base line for evaluation. This was a problem which the Third London Airport study managed to avoid by virtue of its terms of reference, but it is a day-to-day one in transportation evaluation. The difficulties arise when conditions on the transport network are forecast over some very long future time span. If we assume that demand for trips is unresponsive to conditions, then a future situation of extreme congestion will usually be projected. It will be objected that such a procedure is foolish, that demand will respond as the cost of travel goes up, hence this procedure will necessarily give a misleading picture of benefits. In most circumstances it would probably grossly overstate them.

So much is obvious, but what is less obvious is what precisely should be done about it. The demand forecasting procedures developed for urban areas allow some response in terms of modification of mode choice and trip pattern (including direction and length), but reactions in terms of numbers of trips, for each generating unit, household or firm, or changes in the number of generators (i.e. response in terms of land use), cannot currently be modelled, since the necessary relationships have not been established. (Some models, however, allow the number of intra-zonal trips to vary with the result that trips appearing on the modelled network do vary in numbers.) Because of this, the analyst trying to define a base network and land-use pattern for an urban area against which to set a new network has no very clear guidelines to proceed along in order to find a do-nothing which looks sensible, but which does not beg too many expenditure questions, i.e. does not itself involve a significant amount of expenditure. Through accident or design, it is not difficult to stumble across a 'good' scheme by assuming a bad do-nothing and not looking too hard for intermediary solutions. But it is difficult to devise specific rules for finding a satisfactory solution.

The second problem is similar to that discussed: the evaluation of congestion relief when traffic is diverted from road to public transport. A commonly used method of doing this simply abstracts the diverted traffic from road and estimates the vehicle speed change and the resultant change in generalised cost. This may, on busy networks, produce very high estimates of benefit. Such a procedure not only implies a zero elasticity of demand for road use but also the absence of policy measures to restrain traffic. If the volume of vehicle trips is kept constant by policy (i.e. central area parking control), trips diverted from train to road displaces existing road trips and trips diverted to public transport are replaced by other vehicle trips. The (dis)benefits are solely those of trip de-generation or generation. The solutions here may again seem obvious, but in practice they are extremely difficult to apply, partly because of the complexity of the demand relationships on a complex urban network and partly because restraint policies are highly political and cannot be automatically assumed to adjust to a forecast change in traffic conditions as in principle they should. As a result of these traffic and political forecasting uncertainties, benefit estimates can be made only within very broad limits in the majority of cases.

A further problem arises in a network such as London's public transport system if it is improved in one part and large increases in traffic are expected to ensue. Now such increases in traffic may be estimated by various rough and ready comparisons between the area to be served by the improvement and other similar areas, or by more sophisticated means. But it would not normally be practical to derive them from a total London model. This means that very little can be said in detail about what the behavioural changes are which underly the traffic increase which it is expected will occur, with the result that no information is available to shed light on the significance of the change in revenue to the operator: is this a net benefit, or a transfer from other parts of his undertaking? Typically, the by-and-large assumption that costs will be saved elsewhere in proportion to their loss of traffic (the usual assumption of cost–benefit analysis) is made, but it is a particularly dubious one in this particular context. A judgement on this may, however, dominate a particular evaluation.

Finally, there are problems arising on the cost side. That of capital cost estimation, especially for urban schemes, is severe but is of widespread occurrence in and out of the transport sector. The second is more specialised. Many schemes, both inter-urban and urban, present problems on the cost side because of their use of land. Problems have arisen mainly from the interaction between economic evaluation on the one hand and another more general social evaluation system, that underlying planning controls. These controls, in both urban and rural contexts represent very broad judgements on the difference between private and social valuation of different land uses. While economists may find it easy to sketch out a priori justifications for such control in terms of externalities of various kinds, it is not in practice feasible to identify specific costs or benefits arising from changes in land allocation in the way necessary for economic evaluation. The problem may be that of finding the social value of land in Green Belt use, or inner area land, where in neither circumstance is there a clearly relevant market value which might represent its private valuation, still less a value clearly relevant for social cost–benefit analysis.

Two general points may be made on the basis of these brief comments: first, it is not easy to come to any general conclusion on what the most important benefit or cost items or underlying behavioural assumptions are, identify a small number of weaknesses in the way they are at the moment treated and concentrate efforts on remedying these weaknesses. The issue of congestion costs dominates the case for certain types of public transport scheme but features very little in others; the value of time may dominate an inter-urban highways scheme but feature trivially in an urban scheme.

The second point is that the 'economic' approach can only be applied with care and circumspection. On the one hand the issues are so tricky that it is not easy for the day-to-day practitioner to sort them out and on the other, even when conceptually the points are not difficult and where the basic techniques and ideas are of long standing, fairly difficult empirical judgements are necessarily involved.

The difficulties discussed do not solely afflict large schemes – indeed, there is little correlation between difficulty and scheme size until the scale of very large urban networks is reached, when the forecasting problems involved come near to looking insuperable. We cannot therefore confidently delimit certain domains as being easily won territory and others as difficult. If we define as 'easy' problems on which it is possible to give clear-cut advice with a clear conscience, then easy schemes may be found in a variety of circumstances. If we are looking for schemes on which it is very difficult to formulate useful advice we may find them anywhere.

In summary: economic analysis has provided a way of looking at transport proposals, which is undoubtedly illuminating. It gives the analyst confidence (which he would not have, for example, in the field of land-use planning) in his ability to set out the problems at issue and to sort out the identifiable costs and benefits, to structure an appraisal and hence to make progress immediately in determining what work needs to be done. But this general perspective, although sharpened up at conceptual and empirical level over the last ten years, still remains difficult to apply in particular situations. Partly because of the heterogeneity of the transport sector, partly because of the inherent complexity of the economic analysis once this is focused on a specific problem and partly because of the complexity of transport demand and supply factors, the derivation of specific and detailed evaluation procedures remains hazardous. This has important implications for the role of economic analysis in public sector decision taking, in particular, for its suitability as an instrument of routine rather than special investigation.

2 The role of appraisal

Both theoretical and applied studies of the application of economic techniques to the evaluation of public-sector expenditure have been generally silent on the context in which the analysis is to be used. Most textbooks, or applied studies, genuflect to the point that 'the analysis is not everything': a typical statement would be that produced by the Roskill Commission (see

Annex). The implicit assumption of most such references, indeed of a great deal of economic and other analytic writing, is that of a single decision taker to whom advice is offered. This advice, which may extend both to the effects of policies and also to the social value of those effects, he is able to reject if he wishes because one assumes a democracy, not a technocracy. This view of decision taking within a complex government organisation (or because often more than one is concerned, government systems) is of course naive, but it persists, with the effect, it will be argued, that the role of economic or any other similar appraisal is not recognised for what it is. These mistakes do not occur purely in the context of economic analysis. Substitutes for economic evaluation, such as the various matrix methods now proposed for land-use planning, similarly concentrate on a single major decision – the acceptance of a strategy – and are completely unclear about the nature of the total decision process which physical planning must involve, in particular the follow-up, implementation and modification of the original intentions of the land-use plan.

In the real world, decision processes are complex, involving not only the interplay between various parts of an organisation, but also interaction between organisations and between organisations and the outside factors affecting them. They typically last a long time and involve a great number of stages. Decisions vary not only in the magnitude of their consequences in terms of claims on resources, but they also vary a great deal with respect to their immediate consequences. Decisions are not typically firm; they are interim, provisional, subject to availability of funds, to changes in outside factors etc.

In the course of a lengthy decision process, the decisions along the way may be taken with regard to a variety of criteria. The initial decision to consider a road scheme may be set off by a large number of states of the world, and once this decision has been taken, and the next stage is reached, the original states of the world (in which one includes expectations) may no longer exist. These decisions will be delegated to officials of one kind or another; initially perhaps an engineer, mindful of traffic speeds, later to an administrator mindful of local feeling, and at both stages economic analysis may (or may not) give its blessing. Finally the decision will be taken by a politician but his 'decision' or choice is shaped, if not determined, by what has gone before. If he wants a project to be carried out in the field concerned he may be free only to say 'yes' since immediate alternatives will not necessarily be available. But the fact that decision processes are lengthy and complex as such tells us very little about what the task of appraisal is, except that it underlines the point that when we are talking about decision taking in the public sector we are very frequently talking about bureaucratic rather than political processes. These points are scarcely novel; nevertheless, the assumptions underlying much discussion of the relevance of economic methods ignores these points and as a result obscures the tasks which, in the main, appraisal within the public sector may hope to perform.

The implicit assumption of a single decision taker selecting a best set of projects so as to make use of his budget, or to determine the size of it, puts the prime emphasis on choice of projects for execution in a given time period. This type of approach is suitable in certain circumstances, where the external environment, social, technical and economic is changing only slowly. Project definition is a fairly routine matter.

If we introduce change then the emphasis begins to alter. The problem becomes much more one of deciding what kind of schemes to invest in; how to react to changes in technical possibilities or in the legal or financial framework; what general direction policy should take. Those responsible for the expenditures concerned now have a variety of tasks and the appraisal system takes on additional roles. In the case of a programme like road safety, where the three main strands – policy towards vehicle, infrastructure and driver – are interdependent, scheme/policy generation and preparation can be very complex because of interacting possibilities for action. A general strategy has to be selected but its evaluation must necessarily be rather general and sketchy. However searching it is, it cannot guarantee that all the individual schemes it suggests are worthwhile. In these circumstances the appraisal system, if it is working, tells those responsible for the programme if the general direction is wrong. This process may take time; it is essentially a learning process. Schemes must still be selected or rejected, but the implication of any particular selection or rejection goes wider than the scheme concerned. It has implications for the strategy as a whole.

This role of appraisal is extended if we consider the generation of schemes; who thinks up the ideas, how many layers are there of the underlying administrative infrastructure? Those at the periphery of the organisation must have some idea of what schemes to propose. They must know what are likely to be considered good schemes; otherwise it is not worth their while preparing them. The appraisal system tells them this. It can be seen as a means of mutual communication from the centre to the periphery and vice versa. Ideally, the evaluation and conception of schemes should be closely linked processes, each providing information to the other. In brief, the appraisal system performs a variety of functions within the general task of helping decision makers get the best value for money, in whatever terms they define it. What we must now do is attempt to assess how well economic appraisal as it has developed in the transport sector helps in these tasks at the various stages of decision which we have identified.

Two examples

The two examples we will consider both derive from DOE experience, but they do not represent case studies of the parts of the department concerned.

A first example is provided by the relationship between central government on the one hand and local government or semi-independent organisations such as the nationalised industries or transport operators. In many contexts these relationships are conducted in financial terms, but where, as recently, the centre has been operating a subsidy via an infrastructure grant, other criteria have had to be used. How does the cost–benefit framework stand up in these circumstances?

We approach this question by considering the various functions it may perform. First, it can go some way towards defining the terms under which projects are going to be assessed and thus allows sponsoring bodies to prepare justifications in terms which they know in advance are relevant. Second, it can provide a framework for those in receipt of projects to apply sustained and constructive scepticism to the claims of those sponsoring them. Third, it can provide information to the centre, as part of a wider learning process, about the value of projects and the value to be attached to various kinds of scheme.

How well does cost–benefit as it now stands perform these functions? Two points follow directly from our earlier discussion of the state of the art. First, the second, or control, function of cost–benefit analysis is hampered by the discretionary elements which must necessarily exist in any appraisal (or which can only be reduced at immense expense. Why techniques devised to deal with uncertainty are of little help here is explained below). Second, it cannot lay down very precise rules for the execution of appraisal, partly for this reason, and partly for the closely related reason of the gaps in current research evidence, exacerbated in the field of public transport by the large range of types of scheme which are eligible for grant. It has been possible therefore to formulate advice only in very general terms, which is far from telling those on the receiving end what they should do.

Despite these weaknesses, however, it performs the second function by providing the framework for administrators aided by economists to apply judgements on the claims of those sponsoring the projects, on the basis of which advice will be given to Ministers. It does this by encouraging quantification wherever possible, through eliminating double-counting and by providing the evidence which might be useful in coming to subjective views on the value of certain benefit items – together with, where research has been done, checks on such judgements. Economic analysis can provide the framework within which these very general virtues, of which it can claim no monopoly, may be exercised. The conceptual advances referred to in section

1 suggest a comparative advantage in their deployment, at least in this field. Double-counting may be more or less easy to spot: some are still tempted to include both transport time savings *and* the land-value changes they may give rise to. But there are subtler points than this. Economic evaluation, as it has developed in transport, is inexplicit about the changes underlying the benefits as they are measured on the transport network. The value of redistributed or generated trips is estimated not directly, but in relation to the cost change giving rise to them. The argument is that benefit cannot be greater than the original cost change (otherwise the behavioural change concerned would have occurred previously) nor can it be less than zero (otherwise it would not take place). If these arguments hold, then nothing needs to be said about the behaviour itself. Hence precisely what changes are stood proxy for by transport benefits needs some analytic skill to elucidate. The pursuit of real, as opposed to financial effects is another area where economic skills may be of specific value: administrators may be alive to the distinction in principle but not be able to apply it in a specific case. In some cases, such as the correct definition of the opportunity cost of land, the solution may not be obvious even to the skilled analyst.

Carrying out the second function goes some way towards serving also the third function, of providing the department with some feel for what are or are not good types of scheme. Because some schemes are looked at in detail, the demand assumptions criticised and the modelling assessed, the department builds up a store of expertise, and its conventional wisdom about what is good or bad is modified. This function, however, is not always recognised; it tends, for example, to stand in the way of good administration, because even when a scheme looks eligible and satisfactory, we sometimes feel obliged to crawl over it. It creates delays and runs into the sort of difficulties explored in Foster's book (Foster, 1971) in relation to nationalised industry. Nevertheless, this may be the most important function of all. It is partly on the result of evidence, obtained in this way, for example, that the Department has come to the view that within a policy of promoting public transport, large-scale projects of major infrastructure investment are unlikely to be worthwhile, despite the very strong qualitative arguments made in their defence.

Foster has argued that the department always finds it difficult, except in circumstances of acute budget pressure to say *no* directly (if in doubt the obvious response is to postpone a decision). But it does not itself run a transport operation, though it has gained considerably from participation in some local studies. Thus although it may be very difficult to refuse projects which are actually offered for grant, for political or other reasons, if they are accepted on the nod, then no-one is any the wiser. This is not the only channel by which the Department may 'learn' in this general sense, but there

is clearly much to be said for exploiting a function it must in any case perform, by some means or other. A central department has less than perfect
knowledge 'of what is really going on out there' in the system for which it is
responsible. (The situation is different perhaps from that with the BRB and
other Boards since the DOE is responsible for detailed advice and for grant
structures, which presupposes the existence of a central expertise which the
department does not need – though it may like to have – on the operation of
railways.)

Perhaps the main weakness of economic appraisal in the present context,
however, is to be found not in its control function but in the very early
processes of scheme generation. These are fundamental to the impact of the
appraisal system since, as we have pointed out, it is not easy in normal times
to refuse eligible schemes for grant once they have reached an advanced
stage of submission. At the present time, institutional factors such as the
relatively short period of time economic appraisal has been in existence and
the inexperience of local authorities and operators in applying it both combine to reduce the impact of cost–benefit analysis in shaping the ideas
people have about schemes they wish to put forward. These may be reduced
over time partly perhaps through the emphasis within the new TPP system
on option generation. But there are further difficulties which stem from the
nature of economic analysis itself.

Economic evaluation procedures are abstract and unrelated in terminology and categorisation to ordinary language. Their algebraic formulation has helped some but hindered many more. Moreover, various conventions have developed, each suitable for its context, but not always in-
terchangeable. For example, the algebra suitable for inter-urban road evaluation is not easy to apply to urban public transport: in the one case, the
vehicle-mile is the fundamental unit of analysis, in the other the trip. More
fundamentally, the nature of the benefit measure itself gives rise to difficulty.
User benefits are typically measured by combining gains to existing users
(generalised cost savings) with gains to users modifying their behaviour as
the result of a generalised cost change. These benefits, modified by any
adjustments due to pricing failures, are measured 'on the network'. As
pointed out above, the analytic framework in use suggests it is not necessary
to pursue the underlying behavioural changes themselves 'on the ground'
because their value must be bounded by the change in transport costs. This
measurement convention is virtually universal at least in UK practice
because of its immense convenience. The ramification of transport projects
are such that any excuse for not trying to unravel them is welcome.

The convention is adopted essentially because of the difficulties in making
more detailed forecasts. One result of using it, however, has been to divorce
economic evaluation from the underlying travel behaviour and from the

wider planning context within which transport schemes are to be developed. An important consequence is that economic evaluation tends, *even at an analytic level*, to appear as a basically irrelevant hoop through which projects conceived in other ways, must jump. This conflict may be particularly acute in the case of financially-based operators, who may be primarily interested in revenue-generating schemes. But the problem is not confined to this.

Two examples illustrate this point. First, urban planners tend to look at transport as a means of promoting other objectives – these may be expressed in terms of accessibility to certain kinds of facility for certain groups of people, or in terms of the promotion of certain spatial patterns of development. Now it can be shown that economic analysis is compatible with this kind of thinking (and also that much talk of 'planning benefits' additional to 'transport' benefits is double-counting of 'transport' benefits) but that only goes a fraction of the way towards reconciling the two approaches. Thinking about overall objectives, or about desired pattern of growth, may give rise to views on what schemes might be examined. Economic evaluation procedures as presently used do not usually perform this function although they can be adapted to it. Typically, the outputs of the transport study process are not produced in terms helpful for those engaged in related planning activities, except to the extent that vehicle or trip numbers are helpful by themselves. This is in part a failure of forecasting, but it also reflects a failure to use the evaluation process diagnostically, i.e. as a means of searching for good types of project. Thus economic evaluation tends to cut itself off from what should be related and complementary processes. This may arise in another way as the second example shows.

The analytic processes which are now conventionally employed for the study of urban transport projects tend to be set out as a linear sequence with evaluation as a final stage, which is not designed to be diagnostic so much as to pass judgement on the separate processes which have gone before. But this semi-institutional point is made worse by the penchant which economists in transport, and more generally, have had for evaluation procedures based on trade-off behaviour, and their antipathy towards methods of deriving information about personal preferences in other ways. The difficulties of doing this are well known, but the effect is that economic evaluation has an inherent conservative bias – tending to be bad at getting at demands for transport which the present system does not meet very well – but also bad at getting at good schemes even within existing technology (of course an important function of economic analysis is to measure the resource costs of schemes, to which these remarks do not necessarily apply). The relationship between economic evaluation and market research methods remains uneasy.

Our second example is suggested by the inter-urban highway planning process. Trunk highways are planned centrally within an organisational structure very different to that just discussed. The approach taken in applying economic evaluation techniques has, largely as a consequence, been different also. The main aim has been to ensure conformity and comparability within the total organisation – and hence a strict standardisation of evaluation procedures used within it. To this end, various circulars have been issued over the past ten years describing schemes of economic evaluation, in progressively greater detail and complexity, and embodying updated views on underlying traffic as well as economic relationships. The case for conformity is of course strengthened by the relative homogeneity of the schemes concerned.

Despite the progressive elaborations, these procedures contain a number of important simplifying assumptions; for example, the circular issued in 1967 (and subsequently reissued) set out the requirements for estimating a first-year return, i.e. the ratio of first-year benefits to total costs. It is not too difficult to make points about the potential inadequacy of this measure and this particular deficiency has now been removed.

This is a fairly simple matter. But there are very difficult problems in going for an apparently better system of appraisal which stems from the argument in section 1. The central unit is faced with two alternatives. The first is to set out a very simple precise rule, which may then accord ill with the individual situation, and the second is to allow discretion and then to have very great control problems in checking the reasonableness of specific local assumptions.

Unsurprisingly the highways approach has been to tend towards the first of these courses, particularly as for the most part the people working the system are not trained in economic evaluation. This has costs of three kinds. The first stems from the fact that the appraisal system cannot be altered very frequently, not merely because of problems of comprehension, but also because of the need for comparability within the organisation itself. For if improvements are continuously built into the system then effectively the rates of return are calculated in different 'money', yet the task of re-evaluation is a complex and practically impossible one. It is as though depreciation or inflation conventions were being changed annually, when at the same time profits of subsidiaries had to be used as basic monitoring methods of efficiency. The second is, obviously, that the individual evaluation is of poorer quality than it might be. What develops is a conflict between the needs of the organisation for an internal control procedure and the parallel needs of the organisation for best estimates of the value of what it is doing. To the extent that the first need dominates, it has to go outside this internal system for this latter kind of information, i.e. pursue special investigation ad hoc. However, it would be wrong to criticise fairly simple decision rules simply because they fall short of 'best practice'. The advantages of more information at early stages of scheme processing must be set against the high cost of obtaining it in each and every possible case. This 'short-listing' problem has attracted very little attention until recently; the relative merits of engineering rules of thumb and crude economic evaluations remain unexplored.

A third possible cost is devaluation of the whole procedure: those doing it from below must inevitably see it only as a strait-jacket; those assessing the results (who may be external bodies) can use its weaknesses as they please. But a more serious risk of a process of this kind is that it runs the risk of being pseudo-rational, i.e. the process of calculation becomes an end in itself and loses touch with the underlying realities. If general rules of evaluation are to be laid down there is a spectrum of possibilities. On the one hand are evaluations based on what seem to be sensible general assumptions on such matters as the value of time, speed–flow relationships etc. which are common to all highway appraisal processes and which may be justified in *individual* cases as 'best estimates' because, for example, no-one is going to derive a value of time for the M1 as opposed to the M6 (except by virtue of vehicle composition). On the other hand, are procedures based on sets of assumptions which can rarely be justified in the individual case because of the underlying heterogeneity of the situation. The point we are making here is that for institutional reasons it is easy to start at one end and degenerate to the other. Our previous example suggests, however, that in some circumstances no valid point on this spectrum can be found for some categories of scheme.

Not all problems of highway evaluation take the form discussed here; there are many issues which arise at a national level for which national solutions can be imposed and for which a 'best-possible' analysis can be done. An important class of these is design standards. Although design standards do vary with local conditions they do so rather crudely, and with the justification that to go more carefully into the individual cases would be prohibitively time consuming. Standards, within highways and elsewhere, are in general a class of decision which is professionalised rather than politicised (except where safety is involved).

3   **Giving advice**

The problem of 'neutral' advice

The problem of 'neutral' advice is an old problem in economics, but it is perhaps particularly severe in the case of advisory procedures which explicitly go beyond considerations of cost-effectiveness. When the application of economic techniques goes beyond being the instrument of special in-

vestigation, as with TLA, into routine application the problem is exacerbated even more, since the possibility of displaying the underlying value
judgements on which advice is based is no longer open on a case-by-case
basis. At the stage of (apparently) final decision the analysis may be
presented so as to bring out key value judgements in the assessments which
have been made, though there are of course limits to the extent to which that
can be done, but at stages of intermediary decisions, of which there are
many in the decision processes with which we are concerned, value
judgements must inevitably be employed without recourse to the political
process.

This problem is endemic in large-scale government; it has been
exhaustively analysed in the political science literature concerned for example with the meaning of ministerial responsibility. In offering comments on
which advice to Ministers might ultimately be based, or decisions made
which preclude projects being developed sufficiently far for ministerial involvement to occur, the economist is in no different position from the line
administrator, using his 'feel' and 'common sense'. The economist might
add his relative advantage, in such things as spotting double-counting in distinguishing real from financial costs and in checking discounting calculations
and other advantages discussed above, but when he gives advice on values,
which the practitioner of cost–benefit analysis must inevitably do, then he is
doing no more than any other official in applying what seem to him to be
reasonable standards within whatever political guidelines exist. The claim
which economists might make however is that their advice is based on
general principles which can be publicly debated, and empirical work
which can be externally assessed. This may be regarded as a very important
attribute in that it goes some way towards making bureaucratic processes
'responsible' in a wider sense, although, as discussed in section 1, the force
of this point is diminished by the elements of discretion which must even so
enter into any advice that is given.

Traditionally, concern about the value judgements inherent in economic
analysis have centred on questions of distribution of benefits. (Judgements
on the relevance of individual preferences have generally been taken for
granted by economists if not all professions.) Within transport analysis this
issue has all the traditional aspects together with some additional ones
which make it particularly difficult to handle.

This problem arose very early in the practical application of economic appraisal method within MOT, when, as the evidence on the value of leisure
time developed, it became possible to consider differentiating values according to income groups. At that time it seemed to some of the economists involved that a proportional relationship was the valid one. Economists at that
time felt – or at least a majority did – that this issue should not lie dormant

but should be put to the political head of the department. This was done and, as a result, the value of time used within MOT and now DOE for scheme evaluation (but not forecasting, where different considerations apply) has been a single one, no matter what income group is concerned. This rule has been widely, if not unanimously, accepted as being a reasonable one. It also has a great deal of operational convenience.

Nevertheless, it has been argued that this was not the right thing to do — partly on the practical grounds that the evidence was not strong enough to support the proportional relationship, partly because it was thought that this was not an issue which Ministers could sensibly grasp and consider and partly because it was felt that it avoided real distributional issues while appearing to solve them. For because of the nature of transport projects and the small spread of income between parts of the country — such a rule could not have much effect on project choice. The effect of using the average value has been to give the evaluation process a gentle bias and nothing more. It is perhaps for this reason that it has proved acceptable. A similar rule has not been adopted for road accidents, even though the average content of an accident does vary over the country, because the distributional implications (between age rather than income groups) are more sensitive.

The rule, though apparently fairly innocuous, does raise a number of disparate problems. It makes the computation of benefits very complicated in those cases where behaviour is being modelled using a value of time, which is chosen as being that which is believed to be the best estimate of the perceived value not the social valuation. Procedures have to be adopted to ensure that people are not actually estimated as incurring losses (e.g. by apparently taking more expensive routes, in generalised cost terms) when the imposed social value is used. A more subtle effect has been to make the modelling and evaluation process insensitive to certain kinds of issue — arising from heterogeneity of preferences (not necessarily income related) — which an average value tends to smooth over. For example, where 'switching' behaviour occurs, one might expect that those who valued most the change in question would be the first to switch since the value they get would be 'above average'. But if a weighting rule is used which renders the latter out of court, then the incentive to pursue the implication of heterogeneity is diminished. This has reinforced the tendency noted earlier for the evaluation phase to be divorced from earlier analytic processes.

But such a rule might be questioned on quite different grounds; first, while it may be reasonable to adopt it for national decisions such as those on the road programme, there seems less of a case for doing so in the local context, when the allocation of funds to local areas is made on the basis of a different (largely equity) set of criteria. Second, the logic of the rule assumes that final and initial incidence of benefits are the same. This point may not matter in the regional context since the adjustments to the values are for practical reasons broad brush. But it would within a given urban area since there is no general reason when land uses are flexible (in type or intensity) and individuals are mobile that initial and final incidence will be similar. Within a growing or changing area such as London with, in normal times, a large amount of movement through its housing and commercial stock, the potential (not, however, realised in the case of some recent investments to any obvious extent) for benefit shifting is considerable. Indeed the very traffic estimates themselves may depend on it.

Recent studies for example of possible tube extensions in south London have tended to suggest that only significant shifts in the socioeconomic composition of the local population would generate the hoped for traffic levels. In a quite different context, other recent work has suggested (not surprisingly) that the incidence of free fare benefits may also be perverse. But conclusions of this type are particularly tentative because they rest on forecasts of reactions within the socioeconomic or political system of a kind on which evidence is difficult to find. The economic evaluation criteria as currently employed give no guidance on this. In many cases, therefore, the analyst may have to fail to offer advice at all. And finally, there is the question of adjustment of opinion when political heads change, especially when the original decision has not been 'tested' subsequently. On this matter we can only record the presence of difficulty, not its resolution.

Uncertainty

Distributional judgements are inherent in any analysis: so too are beliefs on the relative likelihood of future states of affairs, including both forecasts and values. These do not themselves necessarily entail value judgements, but any summary figure of costs and benefits will do so. The proper treatment of uncertainty, however, seems to be one of the most difficult in the application of analysis to project and policy appraisal. This has important implications for the economic analyst because it means that some of the obvious ways of dealing with the difficulties of economic evaluation, e.g. to propose a range of possible outcomes discussed in section 1 — the necessary uncertainties in evaluation — are not open. Clearly, various commonsense tests can be, and are in fact, carried out; e.g. the sensitivity testing of key variables, trying out extreme values to see if, even on these assumptions, a scheme can be made to change from 'good' to 'bad'. Often such simple procedures can be the basis for firm advice. TLA provided a good example with its treatment of very small time savings. The Heathrow Link provides further examples. But only so much of this can be absorbed. One cannot for each and every evaluation exhaust all the possibilities.

The economist in an advisory role will wish to allow for uncertainty in these ways to make sure his advice holds a reasonable range of assumptions (it may of course not do so). But he has a further interest in having uncertainty explicitly faced. In the 'control' described in the first of our two examples, most would agree that advocacy tends to produce expected outcomes from one end of the spectrum only. The overall probability of many evaluations received is negligible, i.e. all their estimates are 'most favourable', but the absence of a systematic treatment of uncertainty makes it difficult to push this point home. The single figure chosen tends to be the result of a kind of bargaining process in which the proponent has the upper hand.

There are of course more fundamental reactions to uncertainty: for example more information might be obtained, or the scheme or policy concerned redesigned. These are things people can do if they are in control of the total process but it is less easy, if not impossible, to do so in the context of a confrontation over whether or not a given scheme should be given a grant. These are not situations for careful consideration of the frequency distribution of possible values of a given change in generalised cost. But even in less contentious contexts the same kind of gap mentioned above which separates the evaluation criterion from the prior analytic process occurs here, i.e. it nearly always proves impossible to make the fact of uncertainty reflect what it is proposed should be done. The reasons for this are partly political – while there are sometimes advantages in delay which uncertainty may be used to justify, there are equally occasions where firmness and commitment are seen to have political advantage. But the problem is not purely political in that sense; a large part of the problem stems from a widespread preference for long-term plans and long-term (pseudo) commitments.

An example of the problem can be found in the Layfield Report on the GLDP. The economic results were understandably laid on one side since they were *very* limited in scope but firm recommendations were nevertheless made on very little relevant evidence, even on the pattern of traffic flows. Since its publication, its proposals have been rejected by two GLC administrations which have had their own views on what should be done.

Some of these differences are due to broad political views on the value of road investments in relation to other sectoral demands. But underlying these divergences of political view are major uncertainties on traffic growth, environmental values, land-use shifts, investment resources (financial and physical) and planning capability. In the face of these, a key issue (which Layfield only dipped into) is the purpose of any (*very*) long-term plans in this situation. Better perhaps to search for some useful increments but even this is best done in the context of a process which takes more than one possible future into account.

This is in effect another example of the failure of economists to link their's with related analyses. In this context economic approaches have probably been closer to public opinion than some others, in that they have tended to find against large and expensive schemes in urban areas, yet have failed to convince. This is one example of a general characteristic of economic appraisal work, that it has been generally negative, i.e. better at criticising what is proposed rather than leading to proposals itself. Economic thinking frequently suggests a priori alternatives or lines of development, but to make these stick as genuine possibilities requires much more thorough work than a brief comment on the demerits of a particular scheme.

Presentation and intelligibility

A number of relevant points have already been made under this heading, in particular, the abstractness of much of economic analysis and the consequence of the measurement conventions which have been adopted for relating the outputs of appraisal to other parts of the planning process. This has been true even within transport itself. In urban areas, for example, while operators have often benefited from the information flow from land-use transport studies, they have tended to retain their own information systems. This is due partly to institutional factors; it is also due to the fact that the study processes themselves were not conceived primarily with operators' problems in mind. They were addressed to appraisal of large-scale strategies rather than to a continuous process of decision taking on a wide variety of problems.

Within the broader planning field, however, the difficulties are more severe; transport and land-use planning have always been uneasy partners — certainly well before economics entered the scene. The reason for this we need not go into here, but merely to note that economic evaluation procedures have done nothing to bridge existing gaps and may have exacerbated them.

There are some more straightforward presentational problems, to which relatively little attention has been given. The usual form of decision rule in terms of n.p.v. may not, as such, be readily intelligible. It may have to be re-expressed, in political contexts at least, in terms of 'very poor', 'good', or 'bad' value for money. (Terms which may in any case suit the analyst mindful of the tenuousness of some of his assumptions.) But formulations like this might not be helpful even for the politician who accepts the principles on which the advice is based. For example, it might be more useful to him to have a direct measure of the opportunity cost of the funds concerned in terms of houses or other assets which might be invested in instead. The local government member may be faced with choices of that kind, especially if he goes outside the limits of grant eligibility; where he does not, then the opportunity cost can only be expressed within the transport sector itself. He may in addition be helped by disaggregation of final benefits, where these can usefully be provided; he will also be interested in the financial effect per se because of its subsidy and rate poundage implications. He may better grasp the point of, for example, a low return if the point is expressed in financial terms — what the fare would have to be to make the scheme viable. Intuitive judgement operates best on material with which it is familiar.

There are quite different grounds for wanting disaggregated information and judgement. The concept of n.p.v. as a decision rule implicitly assumes that the relevant decision is go or no go on the project concerned. In other words it assumes away the role of the evaluation phase in providing diagnostic information for transport planners, but also for others. Such information may be used for redesign of existing policies or design of related policies. For these purposes components of the overall appraisal, or its underlying assumptions, may be more important. But the point also holds for the analyst himself who may wish to draw general conclusions from the particular analysis and may need specific disaggregation to do this (benefits at different times of day, to different trip purposes or different categories of users). All this can be, and sometimes is, made available. But in general, there is a tendency to lose information rather than gain it in the way in which results are presented. Some progress has been made in terms of producing outputs which indicate the expected spatial distribution of accessibility changes but in general we record this as a neglected area.

Partial evaluation

This again is an old problem; is it worth identifying the rabbit if the stew is mainly horse? Here we would add only a footnote to it, arising out of the earlier parts of the paper. Discussion of this issue has tended to focus on the distortions induced by quantification in the belief that items included in an evaluation which are expressed in money terms gain most weight, the quantified items a little less and the intangibles very little. This would not be the impression of most of those who have been employed in government; the solidity of the intangible in the eyes of those promoting a scheme is a not uncommon delusion. But there is a serious problem here, which arises in transport primarily because transport impacts on the environment in ways which scarcely allow quantification (because the forecasting relationships do not exist, and which certainly cannot be given a monetary weight at the present time, even where in principle they might).

The only point we want to make here is that the problem is to some extent exaggerated by focusing wholly on the final point of decision. In the case of transport assets, in the majority of cases the scheme concerned must earn its keep as a provider of transport benefit. If it does not make a significant contribution here it is unlikely to be worth while at all (there are clearly exceptions). As we have pointed out, economic evaluation is frequently concerned with preliminary stages in longer decision processes. In these circumstances it may be worth saying whether a given scheme is worth promoting, at least to the next stage of analysis. The scheme may at later stages be subject to political judgement, but the decision to prepare and propose it may sensibly be influenced by the more obvious quantifiable factors.

In many cases, the outcome of a partial evaluation is to remove doubts about the importance of a particular item. Evaluation tends to be an iterative process. Rough estimates are first made of the relevant benefits and costs which are progressively firmed up, according to views based largely on the early work on what seem to be the important items. The fact that in a final presentation a partial evaluation in money terms does not appear useful, does not imply that it has not *been* useful in the process of arriving at it. The political debate and subjective argument may be better focused as a result.

4   Concluding comments

An important assumption of this paper has been that economic appraisal must be considered against a very broad backcloth of administrative and political decision taking and its performance judged by a number of different criteria. But having said that, the performance of economic appraisal has not been very easily characterised from the various viewpoints which may be taken. In some contexts it seems most useful as a tool of low-level analysis as a rough check on scheme viability, in others as an instrument of major investigation. The conclusions are not necessarily in conflict. In the Roskill case and that of other very large investments, it might be argued that a large-scale effort to find the right course of action was justified by the scale of the decision. In other situations a quick appraisal using minimum data might be all that might be justified, provided that little hung on the outcome, i.e. that a given, not very expensive, scheme could reasonably be proceeded with, or scrapped.

But the corollary of this is that some areas of decision taking are best left alone. These may be very large-scale decisions where the uncertainties are such that analytic advice contained in a rate of return is both unreliable and unjustifiable and less-grand situations where the available data on forecasts and values is such as to make any evaluation of dubious worth. Many areas of routine decision taking fall into this category, including some major ones.

There are dangers in trying to say something about every decision concerning the allocation of resources, principally from lowering the quality of advice and failing to make significant in-roads into any particular problem involved. The danger of making economic evaluation routine is that maintenance of the system absorbs resources which might be better used in a more innovative way. The former course tends to underplay uncertainties and doubts, the latter is less prone to do so. Furthermore, as we argued earlier, there are inherent difficulties in trying to make cost–benefit a routine exercise.

There are, moreover, positive advantages in failing to provide evaluations of certain kinds of project, e.g. if this results in attention being diverted to the real issues underlying the analytic uncertainty. These may concern lack of knowledge on preferences for a particular kind of benefit: or the scale or type of investment being proposed.

Perhaps the most important single point to emerge from the earlier discussion is that economic appraisal must learn to relate itself to other modes of analysis and other modes of judgement. If it is to survive it will not do so simply because of its inherent excellence as a general idea. Those responsible for appraisal have a major task in linking the forms of output produced by economic analysis with those produced by other approaches and to those on which political judgement can reasonably be expected to bite. Some obvious political demands – e.g. on distributional issues – may be impossible to satisfy. But progress can undoubtedly be made in other directions.

Finally, it is clear that economic skills can contribute to good decision taking in various ways: partly through the application of general analytic skills in setting out a problem clearly, eliminating double-counting etc.; partly through providing advice on possible values of shadow costs, partly through forecasting methods, partly through the analysis of financial costs and the derivation of options. Within transport, until relatively recently, the main intellectual effort has concerned the manipulation of shadow costs and the ever more detailed examination of a narrow range of microeconomic issues, rather than the other phases of planning. Most of this paper would tend to suggest that this balance of effort, of which there are signs of being redressed, has been unfortunate and might now usefully be corrected.

ANNEX

Problems can be analysed by statisticians, operational research workers, systems analysts, economists and other specialists. But however expert in their own fields, they cannot dictate the conclusion. The role is to analyse the problems and suggest lines along which answers may be sought. Both the analysis and the suggested approaches to the answers must be publicly criticised by other experts in the same fields if even informed opinion – quite apart from the public in general – is to have any confidence in conclusions reached with the aid of methods which they will imperfectly understand. The expert evidence at the final series of public hearings has made it abundantly plain that there is no one right view on these matters.

Informed judgement is required at every stage. For example, the choice between the rival views on the value of time – each view argued by experts on the basis of evidence or deduction and each view strongly held by its exponents – in the end has to be a matter of judgement. If the gap is wide and if the outcome turns crucially on that particular point the decision-maker must either back his own judgement in the face of disagreement between the experts or seek fresh knowledge.

Extract from the Final Report of the Commission on the Third London Airport, chapter 3, paragraph 3.9.

REFERENCES

Becker, G. S., 'A Theory of the Allocation of Time', *Economic Journal,* 1965, vol. 75, September, pp. 493–517.

Beesley, M. E. and Foster, C. D., 'The Victoria Line: Social Benefit and Finances', *Journal of the Royal Statistical Society Series A (General),* 1965, vol. 128, part I, pp. 67–88.

Coburn, T. M., Beesley, M. E. and Reynolds, D. J., *The London–Birmingham Motorway, Traffic and Economics,* Part I. 'Traffic Investigation'; Part II. 'Economic Assessment', Road Research Technical Paper No 46, London, HMSO, 1960.

Department of the Environment, *COBA: A Method of Economic Appraisal of Highway Schemes,* London, Department of the Environment, 1972.

De Serpa, A. C., 'A Theory of the Economics of Time', *Economic Journal,* 1971, vol. 81, December, pp. 828–46.

Donnea, F. X. de, 'Consumer Behaviour, Transport Mode Choice and Value of Time; Some Micro-Economic Models', *Regional and Urban Economics,* 1972, vol. 1, February, pp. 355–82.

Evans, Alan W., 'On the Theory of the Valuation and Allocation of Time', *Scottish Journal of Political Economy,* 1972, vol. 19, February, pp. 1–17.

Foster, C. D., *Politics Finance and the Role of Economics,* London 1971.

Foster, C. D. and Beesley, M. E., 'Estimating the Social Benefit of Constructing an Underground Railway in London', *Journal of the Royal Statistical Society, Series A (General),* 1963, vol. 126, part I, pp. 46–92.

Gwilliam, K. M., 'Economic Evaluation of Transport Projects: the State of the Art', *Transportation Planning and Technology,* 1972, vol. 1, December, pp. 123–142.

Harrison, A. J. and Holtermann, S. E., *Economic Appraisal of Transport Projects and Urban Planning Objectives,* Department of the Environment, June 1973.

McIntosh, P. T. and Quarmby, D. A., *Generalised Costs, and the Estimation of Movement Costs and Benefits in Transport Planning,* MAU Note 179, London, Department of the Environment, 1970.

Ministry of Transport, *The Cambrian Coast Line. A Cost/Benefit Analysis of the Retention of Railway Services on the Cambrian Coast Line (Machynlleth–Pwllheli),* London, HMSO, 1969.

– *Report of a Study of Rail Links with Heathrow Airport,* London, HMSO, 1970.

Mishan, E. J., 'Evaluation of life and limb: a theoretical approach', *Journal of Political Economy,* 1971, vol. 79, July/August, pp. 687–705.

Pearce, D. and Nash, C., 'The Evaluation of Urban Motorway Schemes – A Case Study, Southampton', *Urban Studies,* vol. 10, no. 2, June 1973, pp. 129–43.

Quarmby, D. A., 'Estimating the Transport Value of a Barrage Across a Bay', *Regional Studies,* 1970, vol. 4, August, pp. 205–39.

Sugden, R., 'Cost–Benefit Analysis and the Withdrawal of Railway Services', *Bulletin of Economic Research,* 1972, vol. 24, May, pp. 23–32.

Thomas, D. R., 'Cost–Benefit Analysis of Railway Closures', *Chartered Institute of Transport Journal,* 1971, vol. 34, September, pp. 228–33.

10

Roskill revisited

J. B. HEATH

Introduction

Governments seldom look back critically at earlier decisions to try to learn from their experiences; this is generally left to a few parliamentary bodies, the Public Accounts Committee in particular, in the context of public expenditure. In cases where public expenditure has not been incurred, check-backs are even less frequent. This paper is concerned with the continuing saga – coming up to its twentieth anniversary – of a set of decisions about the location, timing and 'need' for a third London airport, and with the principal lessons that may be learnt from the attempt to solve the problem by setting up the Commission on the Third London Airport (the Roskill Commission). Let me start with some important economic aspects concerned with the establishment of the Commission in May 1968.

Was the right question being asked?

The Government has often been criticised for giving the Roskill Commission the wrong terms of reference.[1] The Inquiry had been initiated because of continuing public pressure against an earlier decision to site the new airport at Stansted (some 32 miles north of London),[2] and in the light of studies within the Board of Trade (the Department responsible for civil air transport at that time) which had cast considerable doubt on the earlier decision.[3] The criticism generally made is that the Commission was not directed more explicitly to examine whether there was a 'need' for a third London airport at all.

While the rather curious wording 'the timing of the need' seemed to assume a need, clearly the Commission could have recommended that the timing was 'never'. And although the Commission devoted much thought and study to the question of timing, it was not within an analytical framework that would have permitted it to have said conclusively whether a third London airport was or was not a good use of the nation's resources.

At the time, however, there was a good reason for the assumption of 'need', which derived from the Government's own forecasts of demand and capacity for air passenger and air transport movements. These showed[4] that Heathrow would run out of capacity by the end of 1969 (even on the 'low' forecast the 'saturation' year was 1970), and so the answer to the question of whether a third London airport would be in itself a good investment for the community was thought to be self evident. Since the basis of these forecasts was not published, and since to challenge them within the Government was regarded as 'rocking the boat', and in any event something that the Commission would have to examine, that view of the urgency of the problem prevailed.

Yet the problems of forecasting in air transport should have raised much more fundamental issues than the question of need. First, what was most clearly wrong in the 1967 White Paper was the implied concept of airport capacity. This is a meaningful concept only in highly specific terms, since the variable nature of air transport movements over the day, week, and season of the year means that in the short run capacity is determined by the shape of demand over a period and the tolerance of the system to delays in the peak. In the long run the peak/annual ratio can change with the changing composition of traffic, as can the capacity of passenger terminals, runways and the air traffic control system to handle larger volumes of traffic, while maintaining specific safety standards (which themselves are not necessarily immutable). Capacity, therefore, is not a fixed amount, and 'saturation' would only occur when certain constraints are allowed to bite.

The Roskill Report was of course correct in pointing out that an airport is a system whose capacity is determined by 'where the shoe pinches first', and that over time the system is highly adaptable. A wrong forecast for part of the system can make a large difference. Thus one place where Roskill was in error was in underestimating the rate at which the peak/annual ratio at Gatwick would fall, so that by the time the Civil Aviation Authority (CAA) came to re-examine the forecast early in 1973,[5] Gatwick's annual capacity had effectively increased substantially (because of the more rapid development of off-peak services—largely scheduled services—than had been foreseen).

Secondly, a more fundamental and serious problem is, I believe, only now being fully appreciated. It is that, with our present state of knowledge, long-range demand forecasting in civil air transport is not feasible within a degree of reliability that would be useful for decision making.

The underlying reason for this is that there has been insufficient time in the past for basic relationships (especially price and income elasticities of demand) to stabilise, so that reference to the past in the establishment of any close statistical relationships for predictive purposes are bound to be misleading. New products of major significance are still appearing (new destinations, new fare packages), and so are new means of production (the aircraft), which are an integral part of the product. Successful new products have a rapid initial penetration of the market, with an exponential growth rate that is of course not sustained. Airport demand for air travel is a family of derived demand curves, with products at different stages of their life cycle. Some are reaching saturation, some are coming up to the point of inflection of the product logistic curve, and others are still at the take-off stage. Thus it is hardly surprising that estimates of the price and income elasticities of demand for air travel are all over the place. A recent (as yet unpublished) study by Professor R. de Neufville of all analytically respectable demand studies in air transport show no consistency in the numbers derived, except that in general the price elasticity of demand for business travel is below that for leisure travel. Of course circumstances vary route by route, but that is part of the problem.

Those who study this subject deeply believe that the overall growth curve, which is probably an 'S' shaped logistic like any other product curve, has already passed the point of inflection so that (abstracting from the energy crisis) the aggregate rate of growth is now thought to be declining. But there is a great uncertainty about this, and it is largely guesswork what shaped 'S' curve civil air transport is on, and whereabouts it is on it. The energy crisis at the end of 1973 made matters much worse, and it is still highly uncertain how the long-term trends of demand will have been affected.

These problems are illustrated by some post-Roskill studies. For example the forecast of air passenger movements in the CAA Report[6] for the UK – Continental Europe traffic in 1980 was very different from the Channel Tunnel forecast[7] for air traffic for the same year (adjustments need to be made to put both forecasts on exactly the same footing). The former was based on time-series analysis of air transport movements (depending largely on earlier detailed studies by the British Airports Authority), and the latter (a highly sophisticated and penetrating piece of work)[8] was based on cross-section analysis of total demand. Not surprisingly, even when comparing like with like, the implied price and income elasticities were very different, but it was not self evident which should be preferred: both had considerable justification. Both also had decay factors built in to future growth, which seemed reasonable in the light of their own different approaches, that again were not the same.

If this general diagnosis is correct, we can describe the Roskill venture to forecast demand to 1990 and 2006 by extrapolation (basically from 1969) as not only heroic but probably foolhardy. I would place an equal probability on a wide range of other figures. The close coincidence of several forecasts that have looked far ahead is due to their common methods; the coincidence of several independent forecasts, if they have used basically similar methods and data, is unconvincing.

It is said that a week is a long time in politics; in forecasting demand in civil aviation, 15 years is a long time. It is a very long time if simultaneously one is trying to forecast capacity, and to measure the narrowing gap between the two – too long in my view for credibility. Believing this to be so, it seems to me that the Roskill Commission should not have been asked to recommend a site and the timing for a four-runway airport to serve the London area, but rather it should have been asked to *advise the Government on a strategy for managing the growth of airport capacity in the South East under conditions of uncertainty, in the interests of society as a whole.* What was needed was a strategy that recognised this uncertainty, arising from the inherent problems in the forecasts, and explicitly incorporated it into the way in which the growth of airport capacity should be managed. In the absence of a clear positive indication within a 10–12-year horizon, the question 'is a third London airport necessary at all?' was not, I believe, capable of being answered at the time of the Roskill Commission: nor is it capable of being answered today.

In any event the fact that at a certain date forecasted demand for airport capacity might exceed the forecasted capacity would not of itself demonstrate that that extra capacity should be supplied (even if one believed the forecasts). This would be so only if the extra benefits from so doing were likely to exceed the extra costs, however one might express this (in principle, a positive net present value at an appropriate discount rate). And this was not something over which the Commission was able to devote much time (essentially their analysis was based on minimising net cost rather than maximising the overall net benefit).

Thus with the benefit of hindsight, I believe that the Roskill Commission was set the wrong problem, although what was done would still have been valuable as a major input into the formulation of a strategy for managing demand and the growth of capacity under conditions of uncertainty (on the lines proposed below).

Was the right analytical approach used?

As implied earlier, I believe that the application of social cost–benefit analysis was necessary in this case as a means of identifying the costs and benefits to society of alternative proposals, as indeed did the Commission: but was it *sufficient*? As we all know, the Commission recommended a site at Cublington: the Government chose Foulness, subsequently renamed Maplin, and strongly disagreed with the Commission's recommendation. Should not Roskill have taken his analysis one stage further to incorporate the preferences of those who would be most closely concerned with making the decision? (The outcome would not have been

Cublington, but it may not have been Foulness either.)

There is an interesting parallel with the more recent decision concerning the airport at Sydney, Australia. A Federal/State Committee, aided by some former members of the Roskill team, set up to advise on the problem, recommended the expansion of the existing Sydney Airport at Mascot; but in August 1973 the Australian Government rejected this and decided to develop a new site at Galston (35 km NW of Sydney), which was the Committee's fourth choice (Foulness was the Roskill fourth choice also). Evidently it was thought politically inexpedient to expand Mascot, which had Government held marginal constituencies close by – Galston lay within a secure Opposition constituency. (Following further studies, the Galston site was found to be too costly, and subsequently – August 1974 – the Government have decided to reconsider the desirability of expanding Mascot.)

The MIT team that advised the Mexican Government on the most effective strategies for developing new airport capacity at Mexico City adopted an entirely different approach, however, the results of which were accepted by the Mexican authorities. Their studies,[9] which were very limited in scope as compared with those in the UK or Australia, consisted in identifying the utility functions of those most closely concerned with the problem, in relation to six measures of effectiveness: capital cost; capacity (aircraft operations per hour); access time from the airport; number of people seriously injured or killed per aircraft accident; number of people displaced by airport development; number of people subjected to a high noise level. All the judgemental assessments concerning probabilistic impact and preferences were derived from group and individual sessions with the Ministry of Public Works; this enabled the MIT team to derive utility functions for each of the six measures of effectiveness, using consistency checks for validation. Scaling factors were then derived by the careful questioning of decision makers, which effectively were the weights used in trade-offs. Coupled then with the probability density function, the expected utilities of each of the 4096 options were calculated, and the ten best results identified. From this two types of strategy were found to be most effective.

This approach had the advantage of identifying what were the preferences of the decision makers, and of achieving a high degree of involvement of those most closely concerned – even to the extent of installing a computer terminal in the personal office of the President of Mexico. It provided the basis for negotiation between the principal Ministers concerned, and more or less guaranteed acceptance of the conclusions of the study.

But lacking any systematic Roskill-type social cost–benefit analysis, the preferences identified by the MIT team may not have been soundly based. With better information, obtained impartially and tested for validity in a public arena in the Roskill manner, the preferences of those most closely concerned might well have been very different, and their utility functions affected accordingly.

Thus if Roskill took too little account of the preferences of decision makers, perhaps the Mexican approach took too little account of the true costs and benefits to their society of the alternatives open to them. But it may reasonably be argued that the Roskill terms of reference did not include the production of a preference analysis which incorporated the decision makers themselves, and that such an approach in any event would have been so contrary to our normal practice in the UK as to be unacceptable as a technique.[10]

Be that as it may, the case for going further than did Roskill seems strong, especially as there was a change in Government in June 1970, just before the Commission reported. A change from Labour to Conservative could be almost guaranteed to affect the attitude of Ministers to the Report.

But this raises a further question. When the Government rejected the Roskill Commission's recommendation, was this because they disagreed with the analysis of the Commission, with the values, weights or qualitative judgements made or used by them, or did the Government take account of factors not included at all in the Roskill evaluation? The record of events is hard to interpret from this point of view (and the answer is not crucial to this argument).[11] The point is that if the Government and the Commission had had a close and continuing dialogue during the progress of the study, about the underlying assumptions, about the factors to be taken into account, about the value judgements and preferences of those in the Government who would be concerned with the final decision, then the risk of ultimate fundamental disagreement would have been reduced, the two parties would have articulated their own preferences in a more informed manner, and the kind of recommendation made might have been different.

For example, it is perfectly possible that the implicit valuation that the Government placed on the benefit to the nation of preserving the Vale of Aylesbury (in which Cublington is situated) was greatly in excess of that assumed by the Commission. This is not something that would be easy to identify by survey and questionnaire to the nation, and the views of a democratically-elected Government would clearly be relevant in this case. I do not suggest that the Commission should then have accepted the views of the Government, but at least they could have taken them into account.

Thus a sensible stance for the Commission in the event of such a clash would have been to say 'we conclude from all of our enquiries and studies that the best site is X; we have, however, taken a rather different view from the Government in regard to certain matters that we have mentioned in our Report, and if the Government views were to prevail then we believe that the right site would be Y'. In this way the Commission would have preserved its integrity in recommending what it believed to be the optimum, while indicating its views on the site closest to the optimum that the Government would be likely to accept.

Clearly there could have been value to both the Government and the Commission in such a dialogue. Both sides might have been led to change their views – the Government when confronted with the detached analysis and understanding of the Commission, and the Commission when faced with a different set of value judgements to their own. But – regrettably – such a dialogue probably was not feasible. The whole point of the Commission was to take the controversy out of politics and away from the Government; any hint or indication that the Commission was in any way communicating with those in government who might be responsible for the final decision would have condemned the Commission utterly and raised the most serious questions about its impartiality. In this politically charged environment no close and continuing dialogue was possible.

Nor indeed is such a dialogue often possible in other less important cases. In most other cost–benefit studies Ministerial decision makers are simply too busy (even if they had the necessary understanding of the techniques involved) to give their value judgements and to specify their basic assumptions, and much has to be left to the analysts. This is an argument for publication wherever possible, so that the community at large, the experts as well as those likely to be affected by the decision under discussion, can express their views. In this regard the Roskill Commission did all it reasonably could (in a protracted series of public hearings). In retrospect, however, it is clear that Ministers should have been invited to give their views so that at least parts of the dialogue referred to earlier could have been conducted in public. (I doubt, however, whether Ministers would have accepted such an unusual proposal.)

Furthermore, to take the views of Ministers into account is a hazardous procedure since few ministers are offered long periods in office, and Governments may change. Thus attitudes of mind can vary fundamentally over time, as can the willingness of decision makers to pay regard to the results of systematic analysis.

These are cruel dilemmas for analysts and advisers, especially in a major inquiry of the kind undertaken by the Roskill Commission. There is no easy solution.

Was Roskill's analysis sound?

Apart from the points already mentioned, the analysis has, I believe, stood up to its critics, and to the test of time and further work, remarkably well. It would be too tedious to go over once again the arguments put forward by the critics of the Roskill Report, which have now lost their impact, and one hesitates to criticise when one could not have done better in the circumstances — especially when one could not even do better today. Moreover, my own continuing involvement in the controversy inhibits full discussion in some areas, but three topics can be mentioned.

Forecasting

The first topic relates to forecasting. Essentially what the Commission did, as did those who presented evidence to it, was — to a greater or lesser extent — to rely upon the extrapolation from past trends, as modified by experience and special factors (the Commission went further than did other investigators in deriving 'propensities to fly' according to income, and in using these as a basis for forecasting). That all of the five forecasts (to 1985) should have been rather close (although the BEA single figure forecast was somewhat below the others) was not surprising. What was not done, however, was to consider any fundamentally different approach.

Thus the Commission might have derived a forecast that involved taking imaginative leaps forward to the world of 1975, 1981, 1991 and 2006 (the years forecasted by the Commission),[12] and described alternative scenarios as to what civilisation — especially as it affects demand for air transport — might be like at that time. Use of the Delphi technique would be appropriate here. In parallel with this might have been a technological forecast of the characteristics of aircraft, also using Delphi, and a forecast of the regulatory environment that might then prevail. Having identified these scenarios, one could then work back to the present day to examine what changes would be needed if these scenarios were to represent reality, and whether such changes were in prospect or reasonably likely.

To confront forecasts based on projecting past trends into the future with forecasts based on views of the future worked back to the present day could have been instructive and of considerable value to the Commission in arriving at a 'most likely' forecast, for the reconciliation of divergencies between the two approaches would teach one a great deal.

Furthermore, the confrontation with the sophisticated developments in forecasting adopted (much later in time) by the Channel Tunnel Consultants could also have been enlightening and might have strengthened the points made in the Report about the inherent difficulties of forecasting. It might, indeed, have led them to the main argument in this paper, that major uncertainties in forecasting should lead one back to reconsider the whole nature of the problem under discussion and the kinds of solutions one is seeking.

Regional problems

One of Roskill's more difficult tasks was to know how to incorporate in his studies both regional policy considerations and the possibility of a large expansion of regional airports. On the first of these there was a problem of timing, because the South East Joint Planning Team, under the direction of Dr Burns, was undertaking detailed studies to formulate a strategic plan for the South East.[13] Clearly the location and timing of a Third London airport would become a significant part of such a strategy.

It is curious, however, that subsequent studies[14] made only passing reference to a Third London Airport at Maplin. Yet clearly any strategy for the long term must take account of such a major generator of traffc and employment as an airport of the size of Maplin. In view of the continuing uncertainties over Maplin, this must raise a question of the kind of strategic plan that would be appropriate for the South East as a whole.

Before continuing to discuss this topic, let me turn to the second part of the regional problem. I have always regarded the criticism as unfounded that the Roskill studies made little sense because they were conducted in the absence of a National Airports Plan. When the London area airport system caters for some 60 per cent of all air passenger movements in the UK, and for 50 per cent of all civil air transport movements, a National Plan which excluded the London area would have been nonsensical; and one which included the London area would have pre-empted most of the Roskill work and rendered it pointless.

But it is true that a range of options were open to the Government relating to the use of regional airports – especially those peripheral to the London-area system (Southampton, Hurn, Bristol, Birmingham and East Midlands in particular) – which were not fully explored by Roskill, and which could have affected the growth pattern of the London Area Airport system quite significantly. Such options as the development of an airport at East Midlands, which is environmentally and in capacity potentially more satisfactory than the airports at Luton or Stansted, or the development of a green field Midlands site to rationalise the Midlands airport system and to draw off some of the London traffic, are only now being more fully explored.

Yet there is a basic difficulty about this kind of analysis, as there is about the analysis of a regional strategy for the South East. To generate a grand model which will explain statistically the allocation of traffic to all airports in the country, and to forecast the size and geographical distribution of such traffic, is a hazardous procedure. One doubts the credibility of any model to do this reliably, since the determinants of geographical demand would include not only income variables but also accessibility to existing airports and their attractiveness (a complex relationship), as well as the business decisions of tour organisers operating in a highly uncertain business.[15] Since origin and destination surveys have been repeated only for the London area, there can be no time series estimates of propensities to travel by population zone. Yet to rely upon cross-section income data when the nature of demand is of the kind described earlier is also very hazardous.

These problems again raise the question of the appropriate *form* that planning should take, whether relating to regional airports or to regional development as a whole, when such conditions of uncertainty prevail. They reflect back upon the kind of management decisions that should be made, and they emphasise once again the point made earlier that, under conditions of uncertainty, blueprint plans are wholly inappropriate; rather one needs a strategy for the management of national airports and regional development that will allow for change and adaptation as circumstances unfold. One has to achieve a balance between non-intervention on the one hand, and a blueprint that attempts to dictate what will happen in circumstances when control over the major parameters is very weak. To plan for uncertainty and to manage the situations as they arise is always difficult; it is most difficult in government, where Ministers wish to make bold decisions and where civil servants are best at administering agreed policies.

Noise

The third item I wish to discuss is the question of the analysis of aircraft noise. Official studies of aircraft noise have been based upon two field surveys,[16] the second of which resulted in some statistical relationships that were not wholly satisfactory. Indeed some results were perverse (for instance, the effect of the duration of aircraft noise on the degree of annoyance was negative, indicating that the shorter was the exposure time the more was the annoyance produced). Moreover, noise is based upon the population living in an area, and we know that many areas in and around London are recreation-intensive areas where no one lives but many people visit. To give an example, only a handful of people live in Kew Gardens (some of those who work there), yet the day-time noise is continuous and intense. Since few people live there a close analysis of the statistics would indicate that there is no problem, yet clearly this is wrong. Moreover, the conversion from NNI (Noise and Number Index) into cost, undertaken by the Roskill Commission (based upon the opinions of estate agents), while the best they could have done in the circumstances, undoubtedly leaves much to be desired.

These doubts about the significance of noise—cost estimates suggest that they should be treated with considerable caution, that relative measures are likely to be more meaningful than absolutes, and that the outcome of trade-offs between (for example) noise intensity, number of aircraft and duration of noise exposure in their effects on annoyance may be not at all as forecasted. Until better measures are derived probably one has to be fairly pragmatic in approach, sharing the 'burden' of aircraft noise as public pressure dictates. What one wants to avoid is the confrontation experienced recently in Japan where for the last two years noise abatement groups have thwarted the operation of the new airport at Narita (west of Tokyo) by purchasing land near the airport and erecting on it a 190 ft tower.

Yet in an era in which airport authorities in many countries are considering the imposition of a noise tax on noisy aircraft, not to have available authoritative and up-to-date estimates of the cost of noise is bound to lead to considerable arbitrariness in the levels of tax imposed. There is no uniform method of measurement as between countries, and it seems to me that perhaps the International Civil Aviation Organisation (ICAO), which has already made significant developments in the setting of noise standards, should go further into this field, and at the same time national governments should conduct their own detailed studies. Thus it may be right for the Government of Japan to propose raising the required rate of return of Japan Airlines on the Government held equity in order to compensate those living on the ground near the airport from which this airline operates, but how much those on the ground should be compensated cannot be determined unless there are reasonably reliable estimates of noise costs in the first place. This is an area where much more work is needed.

Before conducting further empirical studies, however, there are several questions of a more theoretical nature that require consideration. The first arises because of doubts whether the disutility of aircraft noise for poor persons living in low cost housing is properly measured by the fall in their property prices, as compared with richer people living in more expensive property. Any given percentage depreciation, which might be taken to indicate equal disutility (in fact the percentage depreciation was found by Roskill to fall positively with income level[17]), would result in a lower absolute value. This is a budget constraint type of problem, familiar in other fields, to which there is no easy answer. While it would be right to weight the market-value depreciation more highly for the poor person, because his marginal utility of money is higher, this does not seem an appropriate adjustment for the point at issue (although it is in the right direction).

The second question is whether the disbenefit of aircraft noise in an area not hitherto affected can be adequately represented by estimates of actual property depreciation in an area which has experienced it for a long while. In the latter there is a certain expectation of aircraft noise and people do not move into the area in ignorance of the existence of aircraft noise. In the former situation, however, people may have chosen to live there because it is quiet, and was expected to remain so. They may indeed have an extremely high 'householders' surplus' (a concept closely parallel to consumers' surplus, which Roskill attempted to measure), the reduction of which would be underestimated by the expected fall in property prices.

Moreover, whether or not compensation would actually be paid to those who would suffer aircraft noise at (say) Cublington, might well affect the level of disbenefit. Absence of provision for compensation may create a sense of injustice and outrage that conventional valuations would miss, and hence would underestimate.

All of these cast doubt on whether the measures of aircraft noise at the 'green field' sites attempted by the Roskill Commission were entirely appropriate, even though they were probably the best that could be done at the time.

Was the recommendation right?

The Roskill Commission concluded that there is no ideal site for the third London airport, and that on 'a balanced judgement of all the factors revealed by the massive evidence before us (which) alone can provide a sound basis for our recommendation ... in the overall national interest Cublington should be the site of the third London airport'.[18] This recommendation, which was expressed in 67 paragraphs of reasoning, and which followed 12 chapters of description and analysis, was superbly expressed and difficult to fault. Yet it was quite different in character from that which would have followed from the terms of reference proposed earlier. Having made this proposal, however, there is clearly some obligation to indicate the general form of the recommendations that might follow from it.

A strategy based on uncertainty would involve identifying several feasible ways of meeting the growth in demand, according to various plausible growth rates and other characteristics. As higher growth rates are assumed, so a different range of policies may become appropriate. There will be discontinuities as higher rates lead to system constraints. The cost and benefit implications of each policy would then be evaluated, using probability weightings and the estimation of 'expected monetary values' wherever possible, within the framework of a decision analysis.

In this way a variety of possible activities that might have to be undertaken would be identified. Each principal strategy would be broken down into as many separable stages or decision points as are feasible. Some stages would be common to several strategies.

The recommendation would then relate to the range of activities that require to be undertaken at an early stage, such as planning applications and public enquiries; to investments that should be planned as dual-purpose facilities (in case the primary purpose turns out to be unnecessary) or where they would have some value to society in alternative uses, such as improved road or rail communications to Southend; to the safeguarding of areas or sites in case they should subsequently be required, such as a British Rail link to Heathrow;[19] to the broad planning of possible regional airport requirements; to further R&D that may be required, for example in quiet engine technology; to further policies that should be pursued in any event in relieving existing airports of noisy aircraft through taxes or regulations; and so on.

The recommended policy would then be to make progress with the implementation of the early stages of several strategies, paying particular attention to activities that required time rather than resources (such as architectural design, physical modelling – of the Thames estuary for example, planning and public inquiries). As events unfolded the studies would be updated and prior probability estimates improved (by Bayesian analysis), and some strategies would then be discontinued as it became apparent that that was not the right path for progress. As it became clear that certain sites or areas would not be required they would be released for other purposes.

All this would require continuing management and research, perhaps over an extended period. A stream of decisions would be required as various decision points were reached. Moreover, compensation would be desirable for localities that are forced to suffer the blight of uncertainty until the situation clarified and firm decisions could be made. None of this is at all easy to explain to people, or for Ministers to accept; yet in a large complex project likely to absorb huge resources and involving many people such an approach would, I believe, be justified.

Can the lessons be generalised?

There are several lessons from the Roskill experience that have wider application, but perhaps the most important of them relates to the main theme of this paper – that under conditions of uncertainty one may have to reconsider fundamentally the nature of the project one is undertaking and the character and type of decisions that have to be made.

The paper has focused on market or demand uncertainty (although there is also a strong element of technological uncertainty subsumed within it – the characteristics of aircraft that will be in airline service in 1990, for example), yet technological uncertainty has bedevilled many projects in recent years. For example, the UK nuclear power programme has not exactly been a success – indeed the Chairman of the CEGB described it to the Select Committee on Science and Technology[20] as 'a catastrophe we must not repeat'. Duncan Burn argues[21] that we started off wrong, relying too much on the single source of technological advice from the Atomic Energy Authority (whereas the United States, using about the same volume of resources initially, relied upon competition to indicate the best way ahead).

Be that as it may, it was surely folly in the light of all the technological uncertainties to go straight from a small prototype reactor at Windscale to a massive programme of (eventually) five full-scale Advanced Gas Cooled Reactors (AGRs), ordered between 1966 and 1970. None has yet been made to work, including Dungeness B the first of them, now six years behind schedule. A strategy that recognised the inherent technological uncertainties would have proceeded with more caution, ordering a single intermediate-sized station first, then perhaps a single full-scale station, while relying on conventional power rather longer; or building simultaneously an intermediate-sized station of another basic design to gain experience. But to order five full-scale stations (and then to suffer a total cost penalty for delays and over-runs said to amount to over £900 million) seems the height of folly.

Regrettably there are other examples of a similar kind. The decision to go straight from the use of Strowger step-by-step telephone exchange automatic switching equipment to the all-electronic exchange (the one electronic exchange built for operational purposes in 1962 at Highgate Wood failed to work), and the related decision not to develop and to make use of the intermediate crossbar technology which other countries in North America, Japan and Western Europe were adopting, delayed for several years the time when the UK would have a system comparable in scope and efficiency to that of other advanced countries.[22] Moreover, the use of the British semi-electronic TXE-4 has still to prove itself an appropriate forerunner to the more complex 'System X'.

It is difficult to identify exactly what causes such projects to go wrong. Pursuit of this topic would take us too far from our central theme, but it is worth noting that in a recent Debate in the House of Commons[23] following the presentation of seven Reports of the Public Accounts Committee, at which a number of similar ill-fated projects were discussed, including Concorde and the Erskine Bridge, some Members blamed the system of decision making in Government and argued that the Executive needs to be separated rather more from the Legislature, and its efficiency improved. While this may be part of the answer, the Roskill experience shows that careful and detailed analysis is certainly not a sufficient condition for the effective management of large public projects, and much wider issues are involved.

Concluding comments

The principal problem identified in this paper concerns the management of a large public-sector decision, involving a long gestation period, in conditions of considerable market and technological uncertainty. The principal messages are first, the importance of recognising that such uncertain-

ties may exist in other projects, and secondly if they do, the necessity to incorporate them in formulating the kind of strategy that then becomes
appropriate.

The second problem concerns the conflicts that may arise from fundamental differences in approach and in modes of thinking between analysts,
however wise and sensible they may be, and politicians.

It is easy to be critical in reviewing past experience, especially when – as
in this paper – information and understanding probably not available at the
time is used as the basis of criticism. The impression has been created by
the continued public controversy that the whole project has been mis-
handled. Twice governments have announced firm decisions (in favour of
Stansted in May 1967 and of Maplin in April 1971); both decisions have had
to be fundamentally reconsidered. Was this indeed the 'sadly mismanaged
affair' that Lord Walston claimed[24] and that David McKie evidently agreed
with after a most careful analysis?[25] I believe that this view is exaggerated.

I believe that future political historians looking back on the whole affair
will see that in spite of many rocks strewn in its path, and of several tumbles
that resulted, the project has made progress in the general direction that a
planned response to uncertainty might have indicated. At the time of
writing no firm decisions have been made.[26] Several reviews in depth have
been conducted, forecasts reconsidered, contingency plans developed. Tentative and limited steps have been made in several directions. True it had
not been planned this way, it had not been managed as part of a coherent
strategy, and not everything has been done as a managed strategy would
have suggested. It gives the impression of muddle. But in relation to some
other projects mentioned, no substantial volume of resources has been
irretrievably committed; the issue is still open. In that sense it has been a
success.

One encouraging feature in keeping the project moving in broadly the
right direction has been the democratic process. Both inside and outside
Parliament opposition to the firm and bold approach ('Stansted it is!
Foulness it is!') has – so far – caused more sensible views to prevail. Supporters and opponents have marshalled their forces, with some effect; and
informed common sense seems likely to win. Moreover, the Roskill Commission itself, with its public inquiries and the opportunities for everyone openly to challenge even its own research studies, was an object lesson in public
involvement. (The pity was, however, that decision makers in the Government itself did not present their views in open session – that was a serious
weakness.)

Perhaps the major political lesson from the Roskill affair is that
governments should approach these kinds of projects, involving great market
or technological uncertainties, with much greater caution and humility.

There is an obvious temptation for the ambitious politician to perceive the ultimate solution (be it the all-electronic telephone exchange, a large-scale programme of Advanced Gas Cooled Reactors, a supersonic airliner, or a massive new airport to serve the needs of the capital city for generations to come) and to go straight for it, thereby demonstrating – he believes – firm government, foresight, and a readiness to gamble. Moreover, such a stance removes doubt and uncertainty, planning and execution can proceed in an orderly manner, implementation decisions can be delegated, and the next problem can be faced with a clear mind. Unfortunately the management of large projects under conditions of uncertainty requires continuous attention, and is a constant bother until the issues become clarified with time and experience.

A second political lesson is the value of informed opposition. Not all major government decisions lend themselves to public debate, even within the confines of Parliament. Yet it is important that opportunities be created at the highest levels of decision making for informed alternative views to be expressed. To rely entirely for advice on a single group of policy advisers within a Department, or a single government agency (such as the Atomic Energy Authority or the Post Office), or a single private enterprise is clearly courting disaster if major uncertainties are inherent in the problem under discussion. If informed competition is not inherent in the context of the decision it must be created.

Perhaps the major lesson for analysts is that more attention should be paid to the art of forecasting, with more recognition of the uncertainties involved. Much progress has been made with evaluating the success of macroeconomic forecasting; comparatively little attention has been given to the microfield, perhaps because of its diversity. A readiness to assign explicit probabilities to the outcome of future events would be a beneficial discipline, and combined with formal decision analysis would be a powerful tool for advisers.

Postscript

The above words were written in June 1974. I have made no textual changes, and I believe that what I said is still true (some facts require up-dating however: for instance two of the five AGR Nuclear Power stations at Hinkley B and Hunstanton B are now on stream and technically are thought to be successful; and today – July 1977 – there is still no decision on the long term future supply of capacity at London's airports).

Moreover, examples of failures in major Government decisions continue to present themselves. Let me illustrate my theme from one of them. In July 1974 the Government 'decided that the Electricity Boards should adopt the pressure tube Steam Generating Heavy Water Reactor (SGHWR) for their next nuclear power station orders'.[27] Three years later that decision no longer stands and the question once more is wide open. Yet the Government seemingly went about making that decision in a proper manner. It asked the Nuclear Power Advisory Board for its advice. The NPAB, which had been set up for the purpose of giving such advice in September 1973, was under the Chairmanship of the Secretary of State for Energy, so important were these decisions considered to be. But in the 9 months of its deliberations on this issue there were three different Chairmen since there were three Secretaries of State responsible: Mr Peter Walker MP, Lord Carrington and Mr Eric Varley MP. The story by which a minority view in favour of the SGHWR became the Government's decision, against the wishes of the CEGB which would have to implement that decision, needs to be told – but this is not the place.

It seems to me, therefore, that the prior and fundamental question which needs to be answered in this case is not 'which nuclear power system should be adopted?' but '*how should it be decided* which nuclear power system should be adopted?' This is exactly parallel to the views expressed in the above article in relation to future airport capacity.

This is, however, part of the wider question raised on page 174 above, that it is the system of decision making in Government which is at fault. My own recent work with the NEDO Study of UK Nationalised Industries[28] has convinced me that the deeply disturbing situation which was revealed there could be attributed largely to the system by which we are governed in this country. Stated most briefly, what is at fault is the role of Parliament and its declining effectiveness, the Ministerial system within Government, and the tasks imposed on the Civil Service for which neither their culture nor their training really suits them. Basically this is what is wrong, and the country will not overcome its long term problems until it is put right.

NOTES

1 These were: 'to inquire into the timing of the need for a four-runway airport to cater for the growth of traffic at existing airports serving the London area, to consider the various alternative sites, and to recommend which site should be selected'.

2 That decision was announced in a White Paper 'The Third London Airport', Cmnd 3259, May 1967.

3 There are several books describing the history of the whole affair, of which the most accurate and readable is 'A Sadly Mismanaged Affair' by David McKie (Croom Helm, 1973).

4 'The Third London Airport', *Op. Cit.,* Table 2.

5 'Forecasts of Air Traffic and Capacity at Airports in the London Area', Civil Aviation Authority, May 1973.

6 *Op. cit.,* Table 4.8.

7 'The Channel Tunnel', Cmnd 5430, September 1973; Appendix 9.

8 The study by Cooper and Lybrand referred to and summarised in the contribution to this volume by Mr R. Rees (ch. 11 below).

9 See R. de Neufville and R. L. Keeney, 'Use of Decision Analysis in Airport Development for Mexico City' (in *Analysis of Public Systems*, ed. A. W. Drake, R. L. Keeney and P. M. Morse, 1972); and, by the same authors 'Multiattribute Preference Analysis for Transportation Systems Evaluation', *Journal of Transportation Research,* vol. 7. 1973.

10 An attempt by the present writer when in the Civil Service to take explicit account of constituency voting was considered by the senior administrators concerned to be wholly inappropriate.

11 One lesson is that failure to guarantee monetary compensation for those who would be adversely affected creates bitter opposition, which was clearly important in this case.

12 Commission on the Third London Airport, Report, 1971; Appendix 6, Table 5.

13 Published by HMSO, 1970.

14 Especially 'Strategic Planning in the South East: A first Report of the Monitoring Group', Department of the Environment, March 1973. While this Report gave too little prominance to Maplin and its implications, the DOE Report 'The Maplin Project: Designation areas for the new town', July 1973 did not put the Maplin new town and all that this implies in a regional context. Thus nowhere does the regional significance of the Maplin development seem adequately analysed.

15 For example, Clarksons ran a bus service to enable passengers to fly from Luton Airport, which covered 21 towns, including Halifax, Darlington, Sunderland, Newcastle and Middlesbrough. A decision by them to bus these passengers to Manchester or East Midlands could affect the distribution of air traffic.

16 The first of these was the 'Final Report of the Committee on the Problem of Noise', Cmnd 2056, July 1963 and the second was 'Second Survey of Aircraft Noise Annoyance around London (Heathrow) Airport', HMSO, 1971.

17 Commission on the Third London Airport. Papers and Proceedings; vol. 7, part 2, Table 20.3.

18 Commission on the Third London Airport, Report, 1971; ch. 13.

19 Designated 'BR3' in 'Report of a Study of Rail Links with Heathrow Airport', HMSO, 1970.

20 First Report from the Select Committee on Science and Technology (Session 1973/74), 'The Choice of a Reactor System.'

21 Duncan Burn, *The Political Economy of Nuclear Energy,* Institute of Economic Affairs, 1967.

22 See 'Beyond Babel' by Brenda Maddox, 1972, where this history is described.

23 See Hansard, 3 December 1973.

24 House of Lords debate on Stansted, 11 December 1967.

25 This was the title he chose for his book, *op. cit.*

26 Subsequently (July 1974) the Government published 'Maplin: Review of Airport Project', which contained a reappraisal of earlier forecasts, to 1990, and examined the implications of four alternative ways of managing the expected increase in demand. At the same time they announced that the Maplin Project was cancelled.

27 'Nuclear Reactor Systems for Electricity Generation', Cmnd 5695, July 1974, p. 3.

28 'A Study of UK Nationalised Industries: Their role in the economy and control in the future', NEDO, November 1976.

11

Cost–benefit analysis
in transport

R. REES

Introduction

This paper is concerned with describing and appraising two applications of cost–benefit analysis in the transport sector. Choice of the two simply reflects interest subject to constraints, rather than an obvious logical connection. The only apparent relation they have is their dissimilarity. The first, the cost–benefit analysis of the Channel Tunnel,[1] concerned a single, very large, probably controversial project, which would have supplied a marketed output in competition with existing services; although in 1975 the Government for the time being rejected this proposal, its analysis is nevertheless of continuing interest. The second is an attempt to introduce cost–benefit principles at the grass roots of road investment planning, relates to a large number of small projects, and, though published,[2] is primarily an internal exercise within the Department of the Environment. Discussion of the two proceeds by taking them separately, but an attempt will be made to draw implications common to both of them at the end.

The Channel Tunnel cost–benefit analysis

In broad outline, the analysis was concerned with estimating the social costs and benefits which would arise from the introduction into an existing system, of a new type of cross-channel facility. This involved forecasting the likely demand for tunnel transport services, and the consequent cost and time benefits to travellers; reductions in resources which would otherwise be required to meet the demand by the existing system; and the revenue losses to existing operators arising from the traffic diversion. The analysis was greatly helped by the existence of a large body of detailed and sophisticated work, which has been carried out in evaluating the financial profitability of the tunnel.[3] In addition to the usual kinds of divergences between private profit and social net benefit, there was in this case the further difference that benefits and costs accruing only to UK households and firms were to be considered.[4]

The outcome of the evaluation can be briefly characterised as follows: from the UK point of view the tunnel would have involved an investment[5] of £261 m., which would have resulted in a saving of £156 m. in capital expenditure, and £347 m. in operating costs, on the alternative sea and air services required to meet the demand. The tunnel represents a transport facility which is rather more capital intensive, but with much lower operating costs, than alternative sea and air transport. Thus, simply on the grounds of minimising cost of an overall transport network, construction of the tunnel would appear justified. In addition, there would have been a net gain in consumers' surplus[6] of £49 m., thus increasing the attractiveness of the tunnel.

The remainder of this part of the paper is concerned with examination of the basis for these conclusions. It is convenient to describe and appraise the analysis under five main headings:

(i) demand forecasts
(ii) calculation of user benefits
(iii) calculation of capital and operating-cost savings
(iv) procedure for calculating a net present value
(v) sensitivity analysis of results to changes in assumptions.

Demand forecasts

Two approaches to the forecasting problem are possible. The more general is to regard the decisions on whether to make a trip, the destination, means of transport, and specific route, simultaneously. Thus the choice of destination depends on the time, cost, and other characteristics of the routes by which one gets there, and these, with other characteristics of the possible destinations, influence the decision on whether or not to make a trip. Alternatively, the decisions can be ordered sequentially, with the decision at each stage independent of those which succeed it. First would come the decision on whether or not to make a trip; next the precise destination and holiday type (car tour, package etc.); next the choice of transport; and finally the specific route (where routes may differ only in relation to a particular segment of the journey, e.g. the channel crossing). Thus the decision at each stage constrains the choices at the next. This second approach implies a hierarchy of forecasting models, with the forecast at each stage providing an aggregate to be decomposed among the alternatives at the succeeding one.

The forecasts[7] underlying the cost–benefit analysis essentially adopt the second approach. A justification is attempted by citing the evidence of an in-depth questionnaire inquiry on the household decision process. It appears that people actually make decisions in this sequence. This is hardly conclusive evidence, however, and runs the risk of confusing the apparent process by which decisions are taken with the nature of the decision itself. It is probable that people have information on the possibilities at later stages when they begin the sequence, and it is also likely that they would revise decisions earlier in the sequence if they acquire new information when they consider a decision at a particular stage.

The forecasts take some account of this, as described below. However, the main assumption of their approach is that the total demand for trips abroad is independent of the cross-Channel route decisions, and so will be unaffected by introduction of the tunnel route. The real justification of the assumption must be on grounds of its feasibility. The analysts were confronted with the problem of predicting, on the basis of past data, the effects of a significant change in costs, duration, frequency, and convenience of the Channel crossing. In the past, however, the latter have varied relatively little compared to the variations in demand for foreign travel, and so past data provide no firm basis for prediction. The conservative assumption of no overall 'generation effect' of the tunnel on demand for trips abroad is perhaps, therefore, the most acceptable one. The implications of this are further discussed below.

Given the basic methodology, forecasts were obtained in the following way: forecasts of total trips abroad, disaggregated into holiday and business trips, were made for each of the years 1980 and 1990; a distinction was also made between long holidays, lasting five days or more, and short holidays. The holiday markets were then further disaggregated in each of two ways: first into type of holiday, e.g. package, or car-accompanied; second into country or zone of destination. Finally, given holiday types and destinations, forecasts were made of demand for the various cross-Channel routes.

The forecasts for total holiday demand were based on a cross-sectional analysis of holiday travel data for the year 1971. A large amount of data was collected by questionnaire methods, and the propensity to take a holiday abroad was then related to socioeconomic variables such as income, age, sex, marital status, number of children, occupational category, and so on. Linear regression models were used to quantify the relationships, and then forecasts were made using the resulting equations. In order to do this, it was necessary to forecast the independent variables for 1980 and 1990. For example, the income variable was forecast by assuming a rate of growth of GNP and a constant distribution of income by household. The resulting total forecasts were checked by comparison with an extrapolation of the time-trend of past growth in demand, and were found to be not unreasonable.

It is rarely difficult to find criticisms of any set of forecasts. The following are perhaps the most important in this case:

(*a*) There are well-known objections to using cross-section relationships for making forecasts over time, of which the analysts showed themselves to be somewhat aware, hence the time-trend extrapolation.

(b) The various socioeconomic characteristics can be expected to be highly collinear. Indeed, because not all respondents to the questionnaire gave their incomes, income was regressed on the other characteristics and assigned to them in this way. An implication of collinearity is that the regression estimates of the separate coefficients may not reflect accurately the real influence of each variable taken separately. Hence, if the variables change differentially over time, there may be distortion in the forecasts. The existence and implications of this problem were not considered in the Report.

(c) As well as the issue raised in (a) there could be some doubt about the stability of coefficients estimated on only one year's data.

(d) Finally, no attempt was made to estimate the variance of the forecast errors, even though, as is discussed below, these are important in determining the overall probability distribution of net benefits of the tunnel.

In breaking down the total demand for long and short holidays into holiday type − long holidays into car-accompanied, package, and independent; short into package and others − a similar procedure to that described above was used. The propensity to take a particular holiday type was regressed on socioeconomic characteristics, the resulting relationships then being used, in conjunction with forecasts of the characteristics, to provide breakdowns of the holiday markets in 1980 and 1990. These forecasts are therefore subject again to criticisms (a)–(d).

Analysis of holiday demand by destination was carried out rather differently. The fraction of total holiday traffic going to each country was related to: the number of friends and relatives of holidaymakers in that country (found from questionnaire surveys to be a highly significant variable); length of coastline; climatic conditions; population; and a 'generalised travel cost'. This last variable, appearing for the first time in the analysis, consists of the amount of money spent on average in getting to the holiday destination, plus a money allowance for the travelling time taken. As a result of the analysis of past decisions, it was possible to impute a value of 5p per hour to the latter, implying that travel time was not, on average, of prime importance in choice of holiday country.[8]

At this point it is worth noting that influence of a fall in time and cost of the Channel crossing is, as a result of the specification of the forecasting models, restricted to the choice of holiday destination, and will in any case be very weak. The time-saving will be given very little weight, and the scope for switching from destinations which do not require a Channel crossing, to those which do, is very limited by the nature of the holiday market. This, together with the fact that there is no increased total demand for holidays, and no change in type of holiday, accounts for the very small 'generation effect' of the tunnel, and in turn the rather low value of user benefit in the final table of the cost–benefit analysis.

The forecasts of holidays by type and destination permitted a forecast of total demand for Channel crossings, which then had to be allocated among the various routes: ferries, hovercraft, and tunnel. The basis for this allocation was a regression analysis which related cross-Channel route-choice probability to money cost, service frequency, and time. In the course of this analysis it was found that 'rational' factors of time, service frequency, and cost explain route choice in the past only with a large residual error, which was held to be due to 'imperfect information, route loyalty-cum-inertia, or qualitative preferences'. In other words, because they could not or did not do the sums correctly, or because they have preferences over routes, travellers chose particular routes even when they were not the best on time and cost grounds. This, the analysts called an 'error structure', and incorporated it into the models explaining past route choice.

In forecasting the future route distribution, the tunnel was given specified values for its toll, journey time, and service frequency. Then, given corresponding values for all other possible routes, forecasts of traffic on each route were obtained from the regression equations. However, given the importance of the 'error structure' in explaining past route choices, there is the problem of attributing one to the tunnel. The report is a little inexplicit on this point, but since it states that in all respects other than time, cost, and frequency, the tunnel was treated as an additional Dover–Calais *sea route*, the safest conclusion seems to be that the same error structure was attributed to the tunnel as to the Dover–Calais sea ferry. That is, in terms of 'imperfect information, loyalty-cum-inertia, and qualitative preference', there will be the same propensity to choose the tunnel when it is not best on time, cost, and frequency grounds, and the same propensity not to choose it when it is the best, as for the existing Dover–Calais ferry service.

If this indeed is the assumption of the study, it is a very heroic, and not very plausible, one. It is surely difficult to identify the 'route loyalty-cum-inertia' of a completely new service with that of a long-established route. Moreover, in terms of qualitative preference, the reliability, comfort, and claustrophobia of a train journey through a tunnel would seem to be rather different to the experience of a sea crossing. The problem facing the analysts is clear: given the importance of the 'error structure' in explaining route choice, how does one evaluate this for a facility which doesn't yet exist? It is not difficult to take exception to the solution adopted. Unfortunately, there is insufficient information in the report to allow an estimate of the importance of this factor to the tunnel traffic forecasts.

To conclude the discussion of demand forecasts, we move from the forecasting procedures to the forecasting assumptions. It was necessary to assume future values of:

(i) national income and its distribution by household (required for forecasts of total holiday demand and holiday type)
(ii) population size and socioeconomic structure (forecasts of total holiday demand and type)
(iii) holiday costs, number of friends and relatives abroad, car ownership levels (holiday location)
(iv) the prices, travel times, and frequencies, of tunnel facilities and competing services (holiday location, cross-Channel route choice).

This in itself would be a major forecasting exercise. I do not propose to discuss (ii) and (iii) in this paper. (i) is discussed below. At this point, the problems associated with (iv) can usefully be looked at in some depth.

The analysts viewed the market for cross-Channel transport essentially as a duopoly, with the tunnel on one hand and the ferry operators on the other.[9] In order to predict the final market shares resulting from a given toll, trip duration, and service frequency for the tunnel, it seemed necessary to predict the reactions of the ferry operators. However, the analysts chose a fairly simple duopoly model, since they assumed that the tunnel policies are held completely fixed throughout.[10] Then, fleet operators choose, for any given fleet size, the levels of fares and frequencies which maximise profit; and finally that fleet size is chosen which yields an 11 per cent d.c.f. rate of return. This gives the values of fares and frequency which are used, in conjunction with the values assumed for the tunnel, to predict the final cross-Channel market allocation.

There are two main criticisms of this exercise:

(i) the tunnel toll was set at the level of the 1971 Dover–Calais ferry fare, incorporating various off-peak concessions, adjustments for car size, etc. The basis for this choice is never made clear, and bears no discernible relationship to the economics of the tunnel. Yet it has important consequences. First is that, in the model just discussed, it is an important determinant of the overall allocation of traffic by routes, and therefore has an important influence on the outcome of the cost–benefit analysis. Second, it means that virtually the only type of benefit received by the majority of travellers who divert to the tunnel is a time saving: they will in general not save money. Paradoxically, the travellers who do save money, but not time, are those who continue to travel on existing ferry routes, since they gain from the competitive fare reductions. In the absence of information to the contrary the choice of this toll assumption seems, to the writer, at least, due to the fact that no agreed policy on the tunnel toll yet exists, and so the analysts have had to choose the least contentious guideline they can find.

(ii) The second criticism is that the analysts have carried out the wrong kind of exercise. The particular toll assumption underlines the fact that there is no awareness in the study of the possibility of choosing allocatively efficient prices. There are strong reasons for suspecting that existing ferry fares incorporate insufficient peak/off-peak differentiation, and generate excessive profits overall.[11] To incorporate these features into the tunnel toll assumptions therefore begs a lot of questions. Given the fact that a large part of the ferry capacity is owned by nationalised industries, while there will be a substantial public interest in the tunnel, a subject which should be explored is the question of an allocatively efficient set of prices for the entire network of cross-Channel facilities, and its implications, *via* its effect on demands, for the overall results of the cost—benefit analysis. In other words, there *is* a relationship between pricing and investment.

There are several possible objections to this second criticism. The first would be to call it naive. The fact that existing ferry capacity is largely state-owned has not precluded policies which look very much like straightforward exploitation of monopoly power. There is nothing therefore to suggest that a policy of social-welfare maximisation would be adopted in the future, Monopolies Commission notwithstanding. This is reinforced by the probable presence of a strong private financial interest in any tunnel. This point, however, raises an issue common to all public-enterprise economics: there is still an almost complete separation between practical decision taking in public enterprises, and the rules and criteria developed in the area of economics concerned with optimality of public-sector resource allocation. The defence of the latter also applies here: allocative efficiency matters, and it is important to examine its consequences for any particular area of decision, in order to appraise existing procedures, and identify potential improvements.

A second objection is that although a large part of the cross-Channel facilities are state owned, there would also be sizeable private sector participation. However, this does not so much preclude social-welfare maximisation as change the definition of the problem.[12] There are two possibilities: first, it could simply be assumed that the private sector would be required to observe the optimal pricing policies, either by direct control, or by appropriate tax-subsidy policies; alternatively, the optimum for the public sector of the industry could be sought, taking into account the effect, *via* the consequential decisions of the private sector, on the social welfare of consumers of the private-sector service. In either case, we would expect the pricing system to differ from that assumed by the analysts.

Finally, we have the objection that since the profits on cross-Channel operations accrue to the state, they can be regarded as indirect taxes, and there seems to be no reason for not levying indirect taxes on services which are, in total, fairly price inelastic, and consumed by relatively high-income groups and foreigners. Again, however, this point simply changes the nature of the problem,[13] rather than ruling out social-welfare optimisation. If a specific amount of revenue is required by the Exchequer, then this can be levied by an optimal set of mark-ups on prices, where the characteristic of these mark-ups is that they are inversely proportional to the price elasticities of demand of the services on which they are levied.

It therefore seems to be worthwhile to consider the kind of pricing systems which would be optimal for the entire system of cross-Channel facilities. First, there would be differentiation of prices according to peak characteristics. Something which the Reports stress, but then do not incorporate into their pricing assumptions, is the extreme peakedness of the annual demand pattern; 60 per cent of the annual flow takes place in July, August, and September, and two-thirds of the flow in any week takes place at the weekend. This suggests at least four demand periods. Then, in the absence of indirect taxation and assuming that the private sector is regulated, the optimal pricing system can be taken to be marginal cost based. It is, therefore, likely that midweek and weekend prices in the July/August/September period will cover running costs and capital charges, while the off-season prices will involve running costs only. Given the high degree of capital intensity of the facilities, this is likely to imply large price differentials. Moreover, because of the much lower operating costs, we would expect that off-peak tunnel charges would be well below those of other routes. It should, perhaps, be mentioned that this marginal cost pricing system need not result in financial losses. The total revenue from peak and off-peak tolls for the tunnel will cover total costs, including depreciation and the required rate of return on capital, provided that the capacity of the tunnel is not larger than the rate of peak demand at the appropriate price. Moreover, even if this were so initially, over time peak tolls would have to be raised to restrict demand to capacity and avoid congestion, thus generating net profits over and above the required rate of return, in a way quite consistent with allocative efficiency. Likewise, since long-run marginal costs of ferry services are likely to be constant or rising no losses will result here.

The effect of imposing an overall profit requirement would be to lead to larger rises in prices of less price elastic services, and therefore, assuming that off-peak demand would be more elastic than on-peak, there would be an even greater peak/off-peak differential. Finally, if the private sector were to be left unregulated, and influenced only through prices of the public-sector services, there would optimally be relatively lower prices of those services which have close private sector substitutes. To summarise: the tunnel toll assumption adopted in the study is arbitrary, and ignores the possibility of establishing an allocatively efficient set of prices for cross-Channel services. These prices are likely to be lower in general than those currently prevailing, with a much greater degree of peak/off-peak differentiation. The result of changing the toll assumption in this way would be to increase the benefits to users, and reduce further the capital and operating costs of the alternative services, thus enhancing the attractiveness of the tunnel project.

User benefits

In calculating user benefits resulting from the tunnel, total traffic was divided into holiday, business, and freight. The benefit to each category consisted of a fall in its 'generalised travel cost', the sum of money and time costs.

The table below gives the sums involved.

The time valuations and motoring costs used in deriving these were provided by the DOE; it is not proposed to go into the basis of those valuations here. The following points are worth noting, however:

(i) the cost (both money and time) of 1 mile travelled on the Continent by a British motorist was taken as exactly half that of a mile in the UK. This was based on the view that the Continental journey was 'part of the holiday', and so was less onerous. It was also said to 'reflect' the findings

TABLE 1 *User benefits*

	1980	1990	Present value[1]
	(£m.)	(£m.)	(£m.)
UK holiday passengers	12.4	18.8	108.7
UK business passengers	2.6	7.9	40.9
Freight	3.3	6.6	36.1
Total	18.3	33.3	185.7

Source: Table 7.1, page 42 of [1].
[1] in 1973 at 1973 prices, for years 1973–2030.

of the consultants in the demand forecasts. The latter study did not, however, produce this particular figure, but only the conclusion that 'travel time (on the Continent) is not of prime importance in the choice of holiday, country or region'. This particular value is therefore, likely to be even more arbitrary than most values of time.

(ii) On the other hand time spent crossing the Channel, of direct relevance to the cost–benefit analysis, is valued at the full DOE leisure rate of 23p per hour, thus assuming that travellers do not regard this as 'part of the holiday', or indeed something to be positively enjoyed.

(iii) A problem arose in this study which is common to many transport cost–benefit analyses. In making predictions of route choices, the travel costs which are used are those actually *perceived* by travellers. However, in evaluating the consequent benefits, the values which are used are the estimates of the 'true' travel costs, which in general differ from those which are perceived, due possibly to incomplete information or the inadequate computational ability of travellers. It follows that some travellers will be predicted as switching to the tunnel when they 'shouldn't' have, and some will be predicted as not switching when they should. In the former case, there is actually a disbenefit from the tunnel, and, in the latter case, a loss of potential benefit. The issue here is essentially one of misinformation. Indeed, by computing the sum of disbenefits to erring switchers and potential benefits to erring non-switchers, we obtain a measure of the benefit from providing *correct* information to travellers, which can be compared to the costs of doing so. The case for providing the information can then be evaluated. Indeed, an interesting case could arise in which a project would have a negative net benefit if this information were not provided and a positive net benefit if it were. However, assuming the information not to be provided, it surely has to be accepted, if one accepts as valid the analysis underlying the forecasting, that the loss of benefit predicted for travellers who switch 'wrongly' is a consequence of the project, and should logically be included as a cost. The present study, however, sets these disbenefits at zero, arguing that it is impossible to accept that someone would voluntarily make himself worse off. This is completely at odds with the logic of the forecasting and evaluation procedures on which the study relies quite crucially: the analysts cannot disregard the implications of the procedures when it suits them to do so, without bringing into question the validity of all the results based upon them.

(iv) As described above, the fare used in calculating the generalised travel cost of the tunnel was the Dover–Calais ferry rate, and so the user benefits arising from money savings to tunnel users will be very small.

(v) There is no weight given in the study to other possible sources of benefits to users, particularly greater reliability[14] and comfort from tunnel services across all weather conditions.

The study (in 1973) noted that if the tunnel were certain to be constructed, ferry operators would, from 1975 onwards, reduce their investment in new capacity, in anticipation of lower demand. This in turn would have created shortages and peak congestion on ferry services until the tunnel came into operation. This would have represented a disbenefit to travellers of £15 m., discounted to 1973. The extent of the under-capacity was estimated from the fleet-scheduling model described earlier. The valuation of the loss of benefit was a matter of some difficulty, involving as it did assumptions on the way in which capacity would be rationed. The Report acknowledged the arbitrary nature of the final estimate.

Net capital and operating cost savings

These cost savings represent the difference in capital and operating costs of the ferry and aircraft services with and without the tunnel. Their magnitude therefore depends, first, on the extent of traffic diversion to the tunnel, and second, on the projected capital and operating costs of ships and aircraft. The latter were estimated by projecting information on current costs obtained from operators, on the basis of assumptions on rates of change of prices and wages, and future technology. These costs then played an important part in the fleet-scheduling model, which in turn helped produce the traffic diversion forecasts, as discussed earlier. Hence, errors in the estimates of future costs are not independent of errors in the tunnel traffic forecasts, but rather accentuate them. For example, if the estimate of ferry operating costs were 'too low', this would imply, through the fleet-scheduling model, an underestimate of traffic diversion to the tunnel (ferry fares are lower, given the 11 per cent target return, due to lower costs), and will also undervalue the resources which would be saved by this diversion. Thus, the overall results are likely to be particularly sensitive to the cost estimates.

The calculation of a net present value

The various forecasting exercises and analyses, most of which have been described above, result in six time streams of costs or benefits:

(i) The UK share of the tunnel construction costs, and capital costs of a new rail link

(ii) capital and operating cost savings from slower growth of sea and air transport capacity

(iii) tunnel operating costs

(iv) benefits to UK users, consisting essentially of time savings to those who use sea and air routes

(v) revenue losses to existing operators, representing the extent of the pure transfer from producers to consumers

(vi) disbenefits to UK users arising out of smaller ferry capacity in the period 1975–80.

Each of these streams is discounted at the Treasury test discount rate (t.d.r.) of 10 per cent, and the resulting present values summed to give the net present value of benefits.

To criticise this procedure is essentially to criticise the Treasury doctrine on investment appraisal, a subject on which there is quite an extensive literature. The analysts were bound to follow this doctrine, and so they are guilty only by association. In this context, use of the procedure assumes:

(i) the present value of UK consumption which will be foregone, as a result of the tunnel, is equal to the present value of capital expenditure.

(ii) likewise the present value of UK consumption generated by the capital and operating cost savings is equal to the present value of the expenditure savings.

(iii) the discount rate(s) which would be applied by all travellers to the future stream of benefits projected for them is a uniform 10 per cent.

(iv) the discount rate applied by all transport operators to the revenue losses is a uniform 10 per cent, and these losses correctly measure the future loss in producers' surplus arising from the tunnel.

(v) the discount rate applied by all travellers confronted with reduced quality of service in years 1975–80, to the disbenefits they will incur, is a uniform 10 per cent.

(vi) the distributional implications of the precise incidence of costs and benefits among UK households can be ignored.

The general arguments which could be levelled against these propositions – that household time-preference rates differ from the social opportunity cost of capital, and that market prices in which costs and benefits are measured may not reflect social opportunity costs, are well known and will not be rehearsed here.[15] One particular aspect of the project can, however, be mentioned, which has special bearing on assumption (i). This is that a significant proportion of the funds required for the project (the Report on the financial aspects of the Tunnel says 25 per cent) are expected to be raised abroad. The consequences of this could be quite significant.

To fix ideas, let us consider two extreme cases:

(a) Only financial flows are involved: the inflow of funds simply goes to expand UK foreign currency reserves or replace other foreign borrowing. The future repayments of the loan likewise are made out of reserves or replace other loan repayments. There are therefore no real resource effects.

(*b*) The inflow of funds represents a net addition to foreign borrowing, which results in the finance of a flow of imports of real goods and services. Thus, there is no corresponding loss of UK consumption or investment as a result of capital expenditure on the project in the years in which finance is provided. Thus, other things being equal, the social opportunity cost of the project is below its capital expenditure. However, it is then consistent to assume that future payment of the debt is made at the expense of future real consumption and investment. If, then, the UK time-preference rate on consumption is greater than the interest rate at which it has borrowed from abroad, the present value of foregone future consumption is less than the initial gain in consumption, and so the net opportunity cost of the project is less than the capital expenditure.

In practice, of course, the actual effect may be a combination of these two cases, and this poses considerable difficulties of estimation. Moreover, there could be an objection on conceptual grounds: it is reasonable to assume an increase in aggregate UK foreign borrowing because of the undertaking of a specific project, since an excess of the UK rate of time preference over the interest rate on borrowing abroad indicates that we would gain by expanding our foreign borrowing anyway. Indeed, the logical conclusion of this point is that foreign borrowing should be conducted up to the point at which the rate of time preference equals the interest rate, in which case the latter could be taken as the basis for public-sector discounting. This argument would certainly be true if we could imagine the UK public sector as an agent in a perfectly-competitive international capital market, able to borrow in a generalised way by issuing bonds. However, the international capital market is likely to be too imperfect to enable such a neat solution, and in particular the possibility of loans may be linked with the undertaking of specific projects. In that case, it is preferable to adopt a project-oriented approach, with an attempt to calculate the precise opportunity cost of a project given the extent of its foreign financing, the interest rate on this, and the time-preference rate.

Sensitivity analysis

All the estimates which have been described so far correspond to what the study calls the 'central case'. Tests of the sensitivity of the results for this case to changes in assumptions take two forms:

(i) the consequences for all benefit and cost streams of a lower GNP-growth assumption are set out in the so-called 'low case'. Thus, the central case assumes a UK GNP growth rate of 3.5 per cent p.a. from 1973–90, while the low case assumes a growth rate 20 per cent lower, at 2.8 per cent p.a. The differences in some of the main magnitudes are shown in the table below. The table indicates a high degree of sensitivity of the final result to the growth-rate assumption, essentially reflecting the effect on total holiday demand of variations in the rate of growth. The tunnel project is highly 'geared' in the sense that benefits, particularly the most important single category, operating cost savings, are very sensitive to growth-rate variations whereas costs are not so.

(ii) The second kind of sensitivity analysis took the form of a series of *ceteris paribus* changes in individual assumptions, with a statement of the effect on the internal rate of return (i.r.r.) of the project in both central and low cases:

(a) the assumption of a high-speed rail link could be replaced by a 'low rail-investment strategy', which reduces capital expenditure but so increases journey time that there is no 'material effect' on the i.r.r.

(b) if fleet operators were to replace existing policies by greater use of peak-load pricing and consequent reduction in existing capacity, there is less scope for capital cost savings resulting from the tunnel, and the i.r.r. is marginally reduced.

(c) the present Monopolies Commission inquiry could result in fare reductions on existing services before introduction of the tunnel. This reduces user benefit from the tunnel, since there is less possibility of competitive

TABLE 2   *Sensitivity to GNP growth assumptions*

	Central case	Low case	Unit effect[1]
	£m.	£m.	£m.
Capital cost savings	156.1	129.9	3.7
User benefits	170.9	128.2	6.1
Operating cost savings	347.1	246.6	14.4
Decrease in revenues	121.5	99.9	3.1
Net present value[2]	291.8	147.9	20.6

Source: Tables 8.1 and 8.2, pp. 43, 44 of [1].
[1] Reduction in sum per 0.1 reduction in growth rate.
[2] Not the sum of previous items in this table.

price reaction, and there is a loss of one point on the i.r.r. for each 30 per cent price reduction.

(*d*) An escalation in capital costs of the tunnel of 20 per cent, in real terms, accompanied by a two-year delay in completion, reduces the i.r.r. by 2–3 points.

(*e*) A 20 per cent reduction in future operating costs of ships and aircraft below the levels assumed in the study would reduce the i.r.r. by 2–3 points.

(*f*) Halving user benefits, equivalent to assuming zero values for time savings of UK holiday and business passengers, reduces the i.r.r. by $1\frac{1}{2}$–2 points.

Before going on to more basic criticisms of both aspects of the sensitivity analysis, it could be said that choice of the i.r.r. in which to express sensitivities is curious. For well-known reasons the appropriate criterion for decision is the net present value of the project, and the change in the i.r.r. between assumptions may not be a reliable guide to the change in net present value at 10 per cent. If the elasticity of net present value with respect to the discount rate changes between cases, then a small change in the i.r.r. need not imply a small change in the n.p.v. at 10 per cent. Thus, suppose in the following diagram curve *A* corresponds to a 'favourable' and curve *B* to an 'unfavourable' assumption. Then, because of the change in slope of the curve, the sensitivity of the n.p.v. at 10 per cent is much greater than that of the i.r.r. If further illustration is required, note that when the income growth assumption is changed, the i.r.r. falls by three points from 17.6 per cent to

Figure 1

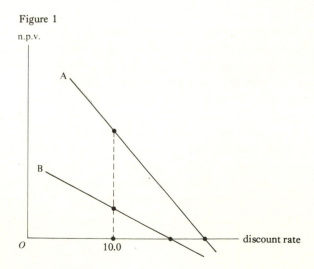

n.p.v.

14.6 per cent, or by about 17 per cent, while the net present value falls from £291.8 m. to £147.9 m., or by about 50 per cent.

A more important point is that the analysis of the effect of varying the GNP growth rate is incomplete. On its own admission, the 'low case' in the Report is more important than the 'central case', because a growth rate of 2.8 per cent per annum is much more consistent with the past performance of the UK than one of 3.5 per cent. However, even the 2.8 per cent rate is no worse than a good average of past UK performance, and even if it is regarded as the central value in the distribution of future UK growth rates, there is a significant probability that the actual growth rate could lie below this. The outcome of the investment in such a situation is, however, left unexplored. Some idea of the consequences may be gained, in a rough and ready way, from the calculations of the 'unit effect' in Table 2. If we assume that there is a simple linear relation between growth rate and net present value of the project, then the unit effect gives the reduction in n.p.v. for each 0.1 point reduction in the growth rate. On this basis, the out-turns would be as in the table below

GNP growth (% per annum)	2.8	2.6	2.4	2.2	2.0
Net present value (£m.)	147.9	106.7	65.5	24.3	−16.9

Little more is intended by these calculations than to show what *could* be true. Given that whatever may be our hopes, our expectations of future growth must include rates in the range 2.2–2.8 per cent with non-zero probabilities, the Report fails to provide information which would allow the sensitivity of the results to these possibilities to be assessed.[16] This leads to the central criticism of the entire sensitivity analysis, which is that it is seriously inadequate for the purpose of presenting to the decision taker the information on which to base an evaluation of the riskiness of the project. The procedure of *ceteris paribus* relaxation of one assumption at a time, with vague information on likelihoods, allows only an impressionistic, and quite possibly wrong, view of the risks associated with the project to be formed. Suppose, for example, there was to be a 2.6 per cent growth rate, a 20 per cent escalation in tunnel construction costs, and a 20 per cent reduction in operating costs of ships and aircraft. From the results as presented, it is not possible to say what the outcome would be, nor how likely this outcome is relative to the more favourable outcomes. A more general approach to the measurement of risks should be taken, rather than that which selects a single 'central case' and then considers piecemeal adjustments to it.

There are three main sources of risk in this kind of cost–benefit analysis:

(i) that arising from the possibility that the hypothesised relationships, for example, those underlying the demand forecasts, may not continue to hold

(ii) that arising from the error variance of the forecasts made from regression relationships

(iii) that arising from the fact that values of independent variables in forecasting relationships, and of crucial valuation parameters, for example operating costs of ship and aircraft, value of time, and prices of competing services, cannot be known with certainty.

In some respects, it could be argued that given choice of the basic forecasting model, we simply have to accept the uncertainties arising from the possibilities (*a*) that it may not be the 'true' model for explaining the past, and (*b*) even if it is so, it may cease to be so in the future. An alternative approach would be to attempt to attach some prior probability of the 'truth' of the model, which could then be used to attach probabilities to the outcomes predicted by it. Where several models are regarded as possibly true, this approach could be extended by postulating a prior probability distribution of models. Such a 'Bayesian' approach to the problem is still relatively undeveloped, however, and most analysts would prefer simply to assume that the model will continue to be true. Given the choice of model, and assuming it is estimated by standard regression methods (as in the present study), it is in general possible to use the estimate of the variance of the distribution of error terms in the equation to obtain the variance of forecasting errors, conditional upon fixed future values of the independent variables. It is then possible to make statements about the interval within which the future value will be, around the forecast value, with a given probability. Increased emphasis on the provision and interpretation of interval forecasts, rather than point forecasts, would greatly increase the general understanding and credibility of forecasting exercises, and of the economists engaged in them.

The interval forecasts just described are themselves conditional on the assumed values of the independent variables. In general, these can only be predicted in terms of a probability distribution rather than a single, certain number. To assume otherwise is to leave out of account a significant aspect of the riskiness of a project. Given these distributions, it is then possible to combine them with the conditional interval forecasts to obtain a revised interval forecast which will incorporate the greater risk inherent in the stochastic nature of the independent variables.[17] Finally, by postulating, where appropriate, particular distributions of valuation parameters, e.g. ships' operating costs, interval estimates can be made of the final net present values of projects.

My basic contention is as follows: adopting this approach to the risks inherent in an investment project will certainly increase the scale and complexity of the analytical work; there will also be 'subjective' elements, such as the derivation of probability distributions of independent variables and valuation parameters. These are, however, differences of degree, and not kind, to existing appraisals. The information on the outcome of an appraisal should be presented to a decision taker in the form of a gamble, which is what the decision is. One should be able to state the odds on whether the net benefits of a project will turn out to be positive or negative, or greater than some alternative. It is both arrogant and wrong to suppose that civil servants and politicians would not 'understand' results so presented. The Channel tunnel sensitivity analysis typifies the kind of incomplete and selective information about risk which often accompanies major investment projects. It is inconceivable that a sensible evaluation of a risky decision could be made on this basis.

Conclusion

This paper has concentrated on the forecasting procedures and assumptions, and problems of cost–benefit analysis specific to this project, rather than general issues such as the appropriateness of considering only UK costs and benefits, the doctrine underlying the discount rate, and measurement of the value of time. It has also ignored what many may regard as the major sin of omission in the Report, namely the question of the amenity and environmental effects of the tunnel. The main points of principle which have been raised concern the price assumptions and treatment of risk in the study. The assumption on the level of the tunnel toll is extremely arbitrary, particularly when contrasted with the sophistication which went into estimation of the ferry operators' competitive responses; and the question of allocatively efficient prices should be pursued. In my view, the sensitivity analysis in no way presents a decision taker with the type and quality of information which is required to evaluate what is essentially a risky decision, and is *unnecessarily* inadequate. These are two areas in which more work should be done before a final decision on the tunnel is made.

The COBA Manual

A point which was mentioned in the previous section, and which forcibly strikes an economist working in the theory of public-sector resource allocation when he comes into contact with the operational realities, is the relatively small area of intersection of theory with practice. The COBA Manual is an attempt to introduce methods of cost–benefit analysis into perhaps the most basic level of road-investment decision taking, that concerned with small-scale projects for road improvement and realignment; improvements and capacity increases of junctions; and small-town by-passes. Such projects would typically have capital costs of between £$\frac{1}{4}$ m. and £10 m. COBA consists of a standard computer programme, for which the planning engineer concerned provides certain input information on the road network before and after the investment, such as traffic flows, congestion, accident levels, etc. The programme simulates the operation of the network, pre- and post-investment, for each of thirty years. It then calculates time and vehicle cost savings, and accident reductions, as between the two situations, evaluates them using standard DOE valuation parameters, and produces a time-stream of net user benefits. These are then discounted to a present value, reduced by the amount of present value of capital expenditure, and the resulting n.p.v. is expressed in a ratio to the latter. The programme permits assessment of different project designs and timings, and also of the effects on a given project of the introduction, up to ten years later, of related schemes. It is also straightforward to test the sensitivity of results to changes in parameters – both input data and valuation parameters.

The COBA procedure is therefore almost the ultimate in routinisation of cost–benefit analysis. It is also a highly decentralised system with the analysis being conducted by those directly concerned with the project, who will often be non-economists, unindoctrinated in the rationale for the procedures they are using (the brief account of the concepts of consumers' surplus and discounting given in the manual perhaps allays doubts but hardly educates). The central control is provided by the choice of the key valuation parameters, as well as of the cut-off ratio of net present value to capital expenditure. Some measure of the scale of the innovation is obtained if COBA is compared to the system it replaces, under which projects were ranked on the basis of the ratio of user benefits in the first year of operation only, to the capital expenditure!

The main technical limitation of COBA is that it can handle neither trip redistribution, i.e. change of destination, nor trip generation, i.e. increased demand for journeys, arising from the investment. It assumes that the number of trips between all origins and destinations is the same in the two situations, and so can only take into account diversion of traffic to different routes between given destinations. This means that it cannot handle two important classes of projects: road construction and improvement schemes in urban or largely urban areas; and major, long-range inter-urban routes, where trip redistribution and generation are important consequences. Presumably this limitation is a matter of time and research effort.

Given the class of projects which it can handle, there are five main comments, some of them critical, which can be made about the COBA procedure. First is the omission from the present value of costs of the project, of the time delays and accident increases which are often experienced in the construction phase of projects such as these. The logic of the consumers' surplus approach requires that they be measured and included; they are unlikely to be a trivial element in the final n.p.v. of many projects, not least because they occur early in time and will be less heavily discounted.

It is interesting to note that because there will be a relatively large number of independent projects of this kind, the averaging which is involved in calculating valuation parameters, traffic flow relationships, etc., is unlikely to involve distortion for the outcome of the programme taken as a whole, because of a law-of-large-numbers effect. It could, on the other hand, matter in the choice between two mutually exclusive localised projects, in areas where the overall average value of, say, the value of time, was untypical. Likewise, some element of redistribution is involved, in that the benefits of projects in areas of high incomes and therefore high time values will be understated, and conversely those in low-income areas will be overstated. Given that workability of the procedure depends on its acceptance by planning engineers, the extent to which its results meet their *a priori* notions of what seems right and sensible may determine its success. The coincidence between results and expectations in turn depends on the extent of local deviations from the overall average, i.e., on the variances of the distributions of the parameters. It could turn out, in fact, that the procedure is overcentralised, and that greater leeway would have to be allowed to local planners to find the valuation parameters appropriate for their areas.

This point also relates to the riskiness of the projects. Since there is a large number of small independent projects, it would seem that risk could be ignored; the operation of the law of large numbers would imply that the variance of benefits of the entire programme would be very small, and so expected value maximisation would be appropriate. However, if the distribution of benefits of a project is not normal, the expected value of benefits is not the same as the most likely value of benefits, and it is far from clear that it is the former and not the latter which is calculated under the procedure.

The main doubts about the COBA procedure, however, arise in relation to the discounting and project-ranking procedures. The procedure has to confront a capital-rationing problem, in which the total budgets are set for some years ahead. Moreover, these budgets are such that projects whose n.p.v.'s are positive when discounted at the t.d.r. of 10 per cent are rejected. The solution adopted is to calculate present values of benefits and costs at 10 per cent, rank projects on the ratio of n.p.v. to capital expenditure, and then apply a cut-off point at a value of the ratio greater than zero.

No justification of this procedure is attempted in the COBA Manual and indeed none is possible: it has no optimality properties whatsoever.[18] First, consider the choice of discount rate. The rationale of the t.d.r. is that it reflects the marginal rate of return on low-risk private-sector investment. But since the capital expenditure of the programme is fixed, this is no longer the relevant opportunity cost of any investment within the programme. Thus, use of the discount rate is inconsistent with the rationale of the t.d.r. Moreover, the fact that projects with positive n.p.v.'s at 10 per cent are rejected means that the shadow prices of the budget constraints in each period exceed 10 per cent. Hence it is inappropriate to evaluate costs and benefits accruing at different points in time at the 10 per cent rate. In the most general case, a specified utility function defined on net benefits at each point in time would be required before the problem of optimal choice could be solved. If, however, the special form of function:

$$U = \sum_{t=0}^{\infty} \rho^t B_t \quad 0 < \rho < 1$$

could be assumed, where B_t is total net annual benefit in year t, then net present values of benefits could be directly computed using the value ρ. The problem is that no one seems prepared to specify a value of ρ.

Secondly, even given the appropriate values of n.p.v.'s, the use of the ratio of n.p.v. to capital expenditure in ranking projects is inappropriate whenever capital expenditures are incurred in more than one period. The use of the present value of capital expenditure in the denominator of the ratio solves the problem of transforming a vector into a scalar, but does so in a way which need not reflect the relative scarcities of capital in each period and the relative demands which projects place on them. It is, in fact, quite easy to construct numerical examples which show that the fact that project A has a higher n.p.v./capital-expenditure ratio than project B is neither necessary nor sufficient for an optimal choice of A.

It is of interest to consider the question of deriving a fairly simple rule for solving these problems,[19] and this can be done by examining explicitly the programming problem underlying them. Suppose that we have some value for ρ in the above equation (Professor Williams suggested basing it upon 10 per cent), together with a specification of projects' capital expenditures, and the total budget, over the planning horizon. Solving the primal programming problem would provide an optimal investment plan; solving the dual programming problem, which has the same information requirement as the primal, would provide a set of shadow prices of capital for each time period, say λ_t, where these have the property that:

$$\frac{\delta \sum_t \rho^t B^*_t}{\delta C_t} \leqslant \lambda_t$$

where B^*_t is the value of benefits in year t arising from the optimal solution, and C_t is the capital ration in year t. Now if capital expenditures of projects are very small relative to the budget, then a close approximation to λ_t, the shadow price of capital in year t, is the present value of benefits of the 'best excluded project', which could be undertaken if the constraint in year t were relaxed. Now, from the so-called 'complementary slackness conditions' of linear programming, it can be shown that the property of any project which should be rejected is that:

$$\Sigma_t \, \rho^t B_t^j - \Sigma_t \, \lambda_t C_t^j < 0 \qquad j = 1, 2, \ldots, n$$

where B_t^j is the benefit in year t per unit of project j, and C_t^j is its per unit capital cost in year t. For practical purposes it could be considered worthwhile to try to obtain some kind of set of estimates of the λ_t, *without* having to go through the procedure of solving the entire problem. The solution suggested by Professor Williams is to assume the λ_t are all equal, and given by an estimate of the present value of benefits of the best excluded project, say, last year. This obviously involves a very strong assumption about the time patterns of benefits, capital expenditures, and budgets over the planning horizon. Nevertheless, the empirical research which could be carried out on past programmes would throw some light on this, and would be a significant step towards improvement in the existing procedures. Note, however, that it would not suffice to base estimates of the λ_t on the returns to the 'best excluded projects' under the existing COBA procedure since, as already pointed out, this has none of the optimality properties of the programming procedure suggested above: we would not be able to say that the 'best excluded project' under COBA is the one which would result from the programming analysis.

Conclusions

The COBA procedure is a significant contribution to solution of the problem of relating apparently optimal decision criteria to actual decision taking in the public sector. Its basic weaknesses relate to the procedures for evaluating and ranking projects, but these are not really of its own making. The attempt to operationalise the criteria set out in the 1967 White Paper [7] serves to bring out very clearly the ambiguities and contradictions inherent in the policy set out there. These weaknesses would, therefore, exist in any set of investment or pricing rules which attempted to do the same thing. That this is not more often brought to our attention is due to the fact that so few attempts are made.

General conclusion

The fact that the main criticisms of the studies do not overlap reflects the basic dissimilarity of the two. The issues of the pricing assumptions and treatment of risk do not arise in the case of COBA, while, because it will presumably not be counted as part of the general transport budget, the question of capital rationing and its effect on the appraisal does not impinge upon the Channel tunnel. However, it is possible to draw some general conclusions on the practice of transport cost—benefit analysis from the two studies. Each is a detailed study carried out within a common framework, consisting of certain centrally-determined valuation parameters and procedures. The defects in these studies relate primarily to this framework, rather than to the detailed attempts to provide the raw material of the evaluations.[20]

The appropriate form of presentation of a project's risks, the consistency of discount rates with capital budgets, the correct calculation of opportunity costs of a project, the allocatively efficient pricing policies of a publicly-owned cross-Channel transport network, are all problems whose correct solutions need to be found centrally. I think it is fair to say that the guidance that project analysts have had on these subjects, when it exists, is either ambiguous and vague, or wrong. And yet the scale and sophistication of the research effort required to improve the evaluation framework common to all projects, is probably no greater than that invested in any one of the larger of them.

NOTES

1 Described in the Report by Cooper and Lybrand Ltd., entitled 'The Channel Tunnel: a United Kingdom transport cost benefit study', HMSO, 1973, and subsequently generally called the Report.

2 The discussion in this paper is based on the 'COBA Manual' which is an internal DOE memorandum. A summary of the procedure has, however, been published and is available from HMSO.

3 This work is described in a series of reports by the consultants. This paper draws particularly heavily on part 2, section 1, Passenger Studies, and the report on the Fleet Scheduling Model.

4 Strictly speaking the study would only justify the 'UK half' of the project, therefore, and overall acceptance of the project would still require it to be acceptable to the French.

  An interesting situation would arise if the desirability of the project altered with the side of the Channel from which it was approached (a possibility which I previously found unlikely, but persuasive arguments from Professor Williams have made me reconsider). Might there then be a case for side-payments?

5 This represents half the tunnel construction costs, plus the cost of a new rail link, respectively £160 m. and £101 m. All figures presented in this paragraph are *present values* at 1973 in January 1973 prices.

6 Arising from time savings plus fare reductions, less revenue losses by ferry operators, this latter being the amount of pure transfer from operators to travellers. The relatively low value for consumers' surplus is commented on later in this paper.

7   A detailed description of these is found in the Report on Passenger Studies.

8   Note that this relates to choice of holiday location primarily within Western Europe, where differences in travel time are relatively small.

9   A description of this part of the analysis is found in the report on the Fleet Scheduling Model.

10 Thus, a toll is assumed for the tunnel which is held unchanged throughout the analysis. There is a single sentence at the end of the analysis to the effect that it would not be worthwhile for the tunnel to enter into a 'price war'. This is a rather puzzling statement, in the light of the high cross-elasticities of demand between the cross-Channel services, given in the report. Did the analysts baulk at the problem of finding a solution to a full-scale duopoly problem? There are further reasons, discussed below, for regarding the toll assumption as unsatisfactory.

11 Thus the report itself tells us that there is over-provision of capacity because of an unwillingness to restrict peak demand sufficiently; and cross-Channel services are currently the subject of a Monopolies Commission inquiry.

12 For a theoretical treatment of this kind of problem, see Rees [5].

13 Again, for a treatment of this problem, see Rees [5].

14 This is measured in terms of the degree of dispersion of actual journey duration about its average value: the greater the dispersion, the less the reliability. At a guess, the tunnel would be more reliable, in this sense, than ferry services, particularly in winter.

15 My views on the correct approach to public sector investment appraisals can be found in Rees [6].

16 Mr D. Barrell, in his very helpful discussion of this paper, made the important point that the Report does not show the extreme sensitivity of the 'high rail-investment strategy' to the growth rate assumption. It appears that even on the 'low case' assumption of 2.8 per cent p.a. growth, the n.p.v. on this investment, *considered separately from the tunnel*, is almost zero. This reinforces the point made here of the uninformative nature of the Report in presenting the risks inherent in the investments to a decision taker.

17 See, for example, Rees and Rees [4], where a procedure is set out for calculating the probability distribution of forecasts from a linear regression model with random independent variables.

18 See, for example, Rees [6], page 38.

19 This paragraph has been added to the paper since the Conference, and was stimulated by some comments from Professor Alan Williams; it is indeed an elaboration of some suggestions he made.

20 In relation to the tunnel-demand forecasts, although I criticised them and pointed out several areas in which they could be questioned, I regard the basic defect as the failure to translate the possible errors and uncertainties, which no forecasting exercise, however good, is without, into a description of the risks associated with the project.

REFERENCES

[1] 'The Channel Tunnel: A United Kingdom transport cost–benefit study', a report by Cooper and Lybrand Associates Ltd., HMSO, London, 1973.

[2] Reports by the Joint Consultants to the Channel Tunnel Company, unpublished. Available on request at the library of the Department of the Environment, 2 Marsham Street, London, SW1.

[3] The 'COBA Manual', Internal Department of Environment document.

[4] J. A. Rees and R. Rees, 'Demand Forecasts and Planning Margins for Water in S.E. England', *Journal of Regional Studies*, 1972.

[5] R. Rees, 'Second Best Rules for Public Enterprise Pricing', *Economica*, 1968.

[6] R. Rees, 'The Economics of Investment Analysis', Civil Service College Occasional Paper 17, HMSO, 1973.

[7] 'Nationalised Industries: A review of financial and economic objectives', Cmnd 3437, HMSO, 1967.

12

Rationalising social expenditure — the arts

M. BLAUG

A careful perusal of the annual reports of the Arts Council since 1946 leaves no doubt that the Council disburses its funds to satisfy a number of more or less clearly defined objectives.[1] These may be summarised as: (1) to diffuse the performing arts (music, opera, ballet, drama and films), and to a lesser extent the visual arts (museums and galleries), throughout the regions of Britain — in a phrase, 'to break the culture monopoly of London'; (2) to diffuse the performing and visual arts among wholly new audiences; (3) to maintain and raise artistic standards in the performing arts; and (4) to encourage the emergence of new art forms as well as new creative artists.

The first question that arises is whether the Arts Council's expenditure pattern actually succeeds in achieving any of its avowed objectives. But that is only the first question. As all four objectives carry some weight in reaching a set of final decisions, what does the Council do when a particular decision scores high in respect of one objective but low in respect of another? After all, any decision designed to achieve multiple ends must involve some order of priorities among ends. But 'score' is a numerical term, and we have yet to demonstrate that any of the four aims of the Council can be quantified, so as to permit us to infer after the event that a certain policy achieved one objective more effectively than another. Our principal task, therefore, is to show that it is at least possible, in principle, to measure the degree of success in achieving these objectives.

Before we proceed, however, we must begin by clearing the ground. The average economist probably feels in his bones that a 'scientific' evaluation of something like public expenditure on the arts is a philosophical, if not a practical, impossibility. But I want to argue that public expenditure on the arts can be evaluated like any other public expenditure. Indeed, in so doing we may come to realise that the problem of multiple ends, which seems to loom so large in respect of the arts, is really a general feature of the evaluation of all public expenditure.

What is cost–effectiveness analysis?

We all know what is meant by cost–*benefit* analysis: it is the attempt to calculate all the direct and indirect costs and benefits of a set of alternative projects or policies, subject only to the proviso that all costs and benefits can be expressed in terms of a common denominator, money. The purpose of the exercise is to choose that project which will maximise a single objective, namely, the excess of monetary benefits over monetary costs as a measure of the aggregate of consumers' surplus. But what do we do when we are concerned to maximise more than one objective and, in particular, when some of these objectives are by their very nature incapable of being reduced to money terms? What we then do is to use what I choose to call 'cost–effectiveness analysis' but which others have sometimes labelled 'systems analysis', 'output budgeting' or 'management by objectives'.[2] In other words, cost–benefit analysis is only a leading species of a much larger genus of evaluation techniques.

Cost–benefit analysis yields a single criterion for choice. Since cost–effectiveness analysis handles activities carried out for multiple objectives, it yields as many choice criteria as there are objectives. To choose at all, we will have to rank the cost–effectiveness ratios in order of importance. Ultimately, therefore, costs and degrees of effectiveness are once again reduced to a common denominator but the yardstick this time is not money but rather the subjective preferences of the decision maker among his stated ends, goals, objectives, etc.

To become a little more specific. Cost–effectiveness analysis always consists of three steps:

(1) specify each of the multiple objectives in such a way that they can be scaled, preferably in cardinal but possibly in ordinal terms (notice that this can always be done, at least in principle, and obviously the very act of choice among alternative activities to achieve multiple objectives implies that it has in fact been done: to choose A over B implies that the outcomes of A and B can be compared and that they have indeed been compared, at least ordinally);

(2) generate alternative policies for achieving the objectives, assess their effectiveness in achieving each of the objectives in terms of a scale, and express these degrees of effectiveness as a proportion of the costs of carrying out the policies (there will be as many of these effectiveness–cost ratios as there are objectives);

and (3) apply the decision maker's 'preference function', indicating his order of priorities among the objectives in terms of numerical weights and choose that policy with the highest weighted effectiveness–cost ratio (if the first step has involved ordinal rather than cardinal scaling, this procedure may fail to yield an unique decision criterion).

No doubt, this sounds very forbidding but all we have really done is to write down in a formal way the implicit logical structure of every decision, whether private or public. It does not matter what the objectives are, or how many there are; provided the means for achieving the objectives are limited – and when they are not, decision making is not a problem worth analysing – the final choice among alternative policies is 'rational' only if it goes through the three steps of cost–effectiveness analysis.

Steps (1) and (2) may present enormous practical difficulties in certain circumstances but, conceptually speaking, they are plain sailing in the sea of positive economics. It is step (3), however, that raises deeper normative questions. How on earth is one supposed to discover a decision maker's preference function among objectives without imposing one's own? Asking him will usually produce a blank stare: if the decision maker is a politician, he is committed first of all to maximising electoral support and that is best secured by blurring objectives, not by revealing them. Nor can we deduce his preference function by studying his past behaviour: he may be inconsistent between decisions; he may have altered his preference function over time as a result of learning-by-doing; besides, circumstances themselves are changing and this itself makes inference difficult. Furthermore, the concept of a single decision maker is, in any case, a convenient fiction; typically, decision making is carried out by a team, whose members may disagree about ends; in consequence, successive policies may express conflicting ends, depending on which member of the team has the upper hand at any moment of time. But if we cannot discover the preference function that underlies policy decisions neither can we evaluate past decisions nor improve future ones.

Further reflections along these lines begin to suggest that there is indeed something wrong with our purist view of cost–effectiveness analysis as a tool for evaluating decision making. In the classic manner à la Robbins, we have implicitly drawn a rigid distinction between means and ends as if the decision makers first choose their goals and then hunt about for policies to achieve them. In point of fact, any decision maker starts with on-going activities and gradually begins to define his objectives in the light of his experience with policies. In other words, decision makers do not try to get what they want; rather they learn to want by appraising what they get. Means and ends are indissolubly related, and evaluation of decision making, or technical advice to decision makers, cannot simply accept the preference function as given.[3]

This view of decision making, so different from the traditional paradigm reflected in our sketch of the three steps that make up cost–effectiveness analysis, has been forcefully argued in recent years by a number of economists and political scientists. A single reference is Braybrooke and

Lindblom, *A Strategy of Decision* (1963), with the revealing subtitle, *Policy Evaluation as a Social Process*.[4] Braybrooke and Lindblom reject all comprehensive approaches to decision making, purporting to lay down global rules for arriving at optimal decisions, and instead advocate what they call 'disjointed incrementalism': it is disjointed because decision making, far from being swallowed whole, is repeatedly attacked in bits and pieces; it is incremental because it considers only a limited range of policies that differ only incrementally from existing ones; 'disjointed incrementalism' does not merely adjust means to ends but also explores ends while applying means, in effect choosing means and ends simultaneously.

It is perfectly clear that Lindblom and Braybrooke have achieved a much more realistic view of the role of advisers to decision makers. Obviously, decision making, particularly public decision making, never achieves more than a third-best solution, if only because the time required to collect adequate information to secure an improvement in 'fine tuning' is the ultimate scarce resource. Nevertheless, it proves useful to keep the three steps of cost–effectiveness analysis in mind as a sort of 'ideal type', while admitting and indeed emphasising that no decision making process in the real world will ever closely correspond to the ideal. The general spirit, if not the letter, of cost–effectiveness analysis does provide a framework for organising our thoughts about the evaluation of real-world decision making.

Having set the stage, we can now turn back to the Arts Council without claiming that we are going to solve all their problems. What I want to do is something more modest: I wish to show that it is possible to apply modern management techniques to the work of the Council. Fortunately, in declaring its objectives, the Council has already gone a long way towards carrying out step (1) of cost–effectiveness analysis. All that is really required is to argue through the logical implications of their stated aims and to show how the objectives could be scaled. Of course, by sticking to the Arts Council, I make things easier for myself. In 1972–73, the Arts Council grant of £14 m. was only just a little less than net government expenditure on 17 national museums and galleries, ignoring additional public funds devoted to local museums and galleries, and we have little basis for delineating the policy objectives that underlie public support for museums and galleries.[5] A further problem area is radio and television. Nevertheless, the Arts Council is the heart of the matter and I will, therefore, confine our attention largely, although not exclusively, to its activities.

Vertical and horizontal diffusion

The first two aims of the Council, as listed above, appear to be fairly similar, involving as they do the gaining of new audiences, either in London or in the provinces. Indeed, the Council seems so far to have concentrated its effort on regional diffusion of the arts in the belief that this would simultaneously achieve both 'vertical' diffusion in terms of new audiences and 'horizontal' diffusion in terms of new regions. But it is much easier to provide the arts for an eager audience which has been barred by distance than it is to create a new demand among members of the public who have hitherto been uninterested in consuming the arts. The Council has, in fact, been more successful in achieving a better geographical distribution of the arts than in attracting a wider cross-section of the population. There is evidence – however imperfect – that audiences all over Britain have shown themselves to be consistently homogeneous in age, education and social background. With hindsight, we may lay down the general rule that a changing composition of audiences does not come about as a simple by-product of increasing provision of the arts. Only a determined policy to attract a different type of audience will successfully achieve vertical diffusion.

The idea of diffusing the arts horizontally to the regions needs to be carefully specified if we are going to evaluate alternative policies of regionalisation. 'The provinces' is a vague term: the cost of encouraging the arts in cities, with a catchment area large enough to provide a ready-made audience, may be far less than that of providing it in small and inaccessible towns. In practice, the Council has, in fact, emphasised large- and medium-sized cities.

Even so, the Council is always faced with the question of whether to implement a policy of horizontal diffusion by extensive touring of London-based companies or by the establishment of permanent Arts Centres in the regions. Though touring is essentially a short-term policy, and the provision of Arts Centres a long-term one, the shortage of funds implies the possibility of conflict between them. In recent years, the balance in terms of expenditures has shifted increasingly towards touring: the goal of meeting an immediate demand, therefore, seems to have been given priority over the aim of investing in the long-term future of the arts outside London. If supplying existing demand is indeed the overriding goal, an obvious first step would be to carry out surveys to determine the catchment area per unit of expenditure. The results could then be compared to the cost of attracting the same number of people by permanent Arts Centres. Unfortunately, the Council so far has failed to adequately survey potential demand and, even more, to pose the issue of touring versus Arts Centres in terms of the costs of meeting a current demand as against a potential demand.

Apart from touring, the arts are also supplied outside London by means of regional theatres and orchestras, directly subsidised by the Arts Council, and by way of the many activities of the Regional Arts Associations, with an annual aggregate budget in 1973–74 of almost £2 m., of which the Arts Council supplies about two thirds. Some local authorities also maintain their own

Arts departments (as well as contributing to the regional associations). This haphazard system of patronage has led both to an arbitrary power and an arbitrary division of responsibilities. Theatres, for example, receive grants from the Arts Council, the local authorities and, to a lesser extent, private industry. Regional Arts Associations also receive money from the same three sources but they act independently of the theatres. The Council has long realised that the aim of horizontal diffusion cannot be realised without more local participation and provision. The ultimate aim, therefore, remains that of local self-sufficiency. But diverse sources of patronage do not necessarily encourage an overall growth of local arts provision unless they are somehow coordinated. The Council has now acquired a Regional Department and money spent on the regions has sharply increased in recent years. But the present administrative structure continues to hinder the development of a comprehensive policy of promoting the arts in the regions.

All this leads to the conclusion that a regional arts policy, comprising the activities of all the local and central agencies involved, including the Arts Council, would seem to be required to rationally underpin the Council's involvement in the horizontal diffusion of the arts. As for the question which is our central concern — how successful has the Council been in achieving its goal of diffusing the arts to the regions? — it cannot be answered without a historical analysis of the provision of the arts outside London since, say, the Second World War, holding constant such factors as regional income levels, regional costs of living, etc., which would have led to an increased provision of the arts in the regions even without the Arts Council. In the absence of such an analysis, therefore, we must leave it as an open question.

Turning now to vertical diffusion, the evidence continues to point overwhelmingly to an educated, middle-class audience, with a conspicuous absence of the working class. The composition of audiences for the arts seems not to have changed significantly during the past 28 years of the Council's existence. Nor is there any indication that a change is now in the making. Even if it were, the Council would hardly be aware of it. It has commissioned only three audience surveys in its entire history, all of which date from the late 1960s,[6] and the only comprehensive survey of London audiences was in fact undertaken privately by Baumol and Bowen.[7]

Actually, it is fair to say that the Council has so far ignored what little evidence there does exist about audiences. Its 1969 Report on opera and ballet contains results of surveys carried out in Leeds, Glasgow and London, which showed an average of 5 per cent of the audience to be manual workers. But the same report blithely talks of opera and ballet attracting a growing audience from a cross-section of the community: 'There is hardly a limit to audience expansion ... Ballet and dance theatre can draw an audience as large as any other branch of the theatre or cinema.'

Information about audiences is clearly of paramount importance to the work of the Council. It is the only way to ascertain the success of a policy of gaining new converts. It is not simply a matter of counting heads. A larger audience may mean more attendances by an identical number of people. The ideal census should show not only the frequency of attendance, age, education, occupation, and distance travelled, but also the level of family income. The distribution of audiences by occupation or by social class does not necessarily reveal the ability of consumers to pay.

Surveys should be taken at a wide range of events. Those which have so far been carried out have been limited in scope, concentrating on opera, ballet and drama. No surveys have yet been undertaken of fringe theatres, poetry readings and jazz events, all of which are being increasingly subsidised. Having discovered the composition of existing audiences, the next step is to find out more about the causes of the apparently limited appeal of the arts. It is here that in-depth interview methods, advocated by the 1969 Mann Report on provincial audiences, would be most useful.

With a limited budget and conflicting goals, the Council must decide on the relative importance of attracting the young, the old, students, the working class, the poor, that is, various categories of people which only partly overlap. Each category of audience could be assigned weighted values, according to the importance attached to attendance within that category. Audiences for each art form could then be compared to the percentage of total subsidy absorbed by each event.

But all this presupposes a detailed specification of aims. For example, if the results of a survey showed that a major part of the subsidy was being spent on a particular art form which had limited appeal, the Council would have to ask itself if the subsidy could be applied more effectively elsewhere. If the objective of the Arts Council is to provide the arts, regardless of who benefits, the answer would be an emphatic No. But if the Council sees its aim as reaching entirely new audiences, positive action in redirecting subsidies might well be more cost-effective.

Both costs and the ability of the consumer to pay must be taken into account when allocating subsidies. Decisions on whether or not to withdraw subsidies will depend on the potential effect on demand. Obviously, such an evaluation depends on the consumer's income and the actual rate at which each set of prices is subsidised.

Take the case of subsidised theatre. To talk of the average subsidy per seat is as meaningless as referring to 'the average price of a seat'. Ticket prices vary with the position of the seats in the theatre. The same level of overall subsidy is compatible with widely differing structures of ticket prices as between cheap and expensive seats in a house. The problem is to find by how much a subsidy has reduced the 'true' cost of seats of different prices.

Without this, there is no way of finding out which section of the audience is benefiting most. This, together with information about audience incomes, would show what proportion of the subsidy is going to whom. It would enable the Council to discriminate more selectively in favour of specific groups.

Ticket-pricing policies are still based largely on conventional rules of thumb among theatre owners and producers. The belief is widely held that further increases in ticket prices would choke off demand. Yet a recent Arts Council report on seat prices concluded that many subsidised provincial theatres had scope to raise their prices; that ticket prices had lagged behind the rise in average earnings since 1963; that middle- and high-priced seats were more frequently sold out than low-priced seats; that higher ticket prices on Friday and Saturday evenings went with larger audiences; and that, in general, audiences were more responsive to events than to prices.[8] Exactly the same phenomena were observed in London for opera, drama and concerts, with the possible exception of the most expensive seats at the Royal Opera House and Sadler's Wells, the Coliseum. The report concludes that: 'in the provinces in particular, the grant [of the Arts Council] is used to keep certain prices below a level at which they could be kept without reducing the size of audiences; and this is the case for all performing arts which we have examined ... In the case of the subsidised London theatres, we would certainly consider it feasible to increase the number of seats sold at middle prices.' Sir Hugh Willat, the secretary-general of the Council, summarises the Report's findings in these words: 'Although certain price increases are recommended ... the council welcomes the fact that there is no recommendation for across the board increases' – which, while strictly correct, hardly does justice to the flavour of the Report. It is difficult to resist the conclusion that the Council has spent a great deal of money to keep seat prices down, in effect subsidising audiences who would have attended artistic events anyway and who would on the whole have been able to pay more.

Vouchers

In general, the Council has shown little flexibility in considering alternative methods of financing the arts. At present, subsidy applications in the performing arts are based on an annual estimate of revenues. There is an unwritten rule that no application is considered if box office receipts account for less than 45–50 per cent of total costs. But the present policies of the Council appear to give producers no incentive to maximise ticket revenues. A company which shows a profit at the end of the year suffers a corresponding cut in subsidy. The Council's own report on orchestral resources suggested that 'too little drive and imagination have been shown in filling the 20 per cent or more of empty seats'.[9] Thus, few British theatres and concert halls lower ticket prices shortly before a performance begins, a standard practice in some American cities. Prom recitals, a well-known method of filling a house and attracting the young with a large number of cheap 'standing' tickets, has so far been rarely attempted outside the field of orchestral concerts. In recent years, the Royal Opera House has been encouraged by a grant from the Midland Bank to experiment with Opera Proms. It is a striking fact that the Arts Council's grant to opera has never been used in this way to fill the Royal Opera House to capacity for the less popular operas and, at the same time, to attract wholly new audiences to opera.

The problem of inappropriate incentives to encourage attendance could be tackled by switching the Council's subsidies from producers to consumers, by means of a 'ticket voucher' scheme.[10] Theatres and concert halls would charge commercial prices, but a certain proportion of seats would be made available for a specific group (children, students, old age pensioners, trade-union members), who would pay for their seats with issued vouchers; the vouchers would then be exchanged by the management for cash from the Arts Council. Alternatively, the Council could undertake to buy seats and offer them directly to selected categories of individuals at a reduced price. This scheme has the enormous advantage of making the selection of beneficiaries as precise as possible.

A drawback of a voucher scheme – apart from possible voucher touting – is that the arts would then become far more consumer oriented. Programmes would passively reflect, instead of actively stimulate, prevailing tastes. In the past, the Council has emphasised the need to subsidise more esoteric art. The crux of the issue, however, is not simply 'arts for the masses' versus 'arts for the elite'. The trade-off is better seen as that of spending more on inducing the uninitiated to start attending artistic events tailored to their untrained tastes, as against spending more on educating existing audiences to demand modern music and poetry. It all depends on which sector of the population the Council considers to be more important, and whether or not 'art for art's sake' is sufficient grounds for a subsidy policy.

A study, commissioned by the Northern Arts Association to examine whether or not its youth voucher scheme was achieving its intended aims, nicely illustrates the point.[11] The scheme was designed to encourage young people between the ages of 15 and 21 to attend artistic events – particularly uncommitted young people who would not attend of their own initiative and in their own time. Anyone under 21 years was eligible to receive a book of vouchers. When presented at any event subsidised by the Northern Arts Association, this entitled the holder to a cut in the ticket price. The scheme was extremely popular. Demand reached some 5,000 voucher-book applications per month. But the report concluded that the goals of the scheme were not being achieved. Only 2–7 per cent of the uptake fitted the description of an ideal user: 'an apprentice or working person who left school at 15, who individually obtains and chooses tickets for arts events'. Results showed that 96 per cent of the users were in full-time education, and 75 per cent attended artistic events in organised school parties. However desirable the attendance of school children may be, the spending of large subsidies on a captive audience was not the express aim of the scheme. In that sense, the scheme was rejected as a failure. All this goes to show that even a voucher scheme needs to be carefully administered to achieve its stated aims. Any subsidy programme which refuses steadfastly to interfere in any way with the artistic policy of the organisations being subsidised is quite likely to end up enriching those who are already converted to the arts. A little less laissez-faire and a little more paternalism may be required to give effect to certain stated aims.

Artistic standards

So much for attempts at vertical or horizontal diffusion. From its earliest days, the Arts Council has been preoccupied with a third aim, namely, raising standards of performances. It is widely held that it is impossible to quantify success in achieving this endeavour because artistic excellence is necessarily a matter of subjective judgement. Moreover, comparison between different productions is seen as being out of the question because a badly-produced and a well-produced performance are virtually different products.

But the issue is not how to convert subjective assessments into objective ones, but rather how to reduce the arbitrariness inherent in all aesthetic judgements. The total impact of a performance on a member of the audience can never be gauged accurately. But many of the contributory factors are purely technical. Lighting, seating, orchestral playing, the standard of acting, the amount of time spent in rehearsal, the quality of the scenery and costumes – these are all matters on which there is likely to be broad agreement among experts. 'Objective knowledge' is merely knowledge about which there is nearly universal agreement. 'Subjective knowledge' is knowledge about which there is usually no agreement whatever. A great many aesthetic judgements fall between these two extremes. Judgements about standards of performance – rather than about the lasting value of what is being performed – tend to lie nearer the objective end of the continuum. A panel of 'experts' could compare two performances in terms of 'better' or 'worse'. Given the costs of producing a 'better' performance, the panel would find itself gradually working towards judgements about 'how much better' or 'how much worse'. In this way the panel would, in fact, be learning to calibrate the quality of productions in relation to the magnitude of their subsidies.

The problem becomes more complicated in practice because the attempt to raise standards of performance tends to pre-empt subsidies that could have been devoted to other objectives. The Arts Council itself certainly recognises a conflict between the cost of raising standards and the cost of attracting new audiences. The policy of subsidising both Covent Garden and Sadler's Wells is a case in point. Though opera sung in English has greater audience appeal, many music critics, rightly or wrongly, regard it as inferior to opera sung in the original language. The Council has accordingly subsidised Covent Garden largely, although not exclusively, to maintain a high standard in the production of opera in the original language (£1,750,000, or 17 per cent of its budget for England in 1972–73), and at the same time has subsidised the Coliseum (£935,000 or 9 per cent of the 1972–73 budget), to encourage more people to go to opera sung in English. As these figures show, opera sung in the original language with front-rank singers is, unfortunately, more expensive to produce than opera in English with English singers. A given subsidy for opera can produce either a modest rise in standards at Covent Garden, or a massive increase in audience size at the Coliseum. Objective measurement does not help us here. To reach a decision, we have to rank our preferences among the two objectives. The Arts Council has never committed itself explicitly on this question. We can infer from its respective subsidies that it gives somewhat greater weight to raising artistic standards. We cannot, however, draw that inference rigorously unless we know (1) how much we will raise standards at Covent Garden by an extra pound of subsidy and (2) how many new opera lovers we can attract at the Coliseum by a given reduction in seat prices. This takes us back to step (1) of cost–effectiveness analysis and illustrates the point that ordinal scaling of objectives is not, in general, sufficient to justify a unique policy.

New art forms

The Arts Council's fourth aim – that of encouraging young artists to experiment with new art forms – has only recently come into prominence. So far, it is apparent that the Council attaches little weight to this objective. Only a minute fraction of expenditure at present goes on direct aid to artists, either in the form of grants to individuals or in commissions of new works. In 1972–73, the total was £126,000.

If the goal is to stimulate the emergence of new art forms, the Council might in principle evaluate the success of its policy by asking not only how many nascent art forms have been encouraged by the provision of a grant, but also how many similar ventures exist without help from the Council. If, on the other hand, the goal is rather to encourage avowedly experimental artists, we run immediately into the problem that those artists requiring financial assistance are precisely the ones who have not yet found public favour and may, indeed, never do so.

It is very difficult to find criteria to distinguish the neglected genius from the neglected charlatan. It is perhaps simpler to earmark a given sum for the goal of encouraging experimental art and to hope for the best. Research councils in the natural and social sciences have long been in the habit of setting aside a fraction of their budget for pure research in some critical area, the outcome of which is totally unpredictable. There is nothing wrong with this. The sum set aside for this purpose automatically provides a measure of the importance assigned to a search for answers that may well not be there. At the moment, the Arts Council devotes about one per cent of its budget to encouraging new art forms. Yet it emphasises this goal in all its annual reports. Unless this is an area where the expenditure of small sums yields enormous results – which we doubt – this appears to be inconsistent.

Museums and galleries

We have so far confined our argument to the Arts Council. But the debate on the ill-fated attempt to institute museum and gallery charges highlights the danger of thinking about the arts in administrative compartments. Various arguments were used by the Conservative Government to justify its decision to impose entrance charges. But the principal one was that if people were able and willing to pay for the pleasure of attending concerts and plays, they ought to be able and willing to pay for museums and galleries: there is no distinction, in principle, between the performing and the visual arts. Some economists, however, have argued that the analogy is not tenable. One function of prices is to ration goods and services that are in scarce supply. If entrance to the opera and theatre were free, excessive demand would almost certainly result. But free entry to museums and galleries in the past has not led to overcrowding. So there is no reason to charge for entry.[12]

This argument has obvious merit. But it does ignore the fact that the visual and performing arts compete with one another for resources. At present, the combined subsidies for both national and local museums and art galleries (about £30 million) exceed the Arts Council's subsidies to the rest of the Arts put together. This, of course, is due to the fact that the visual arts have been freely provided, while box-office revenue finances approximately 45 per cent of the costs of producing the performing arts.

If we assume that the clash between private and social interests is somehow more manifest for the visual than for the performing arts, the argument implies that everyone is willing to pay taxes to guarantee the existence of museums and galleries, though no one is willing as a private citizen to pay to enter a museum or gallery.[13] If museums and galleries were a 'public good', there would be nothing irrational in the willingness to pay taxes to support museums and galleries, while refusing to pay entry charges. But, of course, the 'degree of publicness' of museums and galleries is no greater than that of opera, ballet, theatre, etc.; the consequences of free museums and galleries, therefore, is almost certain to reduce the funds that might be devoted to supporting the performing arts.

To be sure, the role of museums and galleries, in preserving what already exists, is different from that of the live performing arts. Because most major museums and galleries are in London, however, finance for them circumscribes the effort to diffuse the arts throughout the regions, not to mention the effort to stimulate new art forms. Yet how many museums and galleries purchase acquisitions with any attention to public tastes? The tendency of prices to ration what is scarce is only one of its economic functions; another is to reflect consumers' preferences. In that sense, there is a valid economic argument for museum and gallery charges: the funds that now go to subsidise museums and galleries ought perhaps to go to the performing arts because horizontal and vertical diffusion is better satisfied by spending on these than on the visual arts.

Conclusion

Those who are shocked by this assertion are merely exemplifying the widespread tendency towards compartmentalised thinking about the arts. Both the Arts Council and museum charges can only be satisfactorily discussed in terms of public patronage of the arts as a whole. And in assessing such patronage, the technique of 'cost–effectiveness analysis', 'systems analysis', 'output budgeting', 'management by objectives' – it hardly matters what we call it – is just as applicable as it is to defence, health or education, areas in which it has been successfully applied in recent years. It may be impossible to agree on the ultimate value of Stockhausen's works. But it is not impossible to agree whether a 'new music grant' to an orchestra does, or does not, gain new converts to modern music. It may be impossible to reach a national consensus on what the regions 'deserve' by way of subsidy. But it is not impossible to reach a consensus on whether local initiative in the arts is better stimulated by an Arts Council grant to the Regional Arts Associations, or by a matching grant from the Treasury direct to local authorities. And so forth, and so forth.

If this much be granted, the rest of my case follows. Ultimate ends are a matter of value judgements, but means to achieve ends are capable of being objectively assessed. Often, in public-expenditure analysis, the difficulty is that of discovering what the goals really are. The Arts Council, however, as we have noted, has in fact declared its objectives, though not always with sufficient precision. But, having taken the plunge of being quite explicit about its aims, the Council has failed to investigate the degree to which its grants have succeeded in achieving the stated aims. It has neatly avoided the issue of self-evaluation up to now by assuming that the arts cannot be assessed 'objectively'. This confuses aesthetic judgements with the question of measuring the consequences of disbursing funds to the arts by one way rather than another.

I close by conceding that the idea of applying cost–effectiveness analysis to public expenditure on the arts can be made to look like an absurd attempt at 'Utopian social engineering': the problems are too complex and the data required are too great to complete the assignment within one lifetime. But I believe that a beginning can be made in a limited number of areas in the manner of 'piecemeal social engineering': a great deal of perfectly traditional, positive economics – the elasticity of demand for artistic events, comparative cost analysis of alternative methods of providing given art forms, the elasticity of supply of performers, etc. – needs to be done, which would gradually begin to build up a picture of a cost–effective expenditure policy for the arts. It is worth remembering in this connection that the grant to Covent Garden, Sadler's Wells, the National Theatre and the Royal Shakespeare Company together absorb almost 40 per cent of the Arts Council's total budget for England. An application of cost–effectiveness analysis to the problem of, say, opera subsidies, which in principle seems to be perfectly feasible, would therefore make no small contribution to rationalising the total structure of subsidies to the arts in this country.

NOTES

1 The evidence is examined in detail in King, K. and Blaug, M. (1973), 'Does the Arts Council know what it is doing?', *Encounter*, September. See also Blaug, M. and King, K. (1974), 'Is the Arts Council cost–effective?', *New Society*, January 3, an excerpt and terse summary of the present paper.

2 The field of management techniques is a veritable Babel of Tongues. For example, HM Treasury, *Glossary of Management Techniques* (London, HM Stationery Office, 1967), defines cost–effectiveness analysis as 'the cheapest means of accomplishing a defined objective', which misses the point I am making about multiple objectives. Suffice it to say that my definition of cost–effectiveness analysis is not the generally accepted one. Nothing depends, however, on the precise choice of terminology adopted.

3 This is one reason, at any rate, why the idea of value-free social science is apt to be misleading. The moment that social science becomes involved in advising governments, it necessarily ceases to be value-free.

4 See also A. Wildavsky, *The Politics of the Budgetary Process* (Boston, Little Brown, 1964), particularly ch. 5; Y. Dror, *Public Policymaking Reexamined* (San Francisco: Chandler Publishing Company, 1968) and *Ventures in Policy Sciences*

(New York: American Elseviers Publishing Company, 1971). The latter contains a not altogether convincing critique of Braybrooke and Lindblom, and adopts a position midway between the standard view of 'comprehensive rationality' and the Braybrooke–Lindblom view of 'muddling through'. C. E. Lindblom has since developed the argument further in *Intelligence of Democracy* (New York, The Free Press, 1965) and *The Policy Making Process* (Englewood Cliffs, Prentice Hall, 1968).

5 But see Peacock, A. and Godfrey, C. (1974), 'The economics of museums and galleries', *Lloyds Bank Review*, January.

6 See Mann, P. H. (1969), *The Provisional Audience for Drama, Ballet and Opera*, London, The Arts Council; Mann, P. H. (1969), *Report on Opera and Ballet in the United Kingdom, 1966–69*, London, The Arts Council; Mann, P. H. (1970), *Report on Orchestral Resources in Great Britain*, London, The Arts Council.

7 Baumol, W. J. and Bowen, W. G. (1966), *Performing Arts – the Economic Dilemma*, New York, The Twentieth Century Fund.

8 *Report of the Committee of Inquiry Into Seat Prices*, London, The Arts Council, 1973.

9 *Report on Orchestral Resources in Great Britain*, London, The Arts Council, 1970.

10 Peacock, A. T. (1969), 'Welfare Economics and Public Subsidies to the Arts', *The Manchester School of Economic and Social Studies*, December.

11 Durham Business School, 'The Northern Arts Association youth voucher scheme' (Northern Arts Association, 1963, unpublished).

12 Lord Robbins (1971), 'Unsettled questions in the political economy of the arts', *The Three Banks Review*, September.

13 I ignore the fact that many visitors to London museums and galleries are, in fact, tourists. An audience survey conducted in 1971 at the British Museum, the Science Museum and the National Maritime Museum found that as many as a third of all visitors to the British Museum had come from abroad, the figures for the other two museums being 12 and 17 per cent respectively, despite the fact that the survey was conducted outside the summer tourist season. It also transpired that almost a quarter of all visitors were first-time visitors to any national museum and gallery in London and that they were much better educated than the average member of the British population (Digby, P. W. (1974), *Visitors to Three London Museums*, London, HMSO).

13

Rationalising social expenditure – health and social services*

J. W. HURST

Introduction

The Health and Personal Social Services in England (hereafter referred to as HPSS) are financed and run by the public sector. They are therefore candidates for a central planning system to aid in the allocation of resources. In this paper an attempt is made, first, to sketch the ideal information requirements for such a planning system for the services. Secondly, the development of an actual planning system (so far) is described. Thirdly, ways to narrow the considerable gap between the ideal and the actual are suggested.

The paper adopts a partial- rather than a general-equilibrium approach to planning. Problems arising from possible second-best solutions are ignored. The existing institutional and financial arrangements for the HPSS are taken as given, as are the objectives of the services, in so far as these have been specified. Where comparisons are to be made over time it is assumed that the Test Discount Rate for the public sector (10 per cent per annum) will apply. Problems concerning the implementation of plans are ignored. So, also, are problems concerning the relationship between central and local plans.

An attempt to sketch the ideal information requirements for a central planning system

In the most general terms those who run the HPSS must seek to optimise over time the allocation of scarce resources between alternative

* The content of this paper is Crown Copyright and is reproduced by permission of the Controller of Her Majesty's Stationery Office. The opinions expressed in the paper are entirely personal and should not be ascribed to the Department of Health and Social Security. The author is an economic adviser at the Department of Health and Social Security. He wishes to acknowledge the help of his colleagues – in particular Terry Banks, David Pole and Barbara Latter – who are, of course, not responsible for any shortcomings in this paper.

ends subject to a public-expenditure constraint which may vary. In less general terms a number of sub-problems may be identified.

Definition and measurement of output

The problems of defining and measuring the output of health and social services are now the subject of a growing literature. Output may be described at two levels at least. There is the level at which services are rendered to a client and at which market exchange takes place ('intermediate output'). Beyond this there is the impact of services in changing or relieving disease and social problems ('final output'). Most of the difficulties arise in defining and measuring 'final output'. The health services are concerned not only with reducing morbidity and premature mortality but also with population questions, with certain cosmetic aims (in much of dentistry), with custodial care (for example, of insane criminals), with health education and with certain types of manpower training. The social services are concerned with certain problems of social interaction (particularly in the family) and with the care of some members of vulnerable groups (such as the elderly).

So far as ill health alone is concerned, particular diseases differ in severity and duration and each episode may lead to various combinations of pain, disability and premature death. Each of these consequences might be measured along a continuous scale. The health services may intervene in two distinct ways. First, they may prevent or cure disease in varying degrees. Here output has an investment character since the improvement in health is durable (subject to expectation of life). The reduction or removal of the consequences of disease will be joint products. Secondly, the health services may offer palliation or care – the latter provided to substitute for individuals services they can no longer perform for themselves because of temporary or permanent disability. Here output has a consumption character and the products tend to be separable. The existing literature (for example Fanshel and Bush, 1970, and Culyer, Lavers and Williams, 1971) has concentrated almost exclusively on the first of these. There, the output of health services is described in terms of the improved prognosis for individuals following treatment (after allowing for iatrogenic disease). This allows nothing for the second type of output which follows, for example, from the enormous provision of 'hotel' facilities in hospitals and from the care in the community of the permanently disabled.

The prevention or relief of each episode of disease in the individual is not a sufficient basis for measuring output, however. Over the lifetime of individuals multiple pathology is the general case and different diseases are often interdependent. For example, the gains from curing cancer in an individual would be affected by the presence of heart disease. Hence it is necessary to keep the whole individual in view. Moreover, there are likely to be externalities. Quite apart from communicable diseases, the individual's family, his employer (if any) and, indeed, society in general may be crucially affected by his sickness or premature death. These externalities raise the question as to whether the household should not be the basic starting point for measuring output (as in economic theory).

An elementary prerequisite for the measurement of output at any point in time is that the basic facts about the demographic characteristic of the population and about its morbidity and social problems be known. The existence of problems is a necessary, although not a sufficient, condition for services to produce. Other necessary conditions for production to take place (discussed below) are that technology allows something to be done about problems and that patients are able and willing to cooperate in treatment. This suggests that a survey of the 'objective' incidence of morbidity and social problems (including externalities) in the community and the identification of groups at risk is required. More to the point, the survey might address itself to the possibility of changing or relieving such problems.

Definition and measurement of inputs and supply functions
The usual difficulties in describing and quantifying inputs to services are encountered. For example, hospital capital presents problems customarily met in quantifying assets which are durable, specific and often indivisible. These difficulties are not eased by the fact that different vintages of building are often mixed up on the same site. More serious difficulties are encountered in describing and measuring non-HPSS inputs to health and social well-being. Some of these come from the public sector (clean water), some from the private non-household sector (self-medication) and some from the household sector itself (patient's own time and constitution, nursing by relatives, care by volunteers). Information is needed about the availability of all these resources and about their responsiveness to changes in prices and other variables (sometimes with lags) over time.

Definition and measurement of production functions
Detailed knowledge of production functions is needed to allow the relationships between inputs and outputs to be defined – technical efficiency, the possibilities of factor substitution and returns to scale. The usual microeconomic production function theory can be applied to the production of 'intermediate outputs'. More difficult is the definition of the technology for the production of 'final outputs'. Here the economist must turn to disciplines such as epidemiology and sociology. Presumably each particular disease or problem has its own natural history (or probable histories) and is a starting point for investigation, since each differs in its potential for prevention or cure, or the extent to which it generates a demand for care. Each dis-

ease may be dealt with by a variety of packages of services acting in conjunction with the individual's own constitution and time, and other resources in the private sector. Indivisibilities – such as brain surgery – may exist. Public inputs may be either complementary with, or substitutable for, private inputs. Technically efficient methods of combining these inputs need to be defined. There are major uncertainties in these relationships. There is scope for the reduction of this uncertainty by carefully designed and controlled longitudinal medical and social studies. But planners must expect to continue to face uncertainty about technology and must expect to continue to make judgements about questions – essentially – of fact.

The valuation and distribution of outputs

The valuation and distribution of outputs raises ultimate and difficult questions. This paper contains only a personal opinion upon what is finally a political question. The HPSS are paternalistic particularly in their egalitarian aims. For example, the 1944 White Paper 'A National Health Service' (Cmnd 6502, 1944) opened with the statement:

> The Government have announced that they intend to establish a comprehensive health service for everybody in this country. They want to ensure that in future every man and woman and child can rely on getting all the advice and treatment and care which they may need in matters of personal health; that what they get shall be the best medical and other facilities available; that their getting these shall not depend upon whether they can pay for them, or on any other factor irrelevant to the real need – the real need being to bring the country's full resources to bear upon reducing ill-health and promoting good health in all its citizens.

Similar statements may be found elsewhere but they do not help greatly in clarifying the relative value of – say – treatment for the acutely ill and care for the mentally handicapped. It is often said that there should be 'equal treatment for equal need' but this implies unequal treatment for unequal need and the question then becomes 'how unequal?'. The system arrives at valuations but they are implicit. Planning is made easier if judgements are made explicit. Two problems are then forced into the open. First, valuations within the services may not be consistent. Secondly, the valuations within the services may not be consistent with those of consumers. On the first the economist is competent to say little except that consistency is a necessary but not a sufficient condition for an optimum. On the second, however, the welfare economist may be able to offer some ideas about substitutes for the market mechanism.

Although the HPSS are paternalistic, they exist for the benefit of consumers and require information about consumers' preferences. Of course, mechanisms already exist for obtaining such information. First, individuals make their problems and views known at the point of delivery of treatment and the system responds locally and, to a lesser extent, centrally to such information. Secondly, consumers' opinions are conveyed through political channels, through pressure groups and will be conveyed through bodies such as the new community health councils. Unfortunately these mechanisms may not always be adequate to convey detailed and representative information on consumers' preferences, between – say – cure for cancer and care for severe arthritis, to the centre of the system. This suggests that consumer research might be needed. For example sample surveys (embodying some sort of voting system to mimic the price mechanism) might be undertaken. These would be based upon the survey of 'objective' morbidity and social problems mentioned above (p. 223). There would be many difficulties, however, quite apart from what such surveys might cost. Some consumers might be unable to vote and there would be problems in allocating votes to those who were able to vote (should the sick be given the same votes as the well?). There would be difficulties in posing choices. Consumers might find it easier to choose between 'intermediate outputs' where care was concerned (hospital food, for example) than where prevention, cure and perhaps palliation were concerned. These would require knowledge of technical possibilities and judgements of risk better left to 'experts'. In such cases, therefore, choices might be posed in terms of 'final outputs' (perhaps with probabilities attached to allow for attitude to risk). Questions might concern prevention or cure of typical episodes of particular diseases leaving the estimation of pain and disability (although not, perhaps, of the probability of premature death) to consumers. The sub-sample of consumers who have experienced or are experiencing particular diseases might be given special attention. The poor response rate from those beyond the grave, however, would prevent the use of this approach for short diseases with a high fatality rate. Questions about externalities would be desirable but public goods difficulties would have to be overcome. Because of these – and other – difficulties planners may expect to turn, for some time, mainly to sources within services for explicit valuations of HPSS outputs. Ideally these should be such that demand functions for outputs could be defined.

The valuation of inputs

Many of the inputs to the HPSS carry market (though not necessarily competitive market) prices. There are the usual problems in valuing the services of the existing capital stock. Since much of this stock (land apart) is worth little outside the HPSS its cost is negligible unless it has alternative uses within the HPSS in which case the valuation of alternative benefits is necessary. Even the cost of new capital services presents difficulties since much new capital is obtained by upgrading old stock (about which little is known centrally). There are serious practical difficulties in assembling information to cost many of the 'intermediate outputs' of the HPSS, for example, treatment for particular diseases. Problems also arise in pricing inputs to households to help in deciding upon the right distribution of care costs between households and the HPSS (putting aside the broad questions of financing the health services and charging).

Identification of an overall static optimum

If the information and judgements described above can be drawn together it will be possible to define an optimum for each point in time. First, for each pair of HPSS outputs the centre can define the productive possibilities given the optimal deployment of the available inputs under given technology and a given public expenditure constraint. Secondly, for each representative individual with a particular set of problems, risks and relevant externalities, the centre can assess the maximum feasible change in social utility from giving him available outputs (consumption and investment). Between any pair of representative individuals a social utility possibility frontier may be defined. It is assumed that returns from providing services diminish and that satiation can be reached for each individual. Tangency between this frontier and an indifference curve from the social welfare function will indicate a static optimum. The indifference curves will be linear and at 45° to the axes if unequal treatment is given for unequal 'need' but treatment is otherwise given neutrally between in-

Figure 1

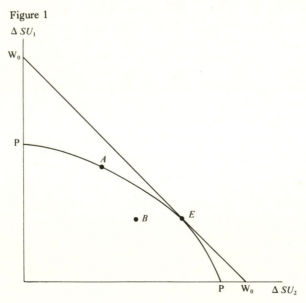

dividuals. Figure 1 illustrates this possibility. ΔSU_1 and ΔSU_2 denote the incremental change in social utility from providing services for individual 1 and individual 2 respectively. PP denotes the social utility possibility frontier and W_0W_0 an indifference curve from the social welfare function. Planners may seek to define only the region around the optimum, at E, and the initial (presumed sub-optimal) state of affairs whether at a point such as A, upon the frontier, or at a point such as B, within it. It is necessary to recognise, however, that even this limited definition of a static optimum will involve considerable uncertainty.

Optimisation over time

If the actual state of the system when planning commences is not optimal, it will be desirable to discover the best path to the optimum. This will require knowledge of the rates of change possible in relevant endogenous variables. The overall optimum will be a moving one, however. It will be affected by changes in exogenous variables such as the population and its problems (from causes outside HPSS), tastes, technology, resources and the available ration of public expenditure. Changes in 'tastes' will follow changes in attitudes and expectations and changes in political parties in power. Changes in 'technology' will follow not only changes in medical practice and in pharmaceuticals but also changes in household behaviour. Since these, and other, shifts will be extremely uncertain, forecasting them may be difficult or impossible. It is necessary to prepare for contingencies, however, for – say – a decade ahead. For example, judging by recent history, it will be particularly important to anticipate changes in medical technology since new inventions have not only changed the use of resources but have also created substantial new demands for new products.

Actual planning information in the Health and Personal Social Services

Existing planning arrangements in the services

There has been central planning in the Health and Personal Social Services since their creation. Both are included in the Public Expenditure Survey System and both are subject to certain types of financial, technical and policy guidance from above. The services work adequately under these arrangements and must continue to work under them for some time to come. But existing planning differs in some major ways from the sort of planning described above. For example, there is little evidence available centrally about final output and a shortage of information with which to analyse the resource implications of policies. There is, therefore, a lack of explicitness centrally about the costs and benefits of decisions.

New planning arrangements in the services

Coinciding with the reorganisation of the National Health Services and the Local Authority Personal Social Services there has been an increased interest in planning within the Department of Health and Social Security (hereafter referred to as DHSS). As outlined in 'Management Arrangements for the Reorganised National Health Service' (DHSS, 1972) the Service is now to develop an annual planning cycle in which the Department itself will make central plans for up to ten years ahead and the districts, areas and regions will make local plans. Local plans will 'flow' upwards and an interactive process will ensue out of which agreed national plans will emerge. In order to produce central plans the Department has set up a Departmental planning system run mainly by the service development divisions within the Department assisted by a small central planning unit. Two major analytical contributions of relevance are being made. The first is the development of a Programme Budget for the HPSS by a mixed team of administrative and professional civil servants (including economists). The second is the development of a series of models including a linear programming model by the Department's operational research unit to investigate the resource consequences of delivering different patterns of care between and within community and hospital services. The remainder of this section is mainly concerned with the contribution to planning of the Programme Budget.

The development of programme budgeting for the Health and Personal Social Services

Programme Budgeting was started in the DHSS in 1971 with the main aim of relating expenditure to objectives and a subsidiary aim of linking expenditure in the Health Services to expenditure in the Personal Social Services. Since then, the aims of the work carried out under this label have broadened somewhat, but despite the recession in the popularity of 'programme budgeting' elsewhere the name has stuck. Initially, attempts were made to devise idealised structures to set out HPSS objectives. But it was soon found that idealised structures could not be costed, nor final output measurements found, so efforts switched to orienting the available data on service activities and costs as much in the direction of objectives as possible. To this end a framework was set up which contained about one dozen main programmes, some based on 'client' (or problem) groups such as the elderly and mentally handicapped, and some based on services, such as those offered by acute hospitals and general practitioners. The framework contained, also, up to two hundred sub-programmes based mainly on services such as in-patient, out-patient or home-help services. For each programme and sub-programme an estimate of its current public expenditure content was made and for most sub-programmes a measure of 'intermediate output' – such as in-patient cases, out-patient attendances or home-help cases – was found. Such budgets were produced retrospectively from 1966/67 for hospital services and from 1968/69 for the remaining services. With the aid of the available price indices, an index of the volume of input for each programme and sub-programme was calculated allowing trends in inputs and 'intermediate outputs' to be compared. A highly summarised version of this Programme Budget for 1971/72 (showing total current expenditure only) is displayed in Table 1. This shows how expenditure has been allocated from the main services of the HPSS (pre-reorganisation) to six major 'client group' programmes, two service-based programmes and an un-

TABLE 1 *Summary programme budget for the health and personal social services**

Current expenditure at November 1972 prices, England, 1971/72. Illustrative figures in £m.

	Programmes	Hospital services	Family practitioner services	Local health services	Personal social services	Other services	Total
I	Primary care and disease detection and prevention		486	21			507
II	Acute	583		23			606
III	Elderly (65+)	112		27	114	6	259
IV	Younger physically handicapped	11			23	13	47
V	Mentally handicapped	73			18	1	92
VI	Mentally ill	145			8	3	156
VII	Children and families	33		21	95	13	162
VIII	Reproduction	142		19			161
IX	Unallocated	100		23	6	44	172
Total		1198	486	133	263	81	2161

* Figures do not total exactly because of rounding to the nearest £m. Care should be taken in interpreting the table. The allocation of expenditure from services to programmes is governed by particular assumptions concerning the definition of programmes, determined often by shortage of information. In particular, the 'true' extent of expenditure on 'client groups' in programmes III–VIII is *understated* since much expenditure upon these groups is included in programmes I, II and IX. Within 'client group' programmes special definitions apply. For example, the elderly who use services for the mentally handicapped are included in programme V and not in programme III. Home nursing and health visiting are included in programme I where attribution of these services to 'client groups' would otherwise be uncertain. The definition of the programmes and the other assumptions on which the figures rest are still under consideration, and the figures should therefore be regarded as purely illustrative.

allocated category. The figures are no more than crude estimates based on institutional accounts devised for purposes other than programme budgeting. Figures 2 and 3 each show examples of trends in inputs and 'intermediate outputs' for sub-programmes. Again the estimates are crude and only provisional conclusions may be drawn. Figure 2 shows that in traumatic and orthopaedic surgery 'intermediate output' (in-patient cases) has been increasing rapidly, probably because of the availability of new techniques. Despite a reduction in the average length of stay per case, input per case appears to have been rising – perhaps because of these new techniques. Figure 3 shows that for the mentally ill in hospital 'intermediate output' (in-patient weeks) has been falling steadily reflecting new methods of treatment which reduce the length of stay in hospital. Input per in-patient week has been rising sharply as a result of a deliberate policy of raising standards in mental illness hospitals. Of course, for neither of these sub-programmes is it possible to distinguish changes in efficiency from changes in the quality of 'intermediate output'.

Achievements and failures of the Programme Budget

As work has developed the Programme Budget has been kept broadly in step with the framework of the new Departmental Planning System. This has enabled the main planning statements, run by the service

Figure 2   Traumatic and orthopaedic surgery: hospital in-patients*.
Indices of input and 'intermediate output' (in-patient cases). 1968/69 = 100.

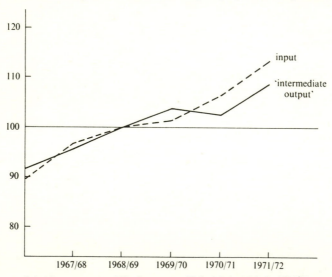

* A sub-programme within Programme II (hospital acute). In 1971/72 current expenditure within it was about £60 million, at November 1972 prices, and 'intermediate output' was 395,000 cases.

development divisions, to be costed in terms of current public expenditure in comprehensive and mutually exclusive categories. Plans are thereby linked with the Public Expenditure Survey System. The information on past trends in the Programme Budget provides a point of departure for considering the future. Past movements in the volume of input are distinguished from movements in relative prices and inflation. Trends in inputs and 'intermediate outputs' are separated. Moreover, to the extent that historic, average costs are approximately equal to future, marginal costs, then the information on real unit costs in the Programme Budget is of direct relevance to decisions on the expansion or contraction of services. Work is now continuing on providing an investment budget and on linking capital and manpower to 'intermediate outputs' on the assumption of fixed technical coefficients and constant returns to scale. Elementary research into the supply of resources is also under way. These developments should enable services to be planned within the constraints set by resources as well as within those set by public expenditure.

Despite these developments there remain a number of shortcomings in the Programme Budget when it is compared with the ideals described above (p. 244ff.). For example, final outputs have not yet been measured centrally,

Figure 3   Mentally ill: hospital in-patients*.
Indices of input and 'intermediate output' (in-patient weeks). 1968/69 = 100.

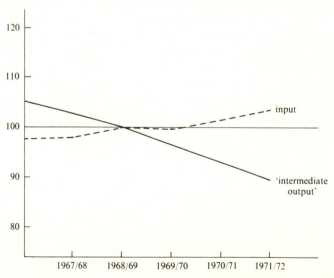

* A sub-programme within Programme VI (mentally ill). Certain elderly, mentally ill patients, most suffering from senile dementia, are excluded from this sub-programme. In 1971/72 current expenditure within it was about £120 million, at November 1972 prices, and 'intermediate output' was 4.4 million in-patient weeks.

nor have certain microeconomic relationships (especially production functions) been quantified. A more serious problem (in view of the initial aims of
programme budgeting) is that the programme structure developed so far
remains in something of a muddle. The structure is based partially on client
groups and partially on services, and the client groups themselves are not
defined in any very systematic fashion. As it is, the same patient with the
same episode of illness (for example, an elderly person, seriously disabled
with arthritis, being referred by a general practitioner to a consultant
orthopaedic surgeon for a hip-replacement operation) might pass through
three different programmes during the one episode of illness. Although the
Programme Budget accounts systematically for all current public-
expenditure costs, it does not account systematically for all the morbidity,
mortality and social problems with which the HPSS deal.

Ways forward
Accounting for ill health and social problems
The gap between the information and analysis that is required
ideally for a planning system and that which is actually available is a large
one. There are, however, ways of continuing the task of closing the gap. One
practicable step is to account properly for ill health and social problems in
comprehensive and mutually exclusive problem groups. A surprising amount
of information is available on morbidity, mortality and (to a lesser extent)
social problems. This allows a rough description of the 'health' of the nation
in terms of the size of groups with particular problems. For example, data
are available on the prevalence of diseases and the incidence of mortality according to the International Classification of Diseases (ICD) – which includes summary diagnostic categories such as 'Infective and Parasitic
Diseases', 'Mental Disorders', 'Diseases of Peripheral Circulatory system',
etc. There is not, to the author's knowledge, a similar classification system
for social problems but no doubt one could be devised for the purpose (for
example, family conflict, delinquency, loneliness, etc.). In many cases these
will be bound up with disease itself (especially mental illness). There are at
least two important advantages of 'diagnostic' information. First, it helps to
point the way not only to the causation of problems but also to the extent to
which services can cure or are needed for care. For example, it is possible to
translate from detailed ICD categories to a classification of disease which indicates the demand for services (Hurtado and Greenlick, 1971). Secondly, it
helps judgements about benefits, since 'diagnostic' groups are likely to differ
in size and in the severity and duration of problems. It is necessary to
supplement 'diagnostic' information, however, with data on age and multiple pathology and possibly on sex, duration of problem, severity of problem
and whether the patient lives alone or with others. These factors help to

determine the returns on prevention and cure and the need for care. Data on all such factors are available on a sample basis, from the General Household Survey (OPCS, 1973) which covers morbidity (self-assessed), use of health and personal social services and other socio-demographic information. Morbidity can be classified by the ICD. Questions are asked which allow a rough distinction to be made between acute and chronic illness and a rough assessment to be made of severity. The General Household Survey (hereafter referred to as GHS) is based on rather a small sample of households. It excludes, therefore, persons in institutions. It is necessary to supplement the GHS, therefore, with age, sex and diagnostic data from other sources such as the Hospital In-patient Inquiry (DHSS, Annual), the Mental Health Enquiry (DHSS, 1972), the Census of Mentally Handicapped Patients (DHSS, 1972), the National Morbidity Survey (OPCS, 1973), the Registrar General's Statistical Review of England and Wales (OPCS, Annual), the Digest of Statistics Analysing Certificates of Incapacity (DHSS, Annual) and Handicapped and Impaired in Great Britain (Harris, 1971). These serve as a check on the GHS as well as covering the population in institutions. There are, of course, a number of difficulties with such proposals. First, certain diseases (such as mental illness) tend to be under-reported in the community and are difficult to measure 'objectively'. Secondly, most statistics contain prevalence at a point in time rather than incidence and duration of illness over a period of time. The former may not record epidemics of acute illness adequately. Moreover, changes for the worse in health often precipitate a demand for services which falls off when the condition stabilises. Thirdly, preventive activities require definitions of groups at risk and existing statistics can only be of partial relevance to these. Lastly, there is a danger that the number of problem groups may become unmanageably large. If groups were defined according to 12 'diagnostic' categories (including purely social problems as a single group) three age categories, chronic or acute, bedridden or mobile, and living alone or with others, then, allowing for empty cells, there would be about 250 groups. For analytical purposes more detail might be required on certain groups: for presentational purposes less. The addition of groups at risk would further complicate the picture. Nonetheless, it would seem to be practicable to bring existing knowledge of morbidity and mortality within the ambit of the planning system in this way. These groups would not, of course, coincide with those containing the representative individuals used above (p. 226), since they are defined on episodes of problems and therefore count individuals with multiple problems more than once. The superiority of the method adopted above (p. 226) will be greater the more important are the interdependencies of problems for individuals.

Linkages between problem groups and services

The definition of problem groups will be of little use if services cannot be linked to them and costed. Fortunately, the GHS, together with other statistical sources named above, allows the services used by each group in a particular period to be measured roughly. This in itself may raise questions about 'unmet need' to add to information about hospital waiting lists. It also enables rough measurements to be made of the way that services are packaged for particular groups although, ideally, this should be studied at a disaggregated level and longitudinally. Finally, problem groups may be costed crudely by using the information already available in the Programme Budget and the assumption that unit costs are identical for all users of services. Where unit costs for particular users are known this information can be incorporated.

Production functions and output measurement

Work has already begun on extending the pioneering studies of Feldstein (Feldstein, 1967) on hospital production functions. Data are available on both inputs and 'intermediate outputs'. The operational research unit's 'balance of care' model uses mainly the assumption of fixed technical coefficients and constant returns to scale, although economies of scale in hospitals have been studied (Coomber and McDonald, 1973). At the University of York a study is being mounted into hospital production functions with variable technical coefficients. It is not yet clear to what extent an engineering approach or an econometric approach to the measurement of these functions is preferable. So far as final output measurement and production functions for 'curing' the problems of the individual and the household are concerned, there remains an unexplored potential for incorporating the findings of epidemiology and social work into the planning framework. Two analytical studies of particular relevance are being conducted – one, into the effectiveness of services for the elderly (Williams and Wright, 1973); the other, based on the National Child Development Study, into the effectiveness of services for children (Alberman and Goldstein, 1970). It remains certain that some technical and final-output questions will remain matters for judgement.

Cost research

When work on the Programme Budget was started current costs for hospital in-patients were not available by hospital specialty. Econometric methods were employed therefore to estimate such specialty costs using data from the routine hospital costing system and methods suggested by Feldstein (Feldstein, 1967). The DHSS routine hospital costing system is now being developed to produce current costs for in-patients by broad specialty groups (such as medicine, surgery and obstetrics). Meanwhile work has begun on estimating diagnostic costs for in-patients both by econometric methods and by direct observation in a few locations. Where capital is concerned rough estimates can be made of the future marginal cost of hospital services, by specialty, in new buildings but, where old buildings can be upgraded or adapted, future marginal costs cannot be estimated centrally until a suitable survey of the hospital stock has been made.

Forecasting and allowing for contingencies

Perhaps the most intractable problem with which planning has to deal is the uncertainty of the future. To some extent forecasting, either by extrapolation of existing trends or by model building, may work. For example, changes in the age structure of the population, the rise or fall of epidemics of chronic disease and even the rate of diffusion of new technology may be reasonably predictable. But the future movement of other variables may be more uncertain. For this reason rigid plans will have a habit of going wrong. The least the planner can do in these circumstances is to build flexibility into planning, encourage an attitude of experimentation and help to prepare the system for shocks.

BIBLIOGRAPHY

BOOKS AND ARTICLES

Alberman, E. D. and Goldstein, H. (1970), 'The "At Risk" register: a statistical evaluation', *British Journal of Preventive and Social Medicine*, vol. 24, no. 3.

Coomber, D. Y. and McDonald, A. G. (1973), 'Operational research service', in *Portfolio for Health*, 2, Nuffield Provincial Hospitals Trust, Oxford University Press.

Culyer, A. J., Lavers, R. J. and Williams, Alan (1971), 'Social indicators: health', in *Social Trends*, no. 2, HMSO.

Fanshel, S. and Bush, J. W. (1970), 'A health status index and its application to health service outcomes', *Journal of the Operations Research Society of America*, vol. 18, no. 6.

Feldstein, M. S. (1967), *Economic analysis for health service efficiency*, North Holland.

Harris, Amelia I. (1971), *Handicapped and Impaired in Great Britain*, Office of Population Censuses and Surveys, HMSO.

Hurtado, A. V. and Greenlick, M. R. (1971), 'A disease classification system for analysis of medical care utilisation, with a note on symptom classification', *Health Services Research*, vol. 6, no. 3.

Williams, Alan and Wright, K. G. (1973), 'Monitoring the care of the elderly', mimeograph.

OFFICIAL PUBLICATIONS

Abbreviations: DHSS: Department of Health and Social Security; OPCS: Office of
    Population Censuses and Surveys.
Cmnd. 6502 (1944), *A National Health Service.*
DHSS (1972), *Census of mentally handicapped patients in hospital in England and
    Wales at the end of 1970,* HMSO.
DHSS (1972), *Management Arrangements for the reorganised National Health Ser-
    vice,* HMSO.
DHSS (1972), *Psychiatric Hospitals and Units in England and Wales.* In-patient
    statistics from the Mental Health Enquiry for the year 1970, HMSO.
DHSS (Annual), *Digest of statistics analysing certificates of incapacity,* Branch
    SR3C.
DHSS (Annual), *Report on hospital in-patient enquiry,* part I, tables, HMSO.
OPCS (1973), *The General Household Survey,* Introductory Report, HMSO.
OPCS (1973), *Morbidity statistics from general practice, second national study,
    preliminary report, method.*
OPCS (Annual), *Registrar General's Statistical Review of England and Wales,*
    part I, HMSO.

14

Rationalising social expenditure — criminal justice systems*

R. W. ANDERSON

The purpose of this paper is to demonstrate the relevance of the standard procedures of applied welfare economics, in effect cost–benefit analysis, to a restricted set of the problems facing those who decide upon the allocation of resources to, and within, the criminal justice system (CJS). Opposition to the application of economic principles to various aspects of social policy is often based on the view that 'X is different'. There was even a time when it was said that water is different. However, path-breaking work on the problems of, *inter alia*, health, education and recreation has shown that these subjects can usefully be tackled by drawing on the most basic concepts of economics – substitution at the margin, opportunity costs, intra-marginal surplus, maximisation subject to constraints etc. This is not less true of crime. Not that the present paper can claim to be breaking new paths. Rather our task is to examine in greater detail an area that has already been considerably explored. More specifically, suggestions will be made as to the design of a cost–benefit analysis of society's efforts to control crime.

The literature effectively begins with the major article by Becker [1], which has stimulated contributions by, among others, Ehrlich [2] and Stigler [3]. Becker asserts that society's decision variables are two: p, the probability that the offender is punished, and f, the value of the punishment to the convicted person. Society's loss-from-offences function is couched in general terms and includes the net damage to society from offences in addition to the social costs of apprehension and of punishment. The function does not lend itself readily to quantification. An interesting feature of the first-order condition for minimising the loss function with respect to p and f is that if the social cost of apprehension is positive, the elasticity of response of

* Acknowledgement is made to the Social Science Research Council for a programme research grant in public sector studies at the Department of Economics and the Institute of Social and Economic Research at the University of York. The author is grateful for comments from Jonathan Baldry as well as from the conference participants themselves.

offences with respect to p exceeds their elasticity of response with respect to f. This should not be taken as support for the view that is sometimes heard that in general a high probability of detection is a more important deterrent than severe punishment. It is interesting to note that Becker shows that at the values of p and f at which loss is minimised only risk-preferrers are induced to offend. Ehrlich [2] shows that if the proportion of an individual's time budget that is devoted to offending depends on the expected return from offending relative to that from legitimate occupations, the elasticity of the time spent in illicit activity with respect to p can only exceed its elasticity with respect to f if the offender is a risk-preferrer. Stigler [3] stresses the need for the structure of punishments to reflect a marginal disincentive to commit the more serious crimes; if the penalty for armed robbery is execution the criminal might as well shoot as many potential witnesses as he conveniently can. Ehrlich makes much the same point when he observes that the practice of imposing concurrent sentences on offenders who have committed several offences since their previous conviction is an incentive to offend repeatedly during this period, since after the first offence the marginal punishment falls to zero, though the probability of apprehension may rise with successive offences.

It is not an aim of this paper to consider what is the appropriate set of punishments for a given set of crimes, though some comments will be made. The aim is to consider how much it is worth spending on crime control with a restricted set of control variables, namely, only the probability of apprehension. What we say therefore has particular relevance to the decisions of those responsible for administering the police; on the whole, they have no power over the punishments imposed on convicts. Although formally p is the decision variable it will not be helpful to think directly in terms of p. The measure of output or benefit is taken as the social value of offences prevented. The programme therefore consists in large measure in finding money values to attach to prevented offences of various kinds.

First it is necessary to say a few words about costs. In assessing the costs of preventing offences it is important to bear in mind that since the benefits are produced by the criminal justice system as a whole, the relevant costs are those of the system as a whole. As an illustration, suppose that the police can prevent crime in two ways: (a) by maintaining a conspicuous presence in crime-prone areas; (b) by detection and apprehension of offenders. The costs of preventive patrol are simply police costs. The effectiveness of preventive patrol does depend on offenders' distaste for exposure to correction agencies, but changes in preventions due to changes in the level of preventive patrolling do not impose additional social costs on parts of the CJS downstream of the police. Actual detection and apprehension of offenders involves their subsequent passage through the correction process, and it is this that brings about the reduction in the value of offences offenders commit in the course of their subsequent careers. The costs of downstream agencies must therefore be counted.

One way of providing the necessary cost information in a systematic way is to simulate the actual behaviour of the system. Blumstein and Larson [4] are the foremost proponents of this approach. First of all, each processing stage in the system is identified. The input to each stage is described by a vector whose *i*th component reflects the yearly flow attributable to characteristic *i*, which would normally be a type of crime but might be any other relevant feature of the flow. Each processing stage is characterised by a vector of cost rates, calculated as average costs to the public purse, but there is no reason why marginal social costs could not be used. The flow of output from that stage is distributed to the elements of the next stage by reference to a vector of branching probabilities. In this way it is possible to trace the downstream costs of an increase in detections, or, more, generally, any change in police practice.

Considerable progress has already been made in elucidating CJS production functions. The consultants Arthur Andersen and Co. have made some estimates of the number and type of future crimes prevented as a result of an offender's detection and process through the CJS as compared with his non-detection [5, 6]. In passing we might observe that it would not do to choose the correctional regime on the criterion of minimising recidivism per unit of social cost. As well as having a rehabilitation effect, punishment may have a deterrent effect. It could be that a regime that is comparatively successful at rehabilitation is comparatively unsuccessful at deterring. Various studies by members of the OR department at Lancaster University [7, 8, 9] have sought to establish the production function of police resources in terms of (*a*) detections and (*b*) preventions. Combination of these two strands would yield a production function for police resources in terms of prevented crimes.

The rule for the police administration is to select the level of operations so as to equate marginal social costs to the whole CJS with the marginal social value of prevented offences. If the police operate within a fixed budget, then the rule must be to maximise the value of prevented offences net of downstream costs, unless the budget is so ample as to enable the marginal equivalence above to be attained. This would be a good point at which to evaluate downstream costs, but this discussion is deferred since it depends upon issues which arise in the attempt to value prevented offences, a problem to which we now turn.

The valuation of offences

Theft is the offence *prima facie* most susceptible to economic analysis. In evaluating the social loss from theft we are at once faced with the problem that since one party's loss is the other's gain, theft is a mere transfer involving no net loss to society as a whole. The implication of this view is that the police should not waste resources trying to prevent theft, but should concentrate on other, socially harmful, offences. If a zero welfare significance is attached to offenders' gains from theft then the social value of the theft is the subjective value to the victim of what is stolen. This value is, of course, negative. Tullock [10], however, points out that theft belongs to an important class of transactions which may be called 'contested transfers': it is because the potential parties to the transaction use their resources to contest the transfer that social costs arise. In the standard case of markets for goods and services the value of the opportunity to produce, exchange and consume a block of output might be measured as the excess of consumers' willingness to pay over the opportunity cost of the resources used to produce the block of output. An interesting question is, what is the analogue for theft?

Shoup and Mehay [11] argue that the alternative legitimate income forgone by offenders is an important element of the social loss from theft. However, they say, since 'as some observers have pointed out, there is a strong empirical relationship between low income and the propensity to commit property crimes, it may be that the typical thief's highest alternative earnings in legitimate activity are below those he can earn in crime'. This leads them to conclude that the amount stolen will overstate offenders' forgone legitimate earnings and therefore their opportunity costs. But this is to ignore certain elements of the opportunity costs (to offenders) of earning the higher illicit income: the risks of capture and the subjective value of punishment must be offset against the additional monetary return from illicit activity.

Perhaps it is possible to justify in the following way the rule that at the margin the amount stolen is equal to thieves' opportunity costs. If we assume offenders to be utility-maximisers it follows that they will continue to steal until at the margin the theft of £1 is just offset by the subjective value of the inputs (including risk, time, capital equipment) they must devote to stealing it.

We now turn to two points raised by Shoup and Mehay in connection with the theft of goods rather than of money.

(1) They say that the money value of loss to the owner of a stolen article may exceed the money value of gain to the thief 'if only because many items have been chosen to fit the tastes and requirements of the owner (e.g. clothes that fit the owner) and have a small probability of being equally serviceable to the thief'. Against this view it can be argued that the opposite might be true. Clothes that the victim has outgrown or con-

siders *démodé* might prove a perfect fit for the offender or conform precisely with his tastes. No presumption can be established either way. In general, however, an individual may be said to value his possessions more highly than the market, otherwise he would sell them on the market. But this might also be true of the thief when he gains illicit possession of these items. For both, therefore, the market value sets a lower limit on subjective valuation of an article.

(2) Thieves are unlikely to reap the full market value of their swag because receivers of stolen goods require a discount to recompense them for the risk and time they devote to finding suitable outlets for it. The significance of this point is that it constitutes a reason why the market value of what is stolen might overstate its subjective value to the offender. Somewhere along the line, however, the stolen goods will be sold to a *bona fide* customer or will displace goods customers would have had to acquire legitimately, i.e., at full market value. Receivers are best regarded as partners in the theft whose function is to provide specialised services. Although the market value of stolen articles may be distributed among offenders other than the actual thieves, there is no reason to believe that it is not captured by the participating offenders taken together. A diagram might aid the exposition.

Offenders have the opportunity to steal goods or money. The market value represents the marginal valuation in each case. The *MC* of stealing goods is everywhere higher than that of stealing money since in order to capture the full market value of goods the services of a receiver have to be engaged at additional cost. It is conceivable that the opposite might be true, but the argument holds good for both cases. In any case it is worth pressing thefts to the point at which the *MC* of stealing £1's worth of goods or money is equal to £1. It is better to add the receivers' turn to thieves' costs than to subtract it from

Figure 1

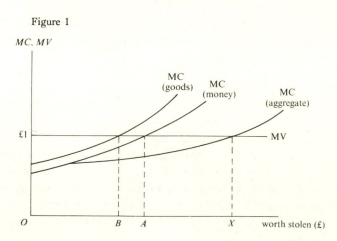

thieves' MV of £1's worth of goods, because the market value of what is stolen is observable and can still be taken to represent the marginal opportunity cost of stealing it. The thieves whose schedules appear in the diagram will commit £OX worth of thefts, £OA of money and £OB (= £AX) of goods.

Although many writers have drawn attention to the fact that potential victims devote large volumes of resources to self-protection and self-insurance, no one has ventured the view that much the same analysis applies to them as to offenders. Potential victims can prevent theft in a variety of ways, e.g. by (a) expenditure on locks, bolts and shutters, (b) employment of security staff and dogs, (c) location of factory or dwelling at places which in the absence of theft would be less preferred, (d) changes in asset-holding patterns, (e) use of time for leisure rather than for producing what is liable to be stolen. If potential victims seek to maximise utility, these theft-prevention measures will be pursued to the point at which £1's worth of some opportunity forgone (whether this represents actual expenditure as in (a) or (b), or subjective value of theft-induced changes as in (c), (d) or (e)) will just forestall the loss of £1 (in expected value terms) through theft.

This analysis of the utility-maximising decisions of offenders and potential victims appears to justify a rule of thumb that where prospective changes in theft are small, the real social cost is equal to (at most) twice the amount stolen. If a zero weight is assigned to offenders' gains the stolen money loses all social value in transfer and the social loss would then be equal to (at most) three times the amount stolen. Alternatively, if offenders are so far to be excluded from society that not even their forgone legitimate earnings are to count as an element of social cost, then the social cost of theft again falls to (at most) twice the amount stolen. It is perhaps interesting to note that even without invoking a zero weighting for offenders' gains, it is possible to provide an economic justification for the view that theft is a social evil, if any were needed. It is also interesting on either assumption about the treatment of offenders' gains and losses, it appears that theft, far from being a mere transfer, may involve social costs of twice the amount stolen at the margin.

We now go beyond exploration of thieves' and victims' behaviour to consider questions arising from theft-prevention by third parties. There is an asymmetry between prevention of legitimate transactions and prevention of theft. If legitimate trading of the marginal unit of a good between producer and consumer is prevented, the social value of the loss per unit is at a minimum. But as the trading of successive intramarginal units of the good is prevented, the social loss per unit rises, at first anyway. If trading in the good is completely stopped, the social loss is consumers' total willingness to pay less the opportunity cost of production. What is the analogue for theft? For offenders the MV of £1 stolen is £1. The MC of stealing £1 in terms of opportunities forgone is likely to rise due to diminishing returns. Equilibrium is achieved when the theft of £1 costs £1. For potential victims there will exist a schedule representing the *MC* of preventing offences. The *MC* of preventing every offence is likely to be high, but there will be a level of offences at which the *MC* is low. Of course, the MC schedules of the two parties will be interdependent, the position of one party's schedule depending on that of the other. What would be the social gain if all offenders became honest overnight and theft were no longer a danger? If £n was the amount stolen before the change, thieves would lose £n, but gain the resources they commit to stealing it £$\sum_{i=1}^{n} MC_i$. But a zero welfare significance attaches to £n since that sum now accrues to victims. Therefore the social value of thieves' gain is £$\sum_{i=1}^{n} MC_i$. If m is the last £ of potential plunder which cannot be prevented without outlay, the gain to potential victims is £$\sum_{i=1}^{m} MC_i$. The implication of this analysis is that the cost of theft has no obvious relationship with the amount stolen. Thieves' opportunity costs, £$\sum_{i=n}^{n} MC_i$, could not be as great as the amount stolen, £n, while potential victims' costs bear no obvious relationship to the amount stolen.

There might well be joint costs on the victims' side. The measures open to householders to prevent personal injury and violation of privacy also prevent loss through theft. It is likely that householders will pursue preventive measures against intrusion generally beyond the point where these are worthwhile solely to reduce expected financial loss. In that case reduction in financial loss is a bonus, gained without cost. However, that does mean that the prevention of a theft saves at most the value of the theft itself, since that is what thieves at the margin are assumed to be willing to forgo.

It is not necessarily correct for the law enforcement agency to concentrate resources exclusively on offences of a type that actually take place. It may be that no offences of the appropriate type will be observed, although – indeed because – potential victims commit resources to prevent them. It is difficult to find good examples: the crown jewels have not been stolen, Fort Knox has never been burgled. These examples are not apt because the potential victims and the law enforcement agency's decision makers are identical, though they may be separate institutionally. But during a period of petrol rationing it might be worthwhile in terms of resource-saving for the police to conduct a blitz against petrol-syphoners in order to dissuade motorists from investing in lockable petrol-caps, a measure which, let us suppose, would forestall all thefts of petrol.

Finally, there is an offence which forms an exception to the general rule that the transfer involved in theft is contested. Most potential victims might go to some trouble to abet this offence. Suspecting that they have been passed a dud £5 note, most people will not scruple to pass it on, since to report the matter is to lose the £5. In this way the loss to victims is widely diffused through a general debauching of the currency. Forgery, therefore, imposes costs only on offenders (apart from those of the mint) so that the marginal social loss from forgery is equal only to the amount of the theft, not more, though we might enter a warning that there may be a threshold beyond which extra forged notes serve to destroy confidence in currency generally, and the social cost of that might be very heavy. In other words, this analysis applies only to the 'small numbers' case.

However, in what has been said so far there has been no analysis of the way in which police action brings about a reduction in the volume of thefts. Suppose that an increase in the probability of apprehension raises offenders' MC of stealing a given amount of money. At the same time, the reduced incidence of criminal activity will result in an increase in the productivity of potential victims' preventive measures and therefore a lowering of their MC schedule. Suppose that as a result of these changes thefts are reduced by the amount £x. If we cleave to the principle that only real opportunity costs and not transfers should be counted, we find the following. The reduction of £x in theft has no welfare significance. Victims' commitment of resources will fall due to the lower cost of effecting the pre-existing preventions, but will rise since it is now worthwhile to commit resources to preventing offences which previously were not worth preventing. It is difficult to say whether the balance of these effects would result in an overall rise or fall in resource commitment. Offenders' resource commitment might similarly rise or fall, there being a reduction of commitment of resources due to a fall in the amount stolen but a rise in the cost of committing the amount of theft that still is committed. Therefore, although police action might reduce the volume of thefts, that would not necessarily reduce the volume of resources committed to contesting the transfer. If, therefore, the criterion of police success is the reduction in resources used to contest the transfer it appears that it might be satisfied just as well by hindering the efforts of potential victims as those of offenders. This appears to be a *reductio ad absurdum* of the proposition that all parties' gains and losses should receive equal weights. However, this absurd possibility is ruled out, albeit rather uneasily, by the distributional considerations adduced above. Most people, however, would want to say that offenders' gains have zero welfare significance. In that case, if the police can reduce thefts by £x by an expenditure of less than that amount, then an improvement in resource allocation is certain to result, whereas an increase in the volume of theft would have a negative social value.

Other crimes

Even more difficult is the problem of valuing crimes involving violence. If a violent act is committed in the course of a robbery, whether to secure swag or expedite escape, special difficulty only arises in assessing the loss to the victim, since we can continue to assume that for offenders the resources used and the expected penalties incurred are balanced against the amount stolen at the margin. Shoup and Mehay [11] deal with the problem by assimilating injury by criminal act to injury by road accident. This solution makes a strong appeal since it sanctions the use of standard figures for road accident losses that are already formulated in most countries, and thus obviates the need for further investigation. The Shoup–Mehay valuations are presented in Table I for illustrative purposes.

The components financial loss plus damage for each crime are given their market values. The loss to the individual from injury is valued as if it had been sustained in a traffic accident and in fact includes only the cost of treatment together with any loss of earnings suffered during recuperation. It must not be supposed, for example, that the social loss from five rapes ($1,000) is to be construed as less than the social loss from one car theft ($1,017), partly because, as the authors report, only 14 per cent of cars stolen are not recovered so that the true car theft figure should be $142 plus a measure of inconvenience, damage, etc., but mainly because these figures do not include warm-blooded costs, which are presumably high in the case of rape and very probably negligible in the case of car theft. The values in the table therefore are minima: for some items the true social value will be near

TABLE 1

Offence	Dollar average personal loss per offence
Robbery	284
Burglary	390
Auto theft	1,017 (142)
Grand theft	239
Petty theft	26
Homicide	93,000
Aggravated assault	200
Forcible rape	200

these values, whereas for others the true social value will be very much higher.

When it comes to assessing these warm-blooded costs, economic analysis cannot yet take us very far. Rape, homicide and pure crimes of violence in general differ from theft in that what the offender gains cannot be measured in the same units as what the victim loses. Victims' loss has no obvious money counterpart. Where actual injury or death are involved road accident figures may be acceptable. But crimes involving threats of violence cannot readily be assimilated to road accidents. Nor perhaps is the fear, as opposed to the physical injury, undergone by those assaulted. Since it is doubtful whether valuations of these 'bads' can be inferred from victims' actual market behaviour, the only obvious solution is to set up an experiment which places victims in simulated market situations in which they are faced by a hypothetical tariff whereby money can be exchanged for changes in the probability of exposure threats and to violence itself – once the initial plunge into the questionnaire method had been taken, quite fine graduations could in principle be valued. Police output could be expressed in terms of these probabilities, and in this way commensurability of input and output could be achieved.

What offenders gain from murder, rape, etc., is also difficult to value. If offenders are aware of the probability of apprehension and of the punishment they are likely to receive, then the expected value of the loss from punishment might serve as a guide, though what relationship this would bear to readily measured variables such as income is not certain. Even if a zero welfare significance is assigned to offenders' gains, it is important to have an estimate of offenders' costs, since these are true social costs which are not incurred if the crime can be prevented.

Special mention must be made of offences against regulations whose aim it is to reduce road accidents, e.g., laws against driving whilst drunk, regulations governing lights, tyres, brakes, etc. The benefits of reducing road accidents are already valued for road investment purposes and there is every reason to use these values here. On the offenders' side difficulty arises because the penalty of suspension from driving might be valued as the consumers' surplus derived from the use of a car during the period of suspension, and that would not be easy to measure. What the offender gains from the offence is the facility and convenience of driving whilst drunk. A rough guide to the value of this might be gleaned from changes in offenders' behaviour in response to changes in the intensity of enforcement of the regulations. For example, the introduction of the breathalyser would have afforded an interesting opportunity. Find a country hostelry which relies for its trade on car-borne tipplers. Divide the catchment area into zones of known population. Conduct a survey to find out the visit rate per thousand population in each such zone. Calculate the distance from the centre of each zone to the hostelry. The travel cost and money equivalent of travel time can then be applied to find the distance–price of the hostelry for each zone. Since there will be a variation of distance–price with visit rate it will be possible to construct a schedule of marginal valuation for the facility. We are now ready to calculate the costs the breathalyser imposes on offenders. Take origin zone, A. Before, the distance–price of OP_a attracted OQ_a visits. Afterwards it might be found that only OQ'_a visits come from zone A. From the MV schedule we infer that the distance–price which would produce that number of trips is OP'_a. The subjective value of the extra risk to those in A is $P_aP'_a$ per trip. The loss of consumers' surplus is P'_aP_aRR'. If no one ever drove whilst drunk P'_a would coincide with P_a and the procedure would correctly show no loss of surplus. But the estimate of the loss would be too low since some visitors might reduce their intake per visit rather than the number of visits. In addition it is necessary to aggregate over zones, and, more difficult, over hostelries. This method is the Clawson method which has most frequently been used to appraise new recreation sites. For a basic use of the method see Smith [17].

Downstream costs of crime prevention

Many of the issues here are straightforward and require little comment. In measuring the costs to be set against the benefits in terms of prevented crimes of offenders' passage through the whole CJS, it is necessary to add court costs of conviction and the costs of punishment to police costs of apprehension and detection. Court costs can be taken as the

Figure 2

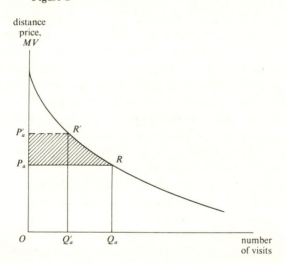

market prices of resources used to handle the relevant increment in throughput, provided all social costs are counted, including opportunity costs of jurors' and witnesses' time and the costs of providing legal representation for defendants, and not merely calls on the public purse.

The treatment of the costs of buildings and staffs used by the prison service could no doubt be assimilated to that of the courts. But the difficulty arises when it is a question of the prisoner-related costs of custody. The problem turns on whether or not offenders are to be included in the definition of society. For instance the change-in-net-output method might be used. Loss is measured by:

> value of prisoners' outside output
> less value of outside consumption
> less value of inside output
> plus value of inside consumption.

This is a measure of what other members of society lose through custody of convicts. In addition, any saving that prisoners undertook outside would have to be subtracted from the above, on the grounds that to save is simply to postpone consumption, not to forgo it, and the benefit to the rest of society is offset by interest payments.

But if prisoners are to be treated as part of society their gains and losses are important too. There are certain affinities between deprivation of life and deprivation of freedom. It might be said that whereas the deceased's loss lies in becoming an ex-member of society, the prisoner's loss consists in becoming a temporary non-member of it. It is tempting to measure what is lost in the same way for each, except that for prisoners the loss would extend over a shorter time span, and not, or not usually, for ever. The loss consists in being denied the opportunity freely to take decisions about production and consumption. In discussing some economic aspects of penal sentencing in Germany, Neu [12] suggests that income (and 'benefit') foregone is a social cost of imprisonment. Mishan [13] objects to the use of income foregone as a measure of the value of life on the grounds that it is not a measure of welfare. On the other hand we can cut the Gordian knot by arguing that a zero value should be placed on offenders' loss of liberty since they voluntarily assume the risks of capture and imprisonment and that their subjective value of these 'bads' is already reflected in the rewards they derive from offending. If we give full weight to their gains and losses at the offending stage it does not seem correct also to count the subjective value of imprisonment.

But if offenders are to be excluded from society, then we need only consider the losses and gains accruing to the rest of society from imprisonment. The net output method outlined above is a measure of this loss. Notice, however, that if the prisoner would have been unemployed the loss might be negative. If prisoners fare no better from the point of view of consumption than the unemployed, inside and outside consumption cancel out. Outside output is zero *ex hypothesi*. Society therefore reaps the fruits of inside production! Furthermore, if the value of outside consumption is taken to be the prisoner's income minus what he spends on others, that might not be a sufficient measure of the resources released by imprisoning a consumer. To the extent that the prisoner releases accommodation subject to a subsidised rent, the value of that accommodation to the remainder of society is not fully captured by the rent payment, but might in certain circumstances be equal to the value of whatever postponement in the construction of a new house is made possible. But if we adopt that figure we must subtract rent payments from the figure for outside consumption.

But society receives another bonus from imprisonment. We have already discussed the benefits in terms of offences prevented or deterred as a result of either an offender's having passed through the CJS or his fear that he might pass through it. The value of offences prevented because the offender is out of circulation has not yet been dealt with. Although this is clearly related to the length of detention, it is nevertheless a downstream benefit to set beside the downstream costs of detecting and apprehending offenders.

Finally, let us say a brief word about fines. Fining as a form of punishment commends itself to Becker [1] on the grounds that fines are simply transfers from offenders to the rest of society and therefore do not involve social loss. Here, then, is a less costly form of punishment than imprisonment. This conclusion survives a change to the assumption that offenders' gains and losses are not to count, for under this assumption the loss incurred by offenders has no significance, while the corresponding gain to the rest of society is equal to the fine. Thus, whereas imprisonment will impose social costs, fining confers a social benefit.

Distributional issues

Much of what has been said up to now has involved distributional value judgments as between offender and victim. There remain one or two other distributional issues.

If offenders' gains are to receive full weight there does not seem to be any good reason to find and return stolen property to its rightful owner, since that in itself is a mere transfer. A justification can, however, be found. Society applies distributional value judgments in the differential taxation of individuals with different incomes. A thief snatching a wallet plunders his victim of after-tax income, unless the latter happens to be a tax-evader. Thieves do not pay tax on the proceeds of criminal activity. The social value of £x stolen is £x if returned to its rightful owner, but only £$(1 - t)x$, where t is the marginal tax rate appropriate to the thief, if left in the hands of the thief. It is therefore worth £tx to recover the stolen money.

Becker [1] refers favourably to the possibility of compensation for offences. Compensation, which is here understood to be generous enough to render the victim indifferent to the offence, could take several forms: (i) offenders compensate society at large, (ii) offenders compensate victims, (iii) society at large compensates victims.

If society at large always compensates victims, there is a problem akin to 'moral hazard' in that potential victims will no longer trouble to make efforts to forestall theft (and other offences), compensation being an acceptable substitute for self-protection and self-insurance. The result might be a great increase in theft and huge transfers to victims. But since compensation is a transfer, it has no welfare significance. Moreover, since it provides an incentive for victims not to commit scarce resources to prevention, is that not a gain to society as a whole? This in turn would induce a lowering of offenders' MC schedules so that they would be able to steal the same amount with fewer resources, although this gain would be offset by the commitment of extra resources, it now being profitable to extend operations to undreamed-of lengths. There are a number of drawbacks to a policy of compensation by society at large: the impossibility of lump-sum transfers, the cost of making and checking legitimate claims, to say nothing of the resources devoted to contesting bogus claims.

Compensation pattern (i) is akin to fines and (ii) is in essence the return of stolen goods to the rightful owner.

Compensation by society at large has been seen by some, notably Thurow [14], as a way out of an equity—efficiency dilemma that arises in allocating a city's police resources to districts which differ in their proneness to crime. Shoup [15] and Dosser [16] pose the question should police resources be deployed so as to equalise the protection given (e.g. equalise crime rates in the two districts) or so as to minimise the total amount of crime. As we have seen, it is doubtful whether compensation can provide a solution.

Concluding remarks

In this paper we have been exploring the possibility of deriving social values for prevented crimes, principally theft. While it is possible to say something about what the various parties' gains and losses are, the question as to which are to be given what weight does not strictly belong to the domain of economic analysis. The most important question is what weight if any to attach to offenders' gains. The final social value of theft has been shown to depend very much on what weights are actually assigned. As for other offences, it is plain that there is still some way to go before money values can be confidently propounded. As we have seen, some components of the loss from crimes of violence can be given reasonable values, but other components, such as the warm-blooded costs, cannot as yet. For these, money values promulgated by elected representatives will have to be used for the time being.

It is important to recognise that the CJS is a *system* and that therefore problems of enumerating costs and benefits must be borne in mind. Finally, the social costs of the system must be carefully identified, as these may diverge markedly from public expenditure.

REFERENCES

[1] Becker, G. S., 'Crime and punishment: an economic approach', *Journal of Political Economy (JPE)*, 1968.

[2] Ehrlich, I., 'Participation in illegitimate activities: a theoretical and empirical investigation', *JPE*, 1973.

[3] Stigler, G. J., 'Optimum enforcement of laws', *JPE*, 1970.

[4] Blumstein, A. and Larson, R., 'Models of a total criminal justice system', *Operations Research*, 1969.

[5] Andersen, A. and Co., 'Some Numerical Estimates of the Effectiveness of the Criminal Justice System', unpublished report to UK Home Office, 1968.

[6] Andersen, A. and Co., untitled, unpublished report to UK Home Office, 1970.

[7] Bryant, J. W., Chambers, M. L., and Falcon, D., 'Patrol Effectiveness and Patrol Deployment', unpublished report to UK Home Office, 1968.

[8] Aspden, P., 'The Application of Mathematical Programming to the Determination of Optimal Police Patrol Deployments', unpublished PhD thesis, Lancaster University, 1971.

[9] Aspden, P., 'Analysis of Beat Patrol Experiment', unpublished report to UK Home Office, 1969.

[10] Tullock, G., 'The welfare costs of tariffs, monopolies and thefts', *Western Economic Journal*, 1967.

[11] Shoup, D. C., and Mehay, S. L., *Program Budgeting for Urban Police Services*, Institute of Government and Public Affairs, UCLA, 1971.

[12] Neu, A. D., 'Penal sentencing in Germany: some economic aspects', *Public Finance*, 1973.

[13] Mishan, E. J., 'Evaluation of life and limb: a theoretical approach', *JPE*, 1971.

[14] Thurow, L. C., 'Equity versus efficiency in law enforcement', *Public Policy*, 1970.

[15] Shoup, C. S., 'Standards for distribution of a free government: crime prevention', *Public Finance*, 1964.

[16] Dosser, D., Notes on Carl S. Shoup's 'Standards for distribution of a free government service: crime prevention', *Public Finance*, 1964.

[17] Smith, R. J., 'The evaluation of recreation benefits: the Clawson method in practice', *Urban Studies*, 1971.

Cost–benefit studies – the way ahead

G. C. CORTI

There are five studies of an applied character in the present volume: a critique (Chapter 1), proposals for new (Chapter 14) and developed (Chapter 13) work, a survey of a current system (Chapter 9) and a reflection on how things passed in some notable cost–benefit studies (Chapter 10). In addition to discussing the five applied essays, I propose to glance at a major application of resource allocation in France [1]. How do these applications measure up to the test of assisting policy formation and decision taking not in some 'real world' that allows all escape from economics, but rather in that observed world in which most of us have to work?

The questions 'can we use cost–benefit analysis?' and 'should we use it?' do not arise discretely in time. But a large proportion of applied economic work allied to policy formation and decision taking inevitably involves forecasting. Prest and Turvey in their survey article of cost–benefit analysis [2] did not deal with problems of forecasting as one topic. Recognising the importance of a view of the future they dealt with its problems under analytical heads such as enumeration and uncertainty. Maurice Peston's short dissertation on risk continues the theoretical consideration of one of these strands, but the temptation to follow down that path will on this occasion be resisted.

Not surprisingly most of the papers touch on the problems of forecasting. Rees's paper concentrates on forecasting in his consideration of the Channel Tunnel studies. His conclusion is that the sensitivity analysis is unnecessarily inadequate and in no way presents the decision taker with the information required to evaluate a risky decision. Good: so the conclusion is more work. More work on what? Rees advocates a model which he describes in another article [3], not in the present collection, for showing the effects simultaneously of forecasting errors, and of variations in independent variable and valuation parameters over their postulated distribution. This model does not deal with the possibility that the hypothesised relationships, for instance those underlying the demand forecasts, may not continue to hold. It does not because this would properly be called uncertainty. Doesn't the decision maker have to face uncertainty however? Because, by definition, objective probabilities cannot be assigned to outcomes it does not mean that some quantification of states of nature embodying altered hypothetical relationships will not assist the decision makers' consciousness that there are new maps of unknown territory. The so-called complete ignorance case is not unknown in the literature of economics [4].

If Rees's conclusion does not satisfy, Heath's — covering some of the same territory above and below ground — is at first sight daunting. Is he saying that forecasting is not worth while because the future is so uncertain? [5] A closer study of the paper corrects any such pessimistic impression. Basing himself mainly — in fact if not in name — on three massive cost—benefit studies: Roskill, the Channel Tunnel and work by the British Airports Authority (BAA) on traffic demand, Heath reaches the conclusion that forecasters should admit far more readily that the degree of confidence they attach to their forecasts is extremely low (assuming this to be a justified conclusion). This process of bringing out the confidence in the forecasts would be assisted if probabilities, including subjective probabilities presumably, had to be assigned. In the course of reaching this conclusion attention is drawn to the interesting phenomenon that the decision makers and their economic advisers, when they first saw one of the studies, that of the BAA, thought it reasonably satisfactory and entirely plausible. Yet when another study, the Channel study, emerged the answers provided by the two for traffic demand were virtually irreconcilable. Small wonder if faced with this technical advice, some decision makers' reaction was to split the difference in the forecasts. Small wonder but large absurdity. It seems rather that three lessons can be drawn from these forecasting experiences; lessons which might be applied with some effect when future large 'lumpy', or system decisions are being contemplated. First, before elaborate studies are launched rough forecasts should be made with the object of illustrating the assumptions, judgements and uncertainties that will have to be built into any later fuller forecasts and upon which much of the analysis of a cost—benefit study will rest. These rough illustrative forecasts should be seen by all concerned: policy advisers, decision takers, legislators, the public if appropriate. This is not to conclude that in every case a large detailed study will not be worth while; it is to conclude that everything should be done to impress on all concerned, at the outset, and uncomfortable though it may be, that doubt will underlie much future work. Now these rough forecasts will inevitably embody the views of the forecasters. It is here that Heath's suggestion about including confidence limits, provided these are overtly recognised to be the result of a subjective process, could assist the decision taker or contemplator. One of the most intractable problems in forecasting is the apparent plausibility of vastly different forecasts. It is quite unnecessary to attribute technical incompetence or moral failure to the forecaster. No matter how objective a frame of mind the forecaster may begin with, he cannot over a period of time avoid being affected by the viewpoint from which he is contemplating the future. There are no independent observers in forecasting. Is the forecaster considering traffic flows from an air transport authority or a body studying an undersea tunnel? The decision maker or his economic adviser will know, but how much allowance should be made for this factor since any forecast the latter makes will be affected by the same phenomenon? Confidence limits should provide some clue to the extent which the forecasters' standpoint and state of mind are influencing his forecasts. The third lesson to be drawn from the experiences described is a standard one for dealing with decisions under conditions of uncertainty. It is worth mentioning because the foregoing has stressed the uncertainty in the forecasts and this can too easily be taken for a 'do-nothing' prescription. The decision taker and the economic, and other specialist, advisers working together – and this has been known to happen – should ask themselves (*a*) what are the inflexibilities in the system being contemplated (that is both the decision system and the subjects under scrutiny) and (*b*) what are the adaptive possibilities as far as solutions are concerned? How far can (*a*) be reduced and (*b*) increased?

Suppose, however, that forecasting, with a due recognition of its pitfalls, is possible so that the future allocation of resources can be visualised. What are the limits of cost–benefit analysis? Should we use it? Where should some fear to tread? In essence that debate goes well beyond cost–benefit analysis and touches on many aspects of how decisions are reached, or how it is believed they should be reached, in our society. That the topic is alive and well is demonstrated by two articles published recently – if prepared some little time earlier. They are by Alan Peacock [6] and Alan Williams [7] respectively. The former wrestles literally with Ralph Turvey on whether or not economists should set themselves up as philosopher kings and concludes that they shouldn't. Agreed, but let's not turn back into the cave, if only to ward against other so-called social scientists (planners?) setting themselves up in that role. Alan Williams treated many curious diseases contracted by sufferers from exposure to cost–benefit that he encountered on his way – some of the cures being pretty miraculous. His prognosis was mildly in favour of cost–benefit analysis and he concluded by quoting Maurice Chevalier: who in the very long run is dead. Agreed again with the spirit of Williams' conclusion: but note that this agreement rests on value judgements and little evidence.

In the present collection we have two strikingly different approaches to the use of analysis in attempts to improve the allocation of resources in areas where the relevance of economics might be questioned. Hurst adopts an apparently modest approach. In outlining the requirements of an ideal information system and seeking to identify and suggest ways of narrowing the gap between ideal and actual, he anchors himself to two points. First there is a planning system in this field and second the objectives of the service (in so far as they have been specified) are known and given. The aim is both deliberately restricted, an improved programme budget rather than a full cost—benefit analysis, and recognisable to the administrator. Not that there is any lack of awareness of these limitations as the discussion of valuation of benefit and distribution of output shows. That discussion brings out difficulties in the way of analysis. The diagram on page 226 shows a social utility frontier between any pair of representative individuals. A social utility frontier in terms of what however? Is it in terms of more or less ill health, of a very close approach to the origins of utility in a choice between pleasure and pain? If so how is the change from a social utility frontier expressed in non-money terms translated into money terms? By means of the pre-existing judgements. This is an application of Bergson's criterion, but as Baumol commented, it 'unfortunately does not come equipped with a kit and a set of instructions for collecting the welfare judgements which it requires' [8]. So it is, of course the acceptability of these very judgements that represents the biggest stumbling block to the application of cost—benefit analysis in fields which are usually thought of as being governed by, say, ethical rather than economic considerations. Further, is not the attempt to frame value judgements in terms of a utility analysis perverse in fields where the underlying political theory, in so far as it was articulated, was more that of a social contract? It is worth taking this detour as Hurst has done because if work in these fields is indeed to be applied it had best be publishable and the points about appropriateness will escape neither potential decision takers nor the beneficiaries, or non-beneficiaries as the case may be, of the service. Such concern should not on the other hand inhibit work designed to improve methods of achieving a given end since in so doing the intrinsic efficiency of that part of the system (its own efficiency if you will) may be improved. Optimality will not be achieved by these methods, but provided the ends are judged right – separately – this improvement in economic efficiency is worth pursuing.

Anderson leads with his chin by labelling his paper as being concerned with the application of cost—benefit analysis to the criminal justice system. The trouble lies in the use of the term 'criminal justice system' being the British system of applying the criminal law (prevention, enforcement and punishment) and not therefore having anything necessarily to do with justice. Avoiding any misunderstanding on this score, we find that Anderson is not concerned merely with increasing the efficiency of achieving given ends. He is concerned to measure the output or benefit of the system and defines this as the social value of offences prevented. There are a number of snags to this. The same problem is encountered as with Hurst's paper. A system of law has evolved in society, in part with the evolution of that society, in part as a function of the very existence of that society. Thus, unless we assume that society has no other dimension but the economic, and that of a utilitarian kind, we are bound to ask whether economic criteria of judgement can suffice. The limitation of the analysis is illustrated by considering the crime aimed at destroying the state. What is the social value of preventing such crimes and how meaningful is any attempt to construct such a sum? The decision taker faced with the realities of Northern Ireland might view such an attempt as scholastic. At the other extreme, however, it can be argued that any attempt to exclude economics from a consideration of the criminal justice system is blinkered since economics will keep creeping in. Naturally, since it is of the fabric of society, as are the laws. Once a start is made on the substitution of economic for non-economic rankings of the value of offences prevented should this not lead to questioning whether economics can and should be limited to valuing an existing system or whether it should not be used more fruitfully as an instrument for analysing whether the existing system is efficient, equitable and just? Consider simply whether the present criminal justice system produces the same results at the same speed for an array of victims and an array of offenders, irrespective of the distribution of their incomes and wealth (victims and offenders including bodies corporate). In short, if an analysis of the criminal justice system is to extend beyond a programme budget or cost–effectiveness type approach it may be prudent to face all the *economic* aspects of the system and the value judgements that back them, together with the other systems of value judgement that are intertwined with them. The analysis would then become an instrument of the political reformer rather than a tool of the decision taker such as the policeman.

Harrison's paper on the other hand is couched in terms correctly – but not exclusively – aimed at the decision taker or good administrator. The essay illustrates the workings of economists with other officials – administrators, planners and other specialists – under a political chief, in a Department of State which is concerned with a multiplicity of decisions. Such testaments are not as common as they might be. It is, therefore, all the more interesting to read Harrison on the applicability of analysis to routine as opposed to special investigations. At this point a short detour on a matter of definition seems warranted. Rees also draws attention to routine analysis, linked with routine decisions, in his discussion of the COBA manual. He proceeds to a criticism of the 1967 White Paper, a topic which by inference attracts the attention of J. S. Flemming also. What is puzzling about both notes is that they do not draw attention to the title of the White Paper – *Nationalised In-dustries: a review of financial and economic objectives* (Cmnd 3437, 1967). Yet Rees is barely concerned with nationalised industries in his considera-tion of COBA or the Channel Tunnel. Flemming approaches the point first on page 45, with his footnote reference to the public/private dichotomy and to the question of whether goods are sold or not, and second on page 49, but in neither instance does he follow through. Altogether criticism of Treasury guidance to project analysts would be likely to be more fruitful if it had regard to the definitions used. Such regard need not of course preclude either analysis of the definitions nor of the extent to which they are being adhered to. At the applied level attention to operational constraints would still be necessary.

Returning to Harrison, it is salutory too for economists to be reminded of the bureaucratic rather than the political nature of the processes economics can be involved in; of the complex nature, not only of policy formation but of day-to-day decision taking with its gradual learning processes and in-terplay of different modes of judgement. In this world of greys the clear cut distinction between analyst and decision maker disappears, the conventional sharp distinction blurs; analyst and decision taker may even be one. Hold hard a minute, however; what is so special about the position of the economist? The problem of income distribution, outlined by Harrison on page 150 of his chapter is the type of issue all too familiar to most officials. Is the value judgement underlying the work so infused with political im-plications that it should go to Ministers? This question has been coped with in the press of business, with delegation of decision taking accepted as part of the style of working. The crucial question then is when should one go to Ministers? The question has two aspects, practical and ethical. As dilemmas on the second front become more acute so they will exert pressures to over-come the practical objections to putting matters to Ministers. Other officials besides economists have some tradition of political neutrality of advice. Of course, there is an element of the mythical in this tradition. But the myth has its value as a reminder of a frontier that we allow to fall at our peril. What distinguishes the economist is his particular expertise, his claim to a body of general principles and empirical work, and his knowledge, therefore, of when and what value judgements underlie his analytical work. His responsibility to himself and to his colleagues is in this last respect to ensure that those judgements are consistent with more political value judgements which have emerged as policy or strategy and further, if as in the case dis-cussed, in the process of learning, doubts emerge as to the applicability and the consequences of a judgement that is guiding a policy, to decide when the time has come that the doubt should be taken to the Minister. The phrases used by Harrison are all too telling: 'not the right thing to do', 'not an issue that

Ministers could grasp' (p. 151). There is ultimately no escape from responsibility in these matters; but can the economists be said to be discharging their function if they leave original decisions around 'untested' too long?

Another instance of the allocation of resources on a substantial scale, utilising shadow pricing of a factor of production, is in train in France. Unlike the situation described by Harrison it is concerned with a single linked sequence of decisions. Following on a report by an inter-Ministerial group under the chairmanship of M. Simon Nora in 1967 [9], a system of 'contrat de programme' was to be established between the French Government and the major public enterprises. These 'contrats' had a certain analogy with the system of financial objectives and principles established in Britain in 1961 and elaborated in 1967; they were designed with both management, in the sense of definition of responsibility, and economic aims in view. A 'Contrat' for Electricité de France was established in 1970 [10]. It specified three objectives for EDF in terms of total or global productivity (*productivité globale des facteurs* – p.g.f. for short), proportion of investment self-financed and rate of return on capital. A constraint is imposed on prices. Then assumptions are defined concerning growth of gross domestic product, demand for electricity, security of supply and general increases in prices in the economy. Consistently with, and in part derived from these objectives and assumptions, an investment programme is then defined for a couple of years within the five years of the 'contrat', the investment programme to be rolled forward in subsequent years. The missing elements, which are not defined, but which are known to exist externally to this system are the principles of pricing and investment appraisal. The former is known to be marginal cost pricing for EDF, whilst investment is appraised relative to a rate, which has been called a time discount rate. All in all an impressive system which should be designed to achieve a more efficient allocation of resources.

The novel part of the system is that of p.g.f. This is defined as the excess over unity of the volume index of output divided by the volume index of use of the factors of production [11]. Use of the individual factors is weighted according to the proportion each represents in the total volume of use of all the factors. At first sight an attractive concept. A measure of cost efficiency is introduced into the objectives and one which takes account of the substitution of the factors of production. Should we adopt this notion in Britain in appraising our nationalised industries objectives and performance? A closer look makes the model even more intriguing. From a first simple assumption that prices correctly represent relative values of products and factors, the idea of substituting shadow pricing is introduced [12]. In practice all that has been done is to revalue assets which produces 'normalised' financial charges (including depreciation). The effect of the revaluation is to argue for a relatively modest target of increase of p.g.f. during the period of the 'contrat'. This has been written into the 'contrat', together with the also rather modest internal financing and rate of return objectives. Now if the enterprise exceeds its objectives it may use any surplus not merely to reduce debt or borrowing, but to increase investment. All other things being equal this last incentive must lead to misallocation of resources provided the original investment programme was optimal with relation to forecast demand at specified prices. The system must also involve distortion in its own terms if no account is taken of the need, say, for a shadow price for any of the labour employed or for a social cost of imported primary fuel (it may be that these potential areas for shadow pricing have been examined and found to be of no account, but there is no evidence of this). So perhaps we should not rush to take over the notion of p.g.f. Since it forms part of a system in being, it should be possible in future years to evaluate it; to see whether the reservations expressed are justified or whether any misallocation of resources is outweighed by other advantages.

So this brings me to a general conclusion to be drawn from a glance at the five British studies and one French case. If we are concerned with improving the allocation of resources, should we not spend more time on assessing whether our efforts and our interventions have truly achieved that end? It is not as if we have not been making efforts. Evidence of the scale of application of cost–benefit studies in Britain over the past few years lies for instance in a dossier of cost–benefit studies which has been built up in the Treasury since 1968. The purpose of this record was to build up a common fund of experience about cost–benefit studies carried out in, with or for Government Departments. With this aim only those studies which were judged to be of more general interest have been recorded. Naturally the process of selection has become stricter as experience has accumulated. Nonetheless an up-to-date count would show over 150 entries in the dossier. Let it be emphasised again that this is not a complete list of studies in Central Government, let alone in local Government or para-statal bodies. Even so, it covers studies ranging from airports and power-stations to straying animals.[1]

If then, our record of effort in applied CBA studies is good – so that any new survey will need an extensive bibliography if it is to do justice to British work – what more is it that I want considered? It is something that economists are not too good at, nor too keen on. It is more evidence of the track record, more studies concerned with trying to evaluate how things have turned out. If we think that CBA will assist decision taking – and personally I believe it can, if it remains within Eckstein's more modest role [13] – why are we not putting more effort into seeing whether and how much it has assisted decision taking? Is it because it is easy to demonstrate that things have changed and the effort of back-checking is not worth while? Or is it because of the intrinsic difficulty of reseparating the roles and actions of the analyst and the decision taker? Against the possibility that it is the second and rather particular difficulty that explains the scarcity of examples of studies of out-turn, let me offer a few questions which we need to try and answer more frequently by tracing the effects and results of cost–benefit studies on public expenditure decisions.

(*a*) Did the analysis help clarify the decision-making process?
(*b*) Did the analysis help or hinder the reaching of a decision?
(*c*) Does the decision appear to have been well- or ill-founded to the extent that it relied on CBA?
(*d*) In turn then, was the CBA well- or ill-founded?
(*e*) How has the project (or lack of it) turned out in terms of the analysis – and in terms of all perceived decision criteria?
(*f*) Was the CBA relevant in the event? (In other words did the analysis identify the presence or absence of all substantial social costs and benefits falling on or to the individuals concerned?)

More answers to these questions might establish economists' part in increasing the good, reducing the bad and avoiding the ugly. If this is my primary conclusion about required developments in applied cost–benefit work, a further conclusion is more widely acknowledged. Four of the five papers under review refer to the difficulties of forecasting under conditions of uncertainty, and the French case pays some attention to the need for adaptability. Heath advocates not merely more recognition of the importance of the phenomenon but the use of specific methods to attempt to deal with uncertainty. I put forward above three prescriptions which could be complementary to Heath's. The conclusion is clear, however; a reorientation of work and a use of supplementary methods, such as confidence limits (with all their ambiguities), is necessary if we are to face uncertainty.

A third and again widely acknowledged, but insufficiently applied conclusion is the need for more apposite enumeration over large areas of public expenditure. Both Hurst's and Rees' notes bring this out, but it is the former, working in a field which is far less trodden by economists than is transport, who has the edge in emphasising the very basic need to build economically relevant information systems. The two preconditions are that the system be relatable to the Public Expenditure Surveys as these evolve and that it be based on an extensive knowledge of the field under consideration. In other words there is no point in adding to the mass of unusable data which is in danger of swamping us all.

Yet a fourth conclusion is not derived from the five papers presented, though the French case offers a connection. There is in it the usual recognition that prices of products and of the factors of production may not present their social values. But the step is hesitant and circumscribed. The use of some general index to revalue assets acknowledges the impact of inflation over a period of time on the different factor inputs (in this it bears in practice some resemblance to the constant purchasing power formula of accountants, but it is justified on more familiar economic arguments as would be expected from its main author). It does nothing, however, to cope with the effect of changes in relative values of the factors nor of outputs. As Godley and Taylor point out in chapter 8 of this volume, at the macro level such shifts bear on the demand on output, on the import as well as the home content of expenditure. So indeed do shifts within the programmes. When at a micro level we bring into play other divergencies between private and social costs, say unemployment (we cannot assume full employment in many micro appraisals) or externalities, we need to consider whether these divergencies involve resource or transfer effects. These problems have been well known to practitioners for some years, but they have been compounded by the advent of faster inflation. It is quite unnecessary to assume a continuation of any particular rate of inflation to assert that the phenomenon has occurred and that we need more published applied studies showing how it has been coped with.

Without some redistribution of effort to allow development along the four lines I have indicated – with all the cautions expressed by the five authors and the cautionary example of the French case – it is not clear that continued published encouragement for applied economic case work on resource allocation can be counted on. It is no light honour for economists to find cost–benefit work treated seriously by a practising politician. Edmund Dell in his book, *Political Responsibility and Industry*, puts some onus on the profession when he advocates the use of cost–benefit analysis as an aid to judgement. 'CBA, for example, may help in systematically opening up a problem.' 'A Minister ... who ... proceeded without further aid ... would simply show poor judgement.' Fortunately, immediately thereafter Dell uses Hobbes' 'equilibrium of the distribution of judgement' to sound what should be a warning not only to Ministers but also to economists.

NOTE

[1] This record of cost–benefit studies has been prepared primarily for use within Government Departments and is not published. However, any researcher considering work in particular fields will wherever possible be put in touch with the authors of extant work in that field. The dossier is an admirable concept and the credit for its initiation lies largely with Alan Williams, Michael Bridgeman and Terry Banks.

REFERENCES

[1] *Lettre de Mission*, Ministers of Finance and Industry to EDF, 23 December 1970.

[2] A. R. Prest and R. Turvey, 'Cost–benefit: A Survey', *Economic Journal*, 1966.

[3] J. A. Rees and R. Rees, 'Demand Forecasts and Planning Margins for Water in S.E. England', *Journal of Regional Studies*, 1972.

[4] W. J. Baumol, *Economic Theory and Operations Analysis*, ch. 24, 1972 ed.

[5] J. Heath, p. 162 above: 'It is that . . . long range demand forecasting is not feasible within a degree of reliability that would be useful for decision making.'

[6] A. Peacock, 'Cost–benefit Analysis and the Political Control of Public Investment', in *Cost Benefit and Cost Effectiveness*, Unwin University Books, 1973.

[7] A. Williams, 'Cost–Benefit Analysis: Bastard Science? and/or Insidious Poison in the Body Politic?', op. cit.

[8] W. J. Baumol, op. cit., ch. 16, p. 404.

[9] Groupe de Travail du Comité Inter Ministeriel des Entreprises Publiques, *Rapport sur les Entreprises, Publiques*, République Française, 1968.

[10] *Lettre de Mission*, ibid.

[11] M. Boiteux, La Notion de Productivité globale des facteurs, Electricité de France, 1973, p. 6.

[12] M. Boiteux, ibid. pp. 4 and 8.

[13] O. Eckstein, 'A Survey of the Theory of Public Expenditure Criteria', in *Public Finances: Needs, Sources and Utilization*, Princeton University Press, 1961.

[14] E. Dell, *Political Responsibility and Industry*, 1973, pp. 230 and 231.

Name index

Subject index